THE SHAKESPEAREAN INTERNATIONAL
YEARBOOK
12: SPECIAL SECTION, SHAKESPEARE IN INDIA

GENERAL EDITORS

Tom Bishop, University of Auckland, Auckland, New Zealand
Alexander C. Y. Huang, George Washington University, Washington, D.C., USA
Graham Bradshaw, Chuo University, Tokyo, Japan (Emeritus)

ADVISORY BOARD

Supriya Chaudhuri, Jadavpur University, Kolkata, India
Natasha Distiller, University of Cape Town, Cape Town,
Republic of South Africa
Jacek Fabiszak, Adam Mickiewicz University, Poznan, Poland
Atsuhiko Hirota, University of Kyoto, Kyoto, Japan
Ton Hoenselaars, Utrecht University, Utrecht, the Netherlands
Peter Holbrook, University of Queensland, Brisbane, Australia
Jean Howard, Columbia University, New York City, USA
Ania Loomba, University of Pennsylvania, Philadelphia, USA
Kate McLuskie, University of Birmingham, Birmingham, UK
Alfredo Michel Modenessi, Universidad Nacional Autónoma de México,
Mexico City, Mexico
Ruth Morse, Université Paris VII, Paris, France
W. B. Worthen, Barnard College, Columbia University, New York City, USA

The Shakespearean International Yearbook

12: Special Section, Shakespeare in India

General Editors
Tom Bishop and Alexander C. Y. Huang

Editor Emeritus
Graham Bradshaw

Special Guest Editor
Sukanta Chaudhuri

ASHGATE

© The editors and contributors, 2012

All rights reserved. No part of this publication may be reproduced, stored in a retrieval system or transmitted in any form or by any means, electronic, mechanical, photocopying, recording or otherwise without the prior permission of the publisher.

The editors and contributors have asserted their right under the Copyright, Designs and Patents Act, 1988, to be identified as the authors of this work.

Published by
Ashgate Publishing Limited
Wey Court East
Union Road
Farnham
Surrey, GU9 7PT
England

Ashgate Publishing Company
Suite 420
101 Cherry Street
Burlington
VT 05401-4405
USA

www.ashgate.com

British Library Cataloguing in Publication Data
The Shakespearean international yearbook.
  Volume 12, Special section. Shakespeare in India.
  1. Shakespeare, William, 1564–1616–Appreciation–India.
  I. Bradshaw, Graham.
  822.3'3-dc23

ISBN 9781409451167 (hbk)
ISBN 9781409451174 (ebk – PDF)
ISBN 9781409471080 (ebk – ePUB)

ISSN 1465-5098

Printed and bound in Great Britain by the
MPG Books Group, UK

Contents

List of Figures	vii
Preface	ix

Part I: Special Section: Shakespeare in India

1   Introduction: Shakespeare in India   3
Sukanta Chaudhuri

2   Impudent Imperialists: Burlesque and the Bard in Nineteenth-Century India   7
Poonam Trivedi

3   "Every college student knows by heart": The Uses of Shakespeare in Colonial Bengal   29
Rangana Banerji

4   Shakespeare in Maharashtra, 1892–1927: A Note on a Trend in Marathi Theatre and Theatre Criticism   43
Aniket Jaaware and Urmila Bhirdikar

5   Story-teller, Poet, Playwright: Three Oriya Translations of Shakespeare (1908–1959)   53
Jatindra K. Nayak

6   "We the globe can compass soon": Tim Supple's *Dream*   65
Ananda Lal

7   Shakespeare in Indian Cinema: Appropriation, Assimilation, and Engagement   83
Rajiva Verma

8   "What bloody man is that?" *Macbeth, Maqbool*, and Shakespeare in India   97
Supriya Chaudhuri

| 9 | Reading Intertextualities in Rituporno Ghosh's *The Last Lear*: The Politics of Recanonization
Paromita Chakravarti | 115 |

Part II

| 10 | "To what base uses we may return": Deconstruction of *Hamlet* in Contemporary Drama
Aneta Mancewicz | 133 |

| 11 | Rethinking Shylock
Andrew Gurr | 153 |

Part III

| 12 | The Field in Review: New Biography Studies, Queer Turns in Theory, and Shakespearean Utility
Rebecca Chapman | 169 |

| 13 | The Field in Review: Textual Studies, Performance Criticism, and Digital Humanities
Niamh J. O'Leary | 195 |

Bibliography   *227*
Notes on Contributors   *245*
Index   *249*

List of Figures

1 *The Merry Merchant of Venice* (June 1898): the "Mounted Mashers" chorus with Jessica on the left played by the author F. J. Fraser. Photo courtesy the ADC, Gaiety Theatre, Simla.   16

2 *The Merry Merchant of Venice* (June 1898): Portia and Bassanio. Photo courtesy of the ADC, Gaiety theatre, Simla.   19

3 *The Merry Merchant of Venice* (June 1898): Portia in lawyer's robes. Photo courtesy the ADC, Gaiety Theatre, Simla.   21

4 *The Merry Merchant of Venice* (June 1898): the full cast. Note Shylock at his shop window (*top right*) and the three brass balls of the pawnbroker's sign (*top middle*). Photo courtesy ADC, Gaiety Theatre, Simla.   23

Preface

From Thomas Carlyle's famous quip about Britain's "Indian Empire" and Shakespeare in 1841 and William Miller's colonial exegesis of the canon in *Shakespeare's King Lear and Indian Politics* (1900) to Tim Supple's multicultural production of *A Midsummer Night's Dream* in English and seven Indian languages (2007), representations of England and India have figured prominently in the history of "cross-lingual exchange," as Sukanta Chaudhuri puts it. *The Shakespearean International Yearbook* is proud to publish a special section on India's engagement with Shakespeare, edited by Chaudhuri. The cluster of essays in the special section represents current scholarship on this important topic. Now in its second decade of publication, the *Yearbook* has featured a special section on a topic of interest in each volume (since 2004) edited by scholars from the United States, South Africa, Australia, New Zealand, the European community, and Japan. Some issues examine the life's work of key Shakespeareans such as the German critic Robert Weimann (2010) and the New Zealand scholar Michael Neill (2011), while others have a thematic focus (such as Shakespeare and Montaigne, the bonds of service, South African Shakespeare, and so on). We are pleased to continue and expand this tradition.

In addition, we are launching a new feature beginning with the present volume in response to the rapid developments in Shakespearean scholarship. "The Field in Review" takes the pulse of Shakespeare studies and serves as a guide to select scholarly monographs and edited collections published about Shakespeare in the previous year as well as resources for teaching and research (such as digital projects). We publish two full-length review essays on different subject areas in this volume. Both authors draw on their respective expertise to provide engaging responses to current scholarship. In her essay, Niamh O'Leary surveys textual studies, performance criticism, and digital humanities. Rebecca Chapman, on the other hand, considers new biography studies, queer turns in theory, and studies of Shakespeare in popular culture and adaptation.

We are also pleased to announce our new advisory board for *The Shakespearean International Yearbook* consisting of leading scholars from the

US, the UK, Australia, the Netherlands, France, Poland, South Africa, India, and Japan. We are deeply honoured and humbled to be able to work with such a distinguished group in the coming years.

For more information including the stylesheet, please consult our website: http://www.ashgate.com/Default.aspx?page=2875. Submissions for consideration for publication should be emailed to siy@ashgate.com.

Tom Bishop
Alexander Huang

General Editors

PART I
SPECIAL SECTION

Shakespeare in India

1 Introduction: Shakespeare in India

Sukanta Chaudhuri

I would perversely ask the reader of the essays in this Special Section to begin by looking at the notes and the works cited in them. Few people will find all the titles intelligible, as they belong to a number of Indian languages besides English (which too is an official language in India). Few again, except Indians, may be able to locate all the places of publication. But all these places have contributed, sometimes extensively, to the world's output of Shakespeareana. Even more significantly, they have published a range of other materials on very different subjects but bearing on the study and performance of Shakespeare.

Outside the Western world, India has the longest and most intense engagement with Shakespeare of any country anywhere. I should say a series of engagements, as Shakespearean traffic was routed through many languages and cultural contexts across the subcontinent, commencing at various dates from the early nineteenth to the early twentieth century. It progressed in parallel on the stage and through the printed word. And needless to say, the cross-lingual exchange was underpinned by direct access to the original English works: a relatively minor strand in the stage encounter, much more important in print, above all in the educational curriculum. Yet, as Poonam Trivedi's essay in this collection brings out, Shakespearean theatre for the colonial English audience had its own creative extensions and transformations. At the opposite, most inclusive end of the spectrum (and time-frame), Tim Supple's celebrated *A Midsummer Night's Dream* weaves seven Indian languages besides English into its fabric. Ananda Lal's essay examines this challenging cultural artefact.

The terms of India's engagement with Shakespeare are endlessly debated, because the evidence is complex and of contrary purport. Thomas Carlyle wrote in 1841:

Consider now, if they asked us, Will you give-up your Indian Empire or your Shakespeare, you English; ... should not we be forced to answer: Indian Empire, or no Indian Empire, we cannot do without Shakespeare![1]

The English genius dodged this weighty choice by placing Shakespeare at the service of Empire. His works became the cornerstone of an education system to service the operation of the Raj, and also condition the colonized population in suitable cultural and ideological terms. Given the notorious difficulty of restricting Shakespeare to a specific ideology, it is not surprising that the effort misfired. English education in general, and Shakespeare in particular, came to foster unsuspected adventures of the intellect, stirrings of a freedom of spirit that came to foster nation-wide stirrings towards political freedom.

Shakespeare was also integrated into the social and cultural resurgence set off across India over this period and (especially in the context of Bengal) often, if controversially, called a "Renaissance." As might be expected, Shakespearean influence was most apparent in drama, where it followed a graded trajectory: from "straight" translation through a range of adaptations—often with radical departures, the Shakespearean connection further obscured by Indian names for the characters; thence to sporadic adoption of Shakespearean lines, themes and motifs; finally to plays that might owe nothing directly to Shakespeare, but that could not have been written without his background presence. Shakespeare has been absorbed in the mother element of modern Indian drama.

Still more remarkably, Shakespeare has impregnated popular and folk theatre across India: sometimes in urban or elite redactions, but also in original reworkings closer to the soil, like Habib Tanvir's celebrated version of *A Midsummer-Night's Dream* using a tribal troupe from central India. Where does one place the Shakespeare performances across rural Bengal by a Marxist group, the Indian People's Theatre Association? And how does one gauge the melding of Shakespearean drama with the virile, often melodramatic, music-rich traditions of the *jatra* in Bengal, *nautanki* in northern India, or *yakshagana* in Karnataka? In yet another direction, Shakespeare penetrated the Parsi theatre, the precursor of the Bollywood film that provided popular urban entertainment across India from the mid-nineteenth to the early twentieth century, and sometimes later.

It is harder to trace a sustained Shakespearean line through Indian cinema, but individual directors have turned so often to the Bard as to practically build up a tradition. Rajiva Verma takes us through the whole sweep of Urdu and Hindi Shakespearean cinema from the colonial to the global age, set against radical shifts of audience, technology, and economics of production.

Other contributors zoom in on particular films. Supriya Chaudhuri examines in detail a celebrated Shakespearean adaptation in recent Indian cinema. Paromita Chakravarti analyses the encounter of stage and screen as viewed in a Shakespearean glass, and reflected in the work of two eminent directors in the two media from two generations. Beyond formal concerns, both essays illustrate how Shakespearean elements can be assimilated to contemporary Indian life. And Chaudhuri, in particular, prompts us to ask how that life, in turn, might illuminate Shakespeare's own problematic contexts.

From the beginning, the pedagogic projection of Shakespeare in India was arguably more extensive than the theatrical, if less productive in creative terms. Far more people encountered Shakespeare in print than on stage; and the greater number did so in the original English texts. (This might have been the single biggest curb on creativity.) But, as Rangana Banerjee's account illustrates, the classroom study of Shakespeare led at least certain privileged groups of students to visit the theatre and even launch productions; while yet others worked Shakespeare into their own writings, in English or the vernacular.

These writings were not exclusively dramatic. Received through the page rather than the stage, Shakespeare was identified as a poet *simpliciter* rather than a specifically dramatic poet. Hence his works could activate complex critical exercises, even entire critical discourses. Aniket Jaaware and Urmila Bhirdikar trace the theoretical ramifications of the rich legacy of Marathi translations of Shakespeare. Infusing Shakespearean themes and characters with the concept of *rasa* and other premises of classical Indian theory, the critics cited by Jaaware and Bhirdikar set up an elaborate discourse of not only literary but moral and philosophic import. This indicates how far Shakespeare had penetrated the social and ethical fabric of the Indian 'Renaissance'.

Yet the entire intellectual edifice rests on translations. Marathi has one of the richest Shakespearean legacies of any Indian language, both textual and theatrical. Its translations are the foundation of a much more complex Shakespearean mindscape. Jatin Nayak's essay provides the contrasting picture in Orissa, where translations are few and the Shakespearean context unfamiliar, so that each rendering is a little discursive island of its own. And yet, as Nayak indicates, the translations reflect the evolution of modern Odiya society, and load the Shakespearean rifts with growing social and ideological concerns.

Eight essays can do scant justice to the range and depth of India's engagement with Shakespeare. But they may serve as markers staking out the extent of Shakespearean territory on the subcontinent.

NOTE

1. Thomas Carlyle, On Heroes, Hero-Worship and the Heroic in History (1841; Oxford: Oxford University Press, 1963), 148.

2 Impudent Imperialists: Burlesque and the Bard in Nineteenth-Century India

Poonam Trivedi

It is commonly accepted that the staging of Shakespeare in English in the colonial period in India was an act of showcasing imperial culture. Like the propagation of English literature, the performance of English drama, particularly Shakespeare, was part of the burden of the empire, of the politics of educating and re-forming native society. Shakespeare and English literature were both consciously used as instruments of political control. As Gauri Viswanathan has demonstrated, the formation and development of the very discipline of English literature was predicated on the needs of the empire.[1]

A prime instance of such an exegesis of Shakespeare in the service of the imperial order is to be found in William Miller's collection of lectures entitled *Shakespeare's King Lear and Indian Politics* (1900). In his preface Miller, who was an eminent educationist and Principal of Madras Christian College, feels impelled to point out that "some of the morals with which *Lear* abounds" have "so direct a bearing on the present condition of India." The play, he says, shows "the moral force of love [in] the body politic," and marks how "fatal disorganization is the sure result if force be withdrawn before 'love' [that is, love of common good] has gained sufficient power." Hence the play cannot but be interpreted as "a warning ... against rushing too fast" towards self-rule! He rhetorically cautions that "As plainly as in the days of Lear, the time is upon us when if there be not such transition as he felt to be required, there will be such phenomena as were rising around him, 'in cities, mutinies; in countries, discord.'" Therefore, Shakespeare's view—if the interpretation given to this drama be correct—must regulate this indispensable transition."[2]

On the stage, too, the performance of English drama, whether amateur or professional, carried an intent to instruct, to reform the taste of the natives. Promoting the cause for a public theatre for Indians in Calcutta in 1832, the *Asiatic Journal* affirmed that "the natives thereby will acquire a taste after European luxury, and advance rapidly in civilisation" (pp. 176–7). In 1835, *The Reformer*, a paper run by Indians, remonstrated that "it is high time that our educated countrymen should substitute for the senses as well as the imagination, whilst they inform and instruct the mind, and improve taste in the place of their ancient rude and gross *Cobies* and *jatras* and *nautches* [indigenous performance forms]" (p. 10).

No engagement with English literature and Shakespeare was free of hegemonic pressure. English teachers famed for their elocutionary skills strove to inculcate authentic pronunciation and intonation; declamation contests in which schools and colleges showed off the fruits of their instruction in the "propah" speaking of English became mandatory. The effect of Macaulay's Minute (1835) and Lord Hardinge's resolution of 1844, assuring preference in selection for governmental positions to Indians who had distinguished themselves in European literature, was that a growing middle class undertook to master English literature—and its performance, elocuting, quoting, spectating, and playing was an integral part of this process. A diary entry of 11 November 1841 by Emily Eden, sister of Governor-General Lord Auckland, notes how "the quantities of baboos" who had crowded the theatre in Calcutta to watch *Macbeth* were all "applauding on the backs of their books."[3] Actor-manager Geoffrey Kendal, in his reminiscences of his Shakespearean tours of India in the 1940s and '50s, remarks that "At one time English plays meant everything; unless you could quote Shakespeare you would not get a job."[4]

Hence it follows that English drama, especially Shakespeare, was performed by the English, professionals and amateurs alike, in the prevailing histrionic style of the period, moving from the classical realism of the eighteenth century to a more emotive histrionic realism and greater emphasis on spectacle among the Victorians. Visiting companies of players were a conduit whereby the mode of performance favored in the metropolis was brought to the colony, to be quickly imitated by local amateurs. The yardstick was always that of London theatre, and reviewers commended players by appellations such as "the Garrick of the East," "the Indian Siddons," and "our own Irving." Shakespeare was almost always performed straight, as "high art": there is no evidence of any Shakespeare performance in English, unlike those in the Indian languages, which was adapted or localized, though often it was edited.

It therefore comes as a surprise, as a shock in fact, to discover that the repertory of the Gaiety Theatre in the summer capital of Simla, reputed to be the "Mecca of amateur English theatre abroad,"[5] performed only one Shakespeare play during its entire existence of over a hundred years—and that was in the burlesque form.[6] In the season of 1898, the Simla Amateur Dramatic Company staged *The Merry Merchant of Venice: A Peep at Shakespeare through the Venetians*. What were the upholders of the empire doing, localizing and travestying the Bard in flagrant opposition to the set dictates of the Empire, and that too in the heart of the Empire in the high noon of imperialism? This is the question this essay poses.

The answer foregrounds an often-forgotten fact of nineteenth-century English theatre: that along with the ideological promotion of Shakespeare and the increasing bardolatry, there was a growing popularity of the Shakespeare burlesque. The nineteenth century was, as Richard W. Schoch has put it, the period of the "burlesque backlash," and Shakespearean burlesques were a specially vibrant yet controversial component of the popular theatre of the time.[7] Stanley Wells, in his preface to the five-volume edition of *Nineteenth Century Shakespeare Burlesques*, notes that Shakespeare was a "natural target"[8] and that beginning with the first English travesty, John Poole's *Hamlet Travestie*, in 1810, roughly twice as many Shakespearean burlesques were written between 1840 and 1870 as in the preceding thirty years.[9] The function of the burlesque was as much to expose the "respectable humbug"[10] of bardolatry as to exploit the cultural capital of a canonical author for a range of theatrical and political possibilities. Burlesques appeared, notes Stanley Wells, about the time when greater attention was being paid to the restoration of the original texts and to historical accuracy in costume and design.[11] He also points out that the restrictive monopoly of the two Theatres Royal, in Drury Lane and Covent Garden, for presenting serious plays, continuing as it did from the Restoration till 1843, had created a pressing demand for more spaces for entertainment.[12] This led to subterfuges to evade the monopoly, and instigated new forms of what was called "illegitimate" drama, which could be licensed through loopholes in the law.

"During the same period [the 1830s] and for the same reasons, dramatic forms evolved as a means of evading the regulations," concludes Wells.[13] Operettas, musicals and burlesques of serious drama developed apace: fast-paced and farcical, mocking the serious but providing the added attraction of songs, dances and, later, choric ensembles. Among the plays of Shakespeare, it was the tragedies, histories, and romances which were the main targets of the burlesque, but *The Merchant* acquired the distinction of being the only comedy to become the butt of travesty. This was possibly because, in the nineteenth century, the character of Shylock had been transformed on stage from the comic caricature of the eighteenth century into a dignified and humanized representative of a persecuted race.[14] With its villain/victim dichotomies sharpened, the character of Shylock, as well as the patriarchal obstacles to romantic love, attracted parodic treatment.

From Francis Talfourd's *Shylock or The Merchant of Venice Preserved* (1849), which became very popular with Robson in the lead role and went through several revisions and editions, to John Brougham's *Much Ado about a Merchant of Venice* (1868) which was an equal success in America, to several shorter pieces especially designed for amateur performance, a tradition of the *Merchant* burlesque had developed in both the amateur and the professional theatre, closely resembling the line of *Hamlet* travesties. In the light of this historical recap, it is perhaps less surprising, almost predictable in fact, that amateur theatricals in Simla, providing entertainment to the English in the isolation of the northern hill town, would take recourse to the lighter delight of a Shakespeare burlesque.

However, *The Merry Merchant of Venice*, written and published by F. J. Fraser of the reputed Pioneer Press at Allahabad, India, in 1895, was designed for more than feckless entertainment. Presented in three acts, it used a basic outline of the plot of Shakespeare's *Merchant* to satirize the class-consciousness, affectations, and make-believe of the ruling class and their imitation-English town of Simla. *The Merry Merchant*, composed as a regular and "respectable" travesty in all its features, has ironically been dismissed for what constitutes its uniqueness—its imperial context. John Gross, in his magisterial survey of the complex cultural identities of Shylock, sees it as one of the "low-comedy versions" which keep "cropping up in unlikely places," and simply a "piece of Anglo-Indian fun."[15] Toby Lelyveld, stage historian of Shylock, judges it not "worth the paper" it was printed on, though it "somehow found [its] way to the stage."[16] It has languished virtually unknown and underestimated not only owing to its distance from the metropolitan centre, but also because English amateur theatre in India remains an undocumented and untheorized phenomenon. A burlesque lives in the topicalities and allusions it can fit into the canonical framework, and comes fully alive only in the process of staging. It thus becomes imperative to venture into the territory of the Empire and gloss its localizations, a task that both Gross and Lelyveld eschew.

Before delving into the details of this Indian-English Shakespearean burlesque, it is worth contextualizing the locale, and social and theatrical set-up which gave rise to it. Of all the theatres established in India by the

English, none was more iconic of the Empire than the Gaiety Theatre in the summer capital of Simla. Established in 1887, after the Chowringhee Theatre in Calcutta (1813) and the Gaiety Bombay (1879), it was directly modelled on the London Gaiety (1868), with gothic arches and awnings, and, more significantly, an attached restaurant-cum-club, all geared to providing a leisured social evening. In Simla, however, the Gaiety carried the added inflection of imperial pride: it was located within the new superstructure of the Town Hall, which also housed a library, reading rooms, a ballroom, and a police station—all symbols of civic authority, and most of them, incidentally, still standing today. Designed as a small bijou theatre, its cosiness contributed to its exclusivity. The journal of Lady Dufferin, Vicereine, records:

> it's a very pretty little place ... and is nicely decorated with pink muslin curtains in each box and gold and white paint. We sit near the stage and not only see the play very well, but all the people in the theatre too, which adds to the amusement.[17]

Amateur English theatricals in Simla had, however, been performed at least since 1838, as the letters of Emily Eden record. They were performed on makeshift stages at the residences of the Viceroy and the Commander General, in the large hall of the Assembly Rooms, and at the Royal Hotel (later Lawries and presently Ladies Park Hotel). Of these venues, the frequently used latter two (the Assembly Rooms and Royal Hotel) were situated in the Lower Bazaar, a distinctly lower-middle-class *Indian* section of the town. We are told that it was "always spoken of as being 'down the khud [hillside]'" by the English and called the "Nautch Gurh [dance hall]" by the Indians, and that the owner, "a Mr. Goad, occupied the one box, and in the pride of ownership could look down upon the Viceroy and Commander-in-Chief sitting in the stalls."[18] No wonder special effort was made to include the new Gaiety Theatre in the civic complex of the Town Hall, located on the spacious Mall Road, set high on the ridge, a few yards down from the imposing Christ Church cathedral. The attempt was simultaneously to assert official authority over the social space of the English stage, and to distance it from Indian hoi polloi.

With the establishment of a custom-built theatre, the Simla Amateur Dramatic Club (ADC) began to flourish. Largely comprising army and government officials, it performed to entertain its members as well as the visiting dignitaries of the summer capital, producing as many as twenty different plays during a season which stretched from April to mid-October. Beginning with 20 members, the ADC, after a hundred years of playing in 1936, had 300 on its rolls. Several Viceroys, Lord Lansdowne for instance, encouraged the theatricals, while some like Lord Lytton, who directed his father Bulwer-Lytton's *Walpole* for the ADC, participated in it wholeheartedly. Amateur performance became a seminal social activity in Simla: both a duty and a diversion, simultaneously intellectual, political and frivolous. "Work and play were inextricably mixed up," was the observation of *The Statesman* (13 July 1913) on Simla society, and soon its ADC was known as "the most famous, the oldest and the best equipped amateur club in the world."[19]

Thus the Gaiety Theatre in Simla holds a central place in the social history of the British Raj: it became symbolic of the fun and frolic, as well as the pomp and exclusivity, of British rule in India. If Simla was developed as a miniscule England ("Everything is so English," wrote Val Prinsep in his 1877 journal, "that … one could fancy oneself in Margate"[20]), its theatricals were all the more so. Malcolm Muggeridge, visiting Simla in 1930, found the plays "authentic English productions; designs by Sahibs for Sahibs without reference to any other consideration—not even the Maharajahs."[21] Nestled among the mountain-tops, performance at Simla was not just a 'playing' but a vicarious reliving: As P. H. Denyer, a celebrant of the Gaiety theatre has let slip, "If Simla provided an escape from the heat and a refuge from Indian problems, amateur theatre took audiences for a time out of India."[22] Since Simla was located way up north, away from the frequented path of travelling English theatre companies, few professional groups performed there. They were also discouraged by the ADC, which zealously guarded its privilege of performing at the Gaiety, and was consequently reluctant to let out the theatre to other groups. The ADC was indeed very energetic in devising its own modes of escapism: it reached its peak in the last decade of the nineteenth century, when it performed more than twenty plays in the season. In 1896, the total number of plays was twenty-nine, with a new play each week, some running eleven nights at a stretch. Given the social climate, it is not surprising to find that little serious drama was enacted, least of all Shakespeare.

When the Gaiety Theatre opened on 30 May 1887, a prologue celebrating the past plays and players of the Simla ADC heralded the show. Asserting that "All the world's a stage," the prologue called for renewed attention:

> To-night, let busy man to pleasure spare,
> The hour New Gaiety claims—abandon care. …
> Has not the fate of men and Empires been
> The common business of the tragic scene? …
> Since plays are but the mirrors of our lives, …
> The stage here offers an amusement chaste …[23]

This was countered by a longer prologue, commonly ascribed to Rudyard Kipling, published in the *Civil and Military Gazette* of 9 June 1887 as a riposte to the distinct vein of self-admiration in the opening prologue. Kipling's ironic retort (if it is indeed his) encapsulates the tensions of the social and political ambience of amateur theatre at the Gaiety in Simla in a tongue-in-cheek manner, and is worth quoting at some length:

> For past performances, methinks, 'twere fit
> To let the patient public give the chit,
> Albeit scarce their memory can score,
> Your triumphs since the season "seventy-four"
> When Lytton ruled the roost, and—so it is sung—
> The Empire and the Amateurs were young.
> You, then as now, were Irvings, Baretts, Keans,
> For you the local Stansfield painted scenes.
> The lenient eyes of Marquises and Earls
> Watched, then as now, your not too girlish girls,
> And deftly praised with diplomatic guile
> The high-strung pathos that provoked a smile,
> Survivors of a score of Simla years—
> Hot for fresh praise and panting for fresh cheers—
> Why tell us this? ...
> Yea, these are gone, and Time, the grim destroyer,
> Already blurs their photos in your foyer, ...
> Belaud the past, and in the praise you paste,
> Praise most yourselves—the Perfect and the chaste.
> Why "chaste" amusement? Do our morals fail,
> Amid the deodars of Annandale? ...
> Great Grundy! Does a sober matron sink
> To infamy through rouge and Indian ink?
> Avaunt the thought. As tribute to your taste,
>   WE CERTIFY THE SIMLA STAGE IS CHASTE.
> Mellowed by age, and cold by tempering Time,
> We find it venerable and sublime. ...
> The audience, not the actors, judge the play, ...
> Who said not "Time will tell" but "Time hath told."[24]

Just as the life and the characters of Simla have been immortalized by Rudyard Kipling in his *Plain Tales from the Hills*, the frivolities and the smugness of the

Simla stage, too, appear to have been exposed by his pungent irony. Kipling was a frequent visitor to Simla during this time as a correspondent of the *Civil and Military Gazette* and the *Pioneer* from 1882 to 1889; he acted as Brisemouche in *A Scrap of Paper*, as did his sister Mrs Fleming in *Lucia di Lammermoor*.

The plays produced at the Simla Gaiety reflect the social mood: farces, satires, comedies, melodramas and musicals, rarely serious drama, and Shakespeare only as burlesque. Simla theatricals are important precisely because they have no Shakespeare: the absence of canonical drama underscoring the position of the theatre as an instrument of cultural showcasing. In Simla, where the English performed primarily for the amusement of other English people, there was little imperative, it seems, for performing and projecting high culture like Shakespeare. The civilizing mission of canonical English literature could be suspended and the unofficial popular stream hold sway: when the guard was off, the colonials could be philistines all. The only known instance of a straight Shakespeare production in Simla, that too in scenes and tableaux termed "a series of representations,"[25] is an open-air *A Midsummer Night's Dream* scheduled at Peterhoff (residence of the Viceroy prior to the Residency, later that of the Commander General of the Armed Forces), which had to be transferred to the ballroom at the Town Hall due to inclement weather. As it was not scheduled at the Gaiety, this was clearly not an ADC production but a charity performance for hospitals in the hills. The only Shakespeare production listed in the *Centenarian*, the record of the hundred years of the Simla ADC, and for which any archival evidence is available, is in the popular burlesque form: *The Merry Merchant of Venice* of June 1898.

As a matter of fact, contrary to the official image of the Simla ADC as the most representative English repertory, burlesques, which were the staple of all amateur clubs, were specially favoured by the ADC too. Lieut.-Col. Newnham-Davis, who has left an account of his personal involvement with the ADC in the 1890s, recalls that:

> a burlesque, put upon the stage regardless of expense, became one of the events of the season; the fairest of Capua's daughters sang in the chorus; and the art of stage-dancing was much cultivated. Elaborate scenic effects were attempted, and one at least of the burlesques played almost as long on its *premiere* as a Drury Lane pantomime does.[26]

He also names a Major Hobday with whom burlesques sprang into prominence, because he could not only write very witty doggerel but was also a clever burlesque actor.

Hence this burlesque Shakespeare, crafted for the Indian English stage, though belonging to the unofficial "Not Shakespeare" stream, was nevertheless true equally to the conventions of the genre, to the company performing it, and to the location embracing it. As lengthy as other, better-known *Merchant* travesties, but more light-hearted, it maintained all the characters and plot outline, taking care to work in the familiar features even as it localized them to the setting of the Indian summer capital. It therefore added more choric songs and dances than the others, along with solos and duets; jettisoned most of the original text, instead using rhymed couplets in parody; set the soliloquies as songs; and introduced a lot of stage business, gags and relentless puns. Not only did it contemporize and transpose the high into the low, but with its polished staging—complete with special effects and live musical accompaniment by the Viceroy's own band—it more than lived up to its subtitle of a "burlesque extravaganza."[27]

The most telling evidence of this Indian/English *Merchant* travesty being in tune with the "mainstream" conventions of the burlesque was that Shylock, as in nearly all early Victorian burlesques of the *Merchant*, was cast as the popular stereotype of the old clothes merchant, who was simultaneously a moneylender and a pawnbroker.[28] He thus became simultaneously a familiar figure, called "Uncle" (1), to the non-official English of moderate means, characterized as the "Indigent Venetians" in the play, who would do anything to gatecrash into Simla high society. His shop displayed the pawnbroker's representative sign of three brass balls over it; he was dressed like all such Shylocks in a long black or brown cloak, tattered hose, three black hats on his head and an "old clo' bag" over his shoulder. He was also meant to have a large nose and a straggling black beard—in all respects true to the type of the Jew in the travesty tradition. There were other instances of borrowing too: as in John Brougham's *Much Ado about a Merchant of Venice*,[29] Antonio was gay and sportive, but here plump and pleasing too, a merry but feckless merchant, who throws out coins to the "indigent Venetians." (In Brougham, he is a compulsive gambler who goes broke and pawns his flesh for himself.) Like Brougham's Americanized version which saw the interpolation of references to "dollars," "Wall Street" (88), "Chicago" (108), "Philadelphia" (112), and so on, the *Merry Merchant* was peppered with Hindustani words and Anglo-Indian usage and references to add flavour to the localization: for example, "p[a]isa" (5), "ek dum" (7), "mitha panis" (8), "chowkidar" (16), "shikared" (20), "bobajees" (20), "katcherry" (21), "gymkhana" (21), "aichi bat" (23), "tiffin-time" (26), along with references to the "Calcutta Turf Club" (14), "Comp'ny John" (20), "Allahabad" (26), and even a whole song which

1 *The Merry Merchant of Venice* (June 1898): the "Mounted Mashers" chorus with Jessica on the left played by the author F. J. Fraser. Photo courtesy the ADC, Gaiety Theatre, Simla.

celebrated the mood of "Kaiko ne?" "Kiswaste ne?" [Why not? Wherefore not?] (23–4). Bassanio, appropriately in the context, was an army subaltern of exceptional romantic fervour in the new "Mounted Mashers" unit (see Figure 1), and Portia a Venetian heiress whose fate, in the clubbing society of Simla, was to be raffled—a thousand tickets at three ducats each—and for whom Bassanio needs to raise a loan to buy the entire lot of raffle tickets. He induces his cousin the merry merchant, Antonio, to borrow the 3,000 ducats from Shylock, and the fatal bond is signed as "a jokelet of the Jew" (12). Talfourd's version too has Shylock making a "merry covenant" (117) for a pound of flesh,[30] while the De Witt shorter sketch has Shylock express similar glee (in Germanic accent): "One pound—cut from your breast / You see, my tears, I like a little chest!" (7).[31]

The test of a burlesque is also in its timeliness and topicality, and the writer, F. J. Fraser, drew on Simla gossip for his material. A dialogue on the difficulties of an Amateur Dramatic Club, again reworking a burlesque convention that highlighted the financial constraints of small theatre groups (as also articulated in the "Argument" of the De Witt sketch), was added early in the play. It exposed some home truths in an amusing manner:

— ADC ? …What's that?…
— A society for clothing the poor. … Next year we are going to have all our plays specially written to suit us. …
— How?
— Well, in each play there are to be twenty principal female parts and each of the twenty lady actresses concerned will have the stage to herself for at least half an hour and a chance of shedding real crocodile tears. … They will be given carte blanche to buy whatever they want in the way of dresses, opera cloaks, fur, fans, feathers, gloves, shoes and stockings.[32]

Songs on the susceptibilities of Simla society provided identifiable targets: Jessica, "Shylock's little lamb" played by the writer Fraser himself, who runs an ice-cream cart because her father does not give her enough money, asks "What sort of season is it going to be?" A smart sergeant replies, "Oh! Just the usual thing! A deal of flirtation and no results." Jessica then quips that Papa should take her to Mussoorie where "there are no ADCs [Amateur Dramatic Clubs, but also the aides-de-camp performing in them] to break an inexperienced girl's heart!"[33] Since the Army had been active in running the Amateur Dramatic Club in Simla, the burlesque had its share of military camp humour too: "A bit like It Ain't half hot Mum!" noted the *Civil and Military*

Gazette in its review of 23 June, 1898, and quoted the following exchange as an example:

> *Bass*: (Aside to Sergeant) Sergeant, what am I to do? I find I have left the Drill Book at home by mistake.
>
> *Serg*: Never mind sir! I am accustomed to help the officers through the parade. You keep near me sir!
>
> *Bass*: Thanks awfully. Now if an anti-Jew riot or a cow-killing row really does take place, what are we to do, and what will my words of command be?
>
> *Serg*: [echoing Dogberry and Verges!] Anything but "Fire" sir! Especially if it be serious.[34]

The mockery of the officers was offset by a duet giving the Subaltern his due, describing the adventures of the Subaltern's heart in a hill station, coping with the ways and manners of the married Captains, the wicked Majors, and the choleric General (9).[35] Other topical allusions included a duet "That shouldn't be done in Simla" references to the races at Annandale and people's obsession with gaming (22),[36] and frequent mention of the club as the centre of social life, entertainment, and gossip (6, 16, 18, 22).

The love stories were handled in a typically comic and breezy manner, critiquing Shakespeare's own patriarchal attitudes as well as the snobbery and restrictions of nineteenth-century Simla: Nerissa functioned as a chaperone, intervening in the first Portia-Bassanio duet and dance, to prevent people from talking and to remind Portia of her father's will (see Figure 2). In Act II in Belmont, she interviews and tries to dissuade six sighing swains who still hold tickets for the Portia lottery. Bassanio finally buys them off for a slight consideration, only to be told by Portia, "You should have offered Simla prices as a proof of the depth of your affection."[37] Another convention of the burlesque was the ludicrous enactment of classic scenes: the casket test was here turned into a raffle. Shylock too has a ticket and runs for the draw. Portia, blindfolded, pulls out number 99, declares it a mistake and inverts it to 66— Bassanio's number (14–15)! Jessica's elopement occasions a serenade, a duet, and a dance *en deshabille*: Lorenzo, Portia's family lawyer with a penchant for the turf, sings "Who's that a snoring?" (16), after which Jessica descends from her window in very light clothing and her hair in curl papers. The two have time to dance before disappearing in a gondola (17–18).

Shylock returns from the club where he has been dining off Brother Jacob— he is a "professional diner-out" too in this burlesque, a "sponge who may be had for 'ball or rout'" (18) and not entirely an outsider to Simla society. But

2 *The Merry Merchant of Venice* (June 1898): Portia and Bassanio. Photo courtesy of the ADC, Gaiety theatre, Simla.

when he sees the rope dangling from Jessica's window, he believes he has been burgled and his daughter murdered. He shouts for the police, but the neighbours rush in to loot "And empty Uncle's shop" (19) in a choric song and dance. While the portrayal of Shylock in *The Merry Merchant* has its share of the "amalgam of farce and pathos" which Michael Shapiro identifies as characteristic of the burlesqued Jews,[38] in comparison with the other travesties, here he is made less vengeful though much more mocked at. The play has been critiqued for its "offensive anti-semitism representing a nadir in late-Victorian Shakespearean burlesque."[39] And while Shylock is abused—called "vile old thief," "old spider," "oily Jew," a "bounder both by birth and education" (4–5), and so on—as in the other travesties, in this he is also ducked in the canal, robbed of his goods and then almost lynched by the choric mob at the end. Yet, he is saved and by the women: Jessica turns up at the right moment and rescues her father from being tarred and feathered by the mob on the directive of the Duke. Portia, who has earlier thwarted his revenge by not allowing Shylock to cut any "inch of fat" along with his pound of flesh, an impossible task given that the corpulent Antonio was "nothing but fat" ... "As fat as butter," as Shylock protests (26), in the end she directs the "quality of mercy" towards Antonio and asks him to forgive the Jew as her fee for saving him—which is spontaneously granted (see Figure 3). Shylock's behaviour in court was a simple comic revenge without malice—"Give me my pound of flesh" (26) and "Give me the ducats, dear" (27)—and he is given no last words of lingering animosity. So there is an ending of "Loving reconciliations all around" (27). Reconciliations at the end were the norm in the *Merchant* travesties, though they often left a touch of the Shakespearean as in Talfourd, with Shylock's confession to the audience: "Although reformed at present, you perhaps / May find him not unwilling to relapse" (150). *The Merry Merchant*, instead, touched a new chord of unequivocal harmonization, turning the mockery into sympathy and, with the revenge forgotten, forgiveness all around. The challenge of infusing a comic caricature with a humanized pathos was for the amateur actors considerable, and the reviews reflect this difficulty. Some reviewers noted how the actor's "attempted imitation of Irving and Beerbohm Tree was feeble" and that he raved and ranted too much even for a burlesque.[40] Others found that though the actor had introduced Shylock as a "raving melodramatic personage" he refined it afterwards into a more acceptable piece of burlesque acting.[41] What is also worth further consideration is why this Indian English burlesque should wish to portray complete unquestioned harmony at the end? Was it because it was scripted for performance not in the "illegitimate" theatres but in official ones of a ruling elite where escapism and fantasy were the norm?

3 *The Merry Merchant of Venice* (June 1898): Portia in lawyer's robes. Photo courtesy the ADC, Gaiety Theatre, Simla.

The reviews in *The Pioneer* (22 June 1898) and the *Civil and Military Gazette* (23 June 1898) particularly commended the music, choric songs, and dances, especially the *pas de deux* between Pierrot and Pierrette—all essential components of a burlesque. But it was the scenery and the representation of Venice at night, with the illuminated Grand Canal in the carnival scene, that stole the show. In terms of its full stage-effect, *The Merry Merchant* came through more as a burlesque musical extravaganza than as a travesty, a subgenre that was rapidly on the rise at the end of the century. As the reviewer of the *Simla News* (23 June 1898) summed up: "many a true word was spoken in jest ... and though it is rather difficult in these burlesques sometimes to hit the happy medium, ... the author seems to have succeeded in this one."

Though the popularity of burlesques was conditioned by their greater suitability for the amateur stage, befitting the "lesser lights" among actors, the few surviving photographs of this production reveal not just the elaborate costumes and sets, the striking tableaux and statuesque stances, but, most of all, the superb confidence of the performers living up to their reputation of the best amateur club, for whom nothing was too low or too high (see Figure 4). Its reputation was validated by the Viceroy Lord Curzon, no less, who complimented the Simla ADC in a farewell speech in October 1905, as one which "vainly endeavours to conceal the genius of the professional under the guise of the amateur."[42] Yet, in parodying the colonial book, these impudent amateurs of the Simla ADC, the very custodians of the cultural and political empire, turned the mighty bard to an in-joke, at the expense of the "empire of letters." Were they not in danger of turning the entire colonial educational enterprise on its head? The populist contestation of bardolatry by the Shakespearean burlesque at the centre could be more disruptive in the colonies, where the nationalist deployment of the poet was more openly promoted.

The recovery of the configuration of this event for the first time, through a gleaning of newspaper notices and reviews, is significant, as there is little surviving evidence of amateur English theatricals of the colonial period. It constitutes a singular moment of popular culture's contestation of the canonical at the very nerve centre of the Indian empire, where, unlike at the ruling centre in London, authority was all in all. It would, however, still remain a curiosity, a mere blip on the colonial radar, were it not for what Linda Hutcheon terms the "transformational potential" of parody which can never be permanently fixed or defined.[43] The fact that *The Merry Merchant* was printed before it was performed indicates that the writer intended it for audiences beyond that of the Simla Gaiety. The *Civil and Military Gazette* of 23 June 1898 notes that the play has had 35 performances. It surely must have received many more—written as

4   *The Merry Merchant of Venice* (June 1898): the full cast. Note Shylock at his shop window (*top right*) and the three brass balls of the pawnbroker's sign (*top middle*). Photo courtesy ADC, Gaiety Theatre, Simla.

a garrison play, it would have been a hot favourite in the circuit of cantonment theatres which stretched across the country from Umballa (Ambala) in the north to Barrackpore in the east, and from Mhow in the west to Pune in the south. Lelyveld's and Gross' summaries and hasty dismissals of the play erase both its local function of critique and its impact on the Indian theatrical scene. English theatre in India was not a mere outpost of the Empire but its extension, exhibiting the same tendencies and fashions. Much of what was happening at the centre was being replicated at the Indian margin, in not just the legitimate but also the "illegitimate" theatre. Modern Indian theatre, which developed largely in imitation of the Western, absorbed all these several tendencies, the hegemonic as well as the popular. Elite Indians—Maharajas and a few civil servants—had the privilege of attending the Gaiety performances.

Further, amateur theatre in Simla was not confined to the English alone. The legion of Indian officers and clerks, who worked for the English summer capital of Simla, had their imaginations, too, caught by the spell of amateur dramatics. Officialdom encouraged mimicry and the formation of dramatic clubs amongst them. Simla Municipal Records show that the first such club, of the "Babus of Government House," was formed in 1893. Soon several other communities set up their own clubs, and on 26 August 1926 a letter in *The Tribune* informs us that "Within a short span of three years, about ten Indian Amateur Dramatic Clubs have sprung up here and, it is reported, that people vie with one another in trying to secure the enviable appointment of secretary to any of these clubs." The Simla ADC at the Gaiety was singularly instrumental in the formation of a playing and playgoing culture amongst the middle class in north India.

The ramifications of this populist amateur English theatrical practice and repertoire, and its mimicry by the Indians, may be seen in the early Indian performances of Shakespeare. These were commonly broad adaptations, almost always with songs and dances written in. A convergence of several lines of influence may be traced: adaptation was intrinsic to indigenous literary culture, as was song and dance in the theatre. But can it not be asserted that their presence in the Indian proscenium theatre received a fillip through the musical burlesque extravaganzas of the Gaiety kind? For instance, in 1915 two musical versions of *The Merchant of Venice* in Bengali, *Sonay Sohaga* and *Saodagar*, with many songs and dances, are known to have been written and performed. In western India, the Parsi, Marathi, and Gujarati theatres had been staging musical adaptations of Shakespeare since the 1860s, among which an adaptation of *Cymbeline* as *Tara* and another of *The Winter's Tale* (both in Marathi), were very popular. In Gujarati, *Saubhagya Sundari* (Blessed

Wife Sundari), a loose amalgam of *Othello*, *Cymbeline*, *As You Like It*, and *Twelfth Night*, acquired such abiding popularity that its main actor and female impersonator, Jayashankar, took on the name of "Sundari"—the Desdemona of the play—as his stage name. The Urdu *Dil Farosh* (1900) by Agha Hashr was a successful Parsi theatre adaptation of the *Merchant*. Though the early Indian adaptations did not consciously parody Shakespeare, several of their amalgamated and hybrid versions were rejected by Indian critics as "travesties" of Shakespeare. Adaptation and burlesque can be seen to function as sliding positions on the same scale.

Stanley Wells refers to *The Merry Merchant* as an example of a burlesque whose obscurity increased in relation to its distance from the metropolitan centre.[44] With a post-colonial intervention, it is possible to relocate to centre stage this neglected but localized "Indian" Shakespeare burlesque. Its performance record allows us to glimpse another more popular stream of Shakespeare performance in English in India, inspired by the theatre of the London Gaiety which, at the close of the nineteenth century, had become the pre-eminent theatre for the burlesque.

The irony of this theatrical and literary genealogy is that the popular vulgarized Shakespeare seems to have bred more offspring than the legitimate. As Stanley Wells reminds us, Shakespeare burlesques "need to be read with an open mind ... they tell us something about their time."[45] Can we not apply the same caveats to our estimation of the early Indian adaptations, which have so far, usually, been derided as "murder most foul"?

NOTES

1. Gauri Viswanathan, *Masks of Conquest: Literary Study and British Rule in India* (New York: Columbia University Press, 1989).
2. William Miller, *Shakespeare's King Lear and Indian Politics* (Madras: G. A. Natesan, 1900), 86–7, 91, 100, 105, and 90–91 respectively.
3. Emily Eden, *Letters From India* (London: Richard Bentley, 1872), 264 5.
4. Geoffrey Kendal, *Shakespeare Wallah* (London: Sidgwick and Jackson, 1986), 161.
5. Lt Col. Newnham-Davis, "Amateurs in Foreign Parts," in *Amateur Clubs and Actors*, ed. W. G. Elliot (London: Edward Arnold, 1898), 221.
6. For an account of the Simla ADC, see P. H. Denyer, *The Centenarian, being a summary of the history of Simla amateur theatricals during the past 100 years* (Simla: Liddells, 1937).
7. Richard W. Schoch, *Not Shakespeare: Bardolatry and Burlesque in the Nineteenth Century* (Cambridge: Cambridge University Press, 2002), 3
8. Stanley Wells, ed., Preface to *Nineteenth Century Burlesques* (London: Diploma Press, 1978), vol. 1, vii.

9. Wells, Introduction to *Nineteenth Century Burlesques*, vol. 3, 52.
10. *Westminster Review*, 18 (1833): 35, quoted by Schoch, 3.
11. Wells, Introduction, vol. 1, xiii.
12. Wells, Introduction, vol. 2, x.
13. Ibid.
14. For the stage history of the play, see James Bulman, *The Merchant of Venice: Shakespeare in Performance* (Manchester: Manchester University Press, 1991).
15. John Gross, *Shylock: A Legend and Its Legacy* (New York: Simon and Schuster, 1992), 220.
16. Toby Lelyveld, *Shylock on the Stage* (Cleveland, OH: The Press of Western Reserve University, 1960), 119.
17. Quoted in Pat Barr and Ray Desmond, *Simla: A Hill Station in British India* (Delhi: B. R. Publishing Corporation, and London: Scolar Press, 1978), 34.
18. Newnham-Davis, 222.
19. Denyer, 20.
20. Quoted by Pamela Kanwar, *Imperial Simla: The Political Culture of the Raj* (Delhi: Oxford University Press, 1990), 1
21. Ibid.
22. Denyer, 10.
23. Edward J. Buck, Simla Past and Present (Calcutta: Thacker, Spink and Co., 1904), 141–2.
24. Ibid., 142–3.
25. Newnham-Davis, 228. Incidentally, Capt. Newnham-Davis was the stage manager for this production.
26. Ibid., 224.
27. F. J. Fraser, *The Merry Merchant of Venice: A Peep at Shakespeare Through the Venetians* (Allahabad: The Pioneer Press, 1895). All citations from this edition, given in the text hereafter.
28. Michael Shapiro traces the roots and development of this type in "Shylock the Old Clothes Man: Victorian Burlesques of The Merchant of Venice," in *Shakespeare's World / World Shakespeares*, ed. Richard Fotheringham, Christa Jansohn, and R. S. White (Newark: University of Delaware Press, 2008), 119–29.
29. John Brougham, *Much Ado about a Merchant of Venice* (New York: Samuel French, n.d.), reprinted in Wells, vol. 5.
30. Francis Talfourd, *Shylock, or the Merchant of Venice Preserved* (London: Thomas Hailes Lacy, 1860), reprinted in Wells, vol. 3.
31. *The (Old Clothes) Merchant of Venice or The Young Judge and Old Jewry, A Burlesque Sketch For the Drawing Room* (New York: De Witt's Acting Plays, no. 331, n.d.).
32. Since burlesques encouraged interpolation of topical names and references, this was an ad-libbed dialogue reported in the review in I, 22 June 1898.
33. Ibid.
34. Several ad-libbed changes from the text in this dialogue, including the last line: as reported in *The Pioneer*, 22 June 1898.
35. Again, this seems to have been added in the Simla Gaiety production, as reported in *The Pioneer*, 22 June 1898.
36. Programme, Simla Gaiety production.

37. Ad-libbed interpolation as reported in the review in the *Civil and Military Gazette*, 23 June 1898
38. Shapiro, 127
39. Jacob Solomon, "Dramatic Burlesques of Shakespeare in Great Britain before 1900" (PhD thesis, University of Pennsylvania, 1975), quoted by Wells, vol. IV, xxiv.
40. *Simla News*, 23 June 1898.
41. *The Pioneer*, 22 June 1898.
42. Denyer, 19.
43. Linda Hutcheon, *Theory of Parody: The Teaching of Twentieth Century Forms* (New York: Methuen, 1985), 20.
44. Wells, Introduction, vol. 4, xxii.
45. Ibid., xxiii.

3 "Every college student knows by heart": The Uses of Shakespeare in Colonial Bengal

Rangana Banerji

I

"Everyone has Shakespeare at home; everyone may open the original text and read it." This extraordinary claim offers a clue to the ubiquitous and universal presence of Shakespeare in Bengal's cultural sphere in the nineteenth century. The remark [in translation] was part of an essay entitled *Shakuntala, Miranda and Desdemona*, authored by Bankimchandra Chattopadhyay (Chatterjee) in 1876. The first formal educational institution on a Western pattern in Calcutta (indeed in Asia), the Hindu College, had been established in 1817, and the University of Calcutta instituted forty years later in 1857. Bankimchandra[1] was amongst the first graduates of the university, taking the BA examination in 1858, for which English was compulsory and an entire paper had been set on *Macbeth*. In the nineteenth century, Shakespeare had been synonymous with the sphere of learning, connoting knowledge, humanity, modernity and exceptional linguistic ability. This essay is concerned with tracing some of the uses to which Shakespearean play-texts were put: pedagogy, entertainment, and the adoption of combative stances by colonial subjects or subalterns.

The spread of educational institutions on the Western model—the various schools, colleges and finally universities in India under British domination—witnessed an astonishing demand for Shakespearean studies. Shakespeare came like a sweetened pill, administering the right dose of morality mixed with a heady draught of universal human nature, resulting in visions of equality and modernity that young Bengali men were only too eager to consume.

Shakespeare came to constitute the coming-of-age of entire generations, since the plays were positioned like rites of passage at the doorway of adulthood.

The politics behind the enthroning of Shakespeare in the college classroom may be glibly explained as a typically "neutral" state apparatus installed by the farsighted colonial powers to keep insurgency in check. The curricular choice in favour of Shakespeare was dictated by the fact that the Bible was feared as a pedagogic tool by the government, which had no wish to offend the religious sentiments of the governed population. Various imperial milestones—for example, Charles Grant's *Observations*, the Charter Act of 1813, Macaulay's Minute and Bentinck's Resolution dated 7 March 1835—mark the road to the establishment of English or Western education in Bengal. By 1835, despite initial official apathy, Western education had been set on a firm footing through the efforts of missionaries and progressive Bengalis alike. We must not lose sight of the economic advantage accruing from English education, along with the more scholarly desire of acquiring the dominant language and literature that paved the way for scripting an astonishing success story of Shakespearean studies.

The rise of educational institutions in Bengal was concomitant with the rise of biographical, historical and psychological studies of Shakespeare's plays. D. L. Richardson, one of the gifted teachers of the newly instituted discipline of English Literature at the Hindu College, was instrumental in deciding the centrality of Shakespeare within the boundaries of the new discipline. In Richardson's *Selections From The British Poets: From The Time Of Chaucer To The Present Day* (1840),[2] the first textbook or anthology of English literary texts in these parts that is justly famous, Shakespeare jostles for space with all the other great English poets. In these early stages of canon formation, it is Richardson's teaching methods, rather than the textbook prepared by him, that seems to have tilted the balance in favour of the Bard. We will investigate later how the techniques and methods employed in analysing the plays helped Bengali youth rediscover issues like race, religion, culture or gender (in the sense of construction of male or female subjects). The ideals of the Enlightenment and notions of rational, scientific advance, bringing in its wake material progress, combined with inspired teaching by the likes of Henry Louis Vivian Derozio and Richardson to contribute to the identity formation of educated young men. Partha Chattopadhyay argues for the transformation of the "spiritual" or "inner" domain through the efforts of these Western-educated Bengali men, that later brought the desired effects of a political or "nationalist" transformation in the "outer" domain of the emergent national state.[3]

An outline of nineteenth-century pedagogic practices is necessary at this stage, before we can focus on the social impact of Shakespeare's plays. The University of Calcutta was instituted in 1857; the first batch of students wrote the BA examination in 1858. The BA course was structured with five components in the following manner *c.* 1860:[4]

- Languages: English was compulsory. Students had to appear for another language out of Greek, Latin, Hebrew, Arabic, Persian, Sanskrit, Bengali, Oriya, Hindi, Urdu, and Burmese
- History
- Mathematics And Natural Philosophy
- Physical Sciences
- Mental And Moral Sciences

If a candidate passed the BA in the first division within five years of passing the Entrance Examination, he was eligible to be examined at the Honours level. On obtaining Honours in any one or more of the five above-mentioned components of study, he was eligible to join the MA course and obtain the degree without further examination or fee. But both were necessary for candidates from other Indian universities, or from universities in Britain.

So far as Shakespearean texts in the syllabi are concerned, Shakespeare was studied at the BA and higher levels. Earlier, at the Entrance and FA (First Arts) levels, common authors included Scott, Milton, Pope, Dryden, Addison, Bacon, Cowper, and Beattie. Only one Shakespearean play was prescribed for close textual study at the BA level, and this was changed every year. The chart below attests to the range of the selection.

1858	*Macbeth*
1859	–
1860	*Julius Caesar*
1861	*King Lear*
1862	*Macbeth*
1863	*Coriolanus*
1864	*Hamlet*
1865	*The Merchant of Venice*
1866	*Othello*
1867	*The Tempest*

At the Honours level, the Shakespearean component consisted of two plays: for example, *Henry IV*, Part I and *Macbeth* in 1864. Barring the first year, when the candidates faced an entire paper on *Macbeth* at the BA level, the paper on Poetry included questions from the prescribed Shakespearean text.

The examination questions being extant, we can form an idea of the in-depth knowledge demanded by the tough standard set by the examiners. Questions were set on the source, on the evidence for dating the play, on characterization and on comprehension, and included passages for explication. For instance, "O what a noble mind is here o'erthrown …" from *Hamlet* (3.1. 153)[5] was set for explanation in 1864. Also included were questions testing the candidate's knowledge of Elizabethan word-usage, like this example on *Coriolanus* in the 1863 BA Examination:

> Explain Shakespeare's use of the following words:
> disgrace   gird   crack   delay   attended
> rapture   misery fond   flaw

Other questions related to textual criticism, taking up well-known emendations and alternative readings. Thus on *Macbeth* in the BA Examination of 1862:

> "Though <u>bladed</u> corn be lodged". What is to be understood by the term bladed, and what emendation has been suggested by the apparent impropriety of the epithet?

In university examinations, the student's grasp over grammar and idiom was tested in every language studied, and English was no exception in this respect.

Sometimes we are startled by the stress on knowledge of the biographical, social and historical background pertaining to Shakespeare, my favourite being the following evidence of a historicist perspective from the BA Examination of 1862:

> It has been asserted that Shakespeare must have received a legal education. On what circumstances is this opinion based? Quote, or refer to, any passages in the play of Macbeth which might be thought to support it.

More commonly, students were expected to construct full-length character studies of favourite characters like Hamlet. That Romantic criticism in the shape of Coleridge and Schlegel formed part of the "horizon of expectations" for mid-century Bengali readers of Shakespeare, we know from the questions set on *Macbeth* in 1858:

i) Shew by an accurate comparison the truth of Schlegel's remark that, in the progress of action, Macbeth is altogether the reverse of Hamlet.

ii) In what words of the Porter-Scene does Coleridge recognise the certain hand of Shakspere [*sic*]? The same words occur in Hamlet, and the same idea in All's Well, &c; quote the lines in both these dramas.

Bankimchandra had appeared for the above-mentioned paper. Whether he had prior acquaintance with Coleridge on Shakespeare, or was alerted to its presence in the examination hall, we do not know. What we know for certain is that, drawing upon Coleridge's analogy with the other arts, he not only made a similar remark in the essay on Shakespearean drama referred to above, but he reversed the analogy:

Shakuntala is a painter's creation; Desdemona a sculptor's construction, lifelike. Desdemona's heart is completely bared and expanded to us. Shakuntala's is expressed through hints only.[6]

The remark is reminiscent of Coleridge's lecture on *The Tempest*, where, while comparing Greek drama with Shakespearean drama, we find the following assertion: "The Shakespearian drama and the Greek drama might be compared to painting & statuary."[7] The comparison, critics say, is almost certainly derived from Schlegel, but whether Bankim was aware of the source is beside the point. He recalled the analogy in the 1876 essay on *Shakuntala, Miranda and Desdemona*, an essay that has won him plaudits for inaugurating comparative literary studies in India.

In this essay, the cultural difference behind the production and appreciation of plays by Shakespeare and Kalidasa is foregrounded by Bankimchandra. The location from which he is indulging in such literary estimates makes Bankim particularly alert to the value he is inscribing in Shakespearean texts. As texts produced by the dominant culture and disseminated by its educational institutions, *The Tempest* and *Othello* are stamped with critical approval. But the superior/inferior binary opposition between Shakespeare's and Kalidasa's texts almost collapses when, by focussing on the creation of feminine subjectivity in different cultural matrices, he claims for the indigenous play-text a certain inherent strength. The strategy adopted by Bankim is to claim the private sphere of desires and affections as equal in status in the two cultures reflected in the plays under discussion.

Secure in the claim of equality, Bankim does not hesitate to point out what he considers a defect in Shakuntala's characterization by Victorian standards:

her coyness mixed with artfulness. He takes pains to point out that the contrast between the trusting openness of Miranda and the cunning hide-and-seek in Shakuntala is not simply due to the difference in cultures or countries of their production. "It is not as though Shakuntala is shy because she is of this land, or that Miranda and Juliet, being shameless English girls, open their hearts."[8] He ascribes the contrast to the different contexts producing such behaviour: Shakuntala, unlike Miranda, is a hermit's daughter: a sport or brief dalliance with the king, and she is obscured by Dushyanta, "a mere lotus in an elephant's snout."[9] Stressing the artistic excellence of Kalidasa, Bankim adds: "The creator of Shakuntala is in no way inferior to the poet of *The Tempest*."[10]

Later in the same essay, influenced no doubt by the Aristotelian valorization of tragedy so common in his age, he finds faults with the characterization of Shakuntala. Now she is found wanting when compared with Desdemona's fortitude in the face of humiliation and desertion by her husband. The comparison is between two disparate entities, "the ocean with the garden," drama with narrative poetry. Bankim goes on to dismiss both Kalidasa's creation and *The Tempest* as beautiful narrative romances: "Desdemona's characterization reaches a completeness that Miranda's and Shakuntala's do not."[11]

Shakuntala's reactions are brought out indirectly, through hints (though we might argue that Shakespeare too leaves us with plenty of such in-built stage directions)—often in speeches by other characters, while no hints are employed in portraying the real distress of Desdemona. Without concerning ourselves with the accuracy or inaccuracy of such insights by Bankimchandra, we may briefly review the scene in contemporary Bengal to discover what facilitated the appearance of such an estimate. The essay betrays the long-held notion that Shakespearean tragedies are the parameters by which all drama should be judged.

II

Theatres multiply like mushrooms

The acting of Shakespearean scenes, or even entire plays, had become a rage amongst Westernized Bengali youth. As an early occurrence of theatre on the Western model, we find the simultaneous staging of scenes from *Julius Caesar* and Bhavabhuti's *Uttararamacharit* (translated into English by H. H. Wilson) at Prasanna Kumar Tagore's "Hindu Theatre" in 1831. Shakespearean drama then took off in a big way, while the staging of indigenous plays was neglected. Thus, in the Bengali newspaper *Samachar Chandrika* of 9 February 1857, we come across a lament that contemporary students show reverence for English drama but not at all for Sanskrit or Bengali plays: "Every year, students put up performances of the famous English poet Shakespeare's plays, but no one attempts anything similar in Bengali."[12] This observation on the current dramatic scene in Bengal comes in the wake of another memorable comment by Jatindramohan Tagore. In a letter to Michael Madhusudan Dutt, he had observed, "Now theatres are mushrooming all over our country."[13]

The large-scale growth of theatres is closely linked to the syllabi and pedagogy of the new educational institutions in Bengal on the Western model. The plays were also performed by students at annual concerts, and records exist to show that the students of Drummond's Dhurrumtollah Academy were reciting selected passages from Shakespeare in 1822. "A boy of the name Derozio gave a good conception of Shylock," we are told.[14] (Later, Derozio became a teacher at the Hindu College and also a poet, penning a couple of sonnets on Shakespeare among other things.) From 1827 onwards, the tradition of enacting scenes from Shakespearean plays began at the Hindu College. Entire plays were performed by amateur companies composed of students of other schools in Calcutta, like the performance of *Julius Caesar* in 1852 at the Metropolitan Academy. This tradition continued unabated through the nineteenth century.

We are lucky to possess information about the teaching of Shakespeare from reminiscences of the alumni of such institutions. Rajnarain Bose, alumnus of Hindu college, gives us details of the final-year syllabus.[15] Students in the final year or the "First Class" read *Macbeth*, *King Lear*, *Othello*, and *Hamlet*, in addition to texts by Bacon, Milton, Pope, Gray, and Young. Bose admitted that, although he was astounded by the powers of Shakespeare and Milton, his love was reserved for Spenser, Thomson, and Byron. Bose also passes on to us anecdotes about the teaching of Shakespeare by D. L. Richardson, the famous successor to Derozio at the Hindu College. Macaulay is said to have remarked that he could forget everything about his Indian sojourn, except for Richardson's reading of Shakespeare.

Richardson's gloss on "hoar leaves" in *Hamlet* 4.7.139 demonstrates how closely the texts were read in class. He is said to have explained that since leaves are reflected in water from below, the colour is "hoar" and not green. We have noticed this kind of close reading earlier in conjunction with the questions set at Calcutta University. Richardson was an exceptionally gifted teacher who also seems to have practised the explication of dramatic texts as "plays-in-performance." He believed that students would learn to recite Shakespearean verse correctly from the theatre. When students visited his house, he would ask them "Are you going to the theatre to-day?" and occasionally distribute passes for plays at thriving Calcutta theatres like the Sans Souci. Bose states that Richardson often attended rehearsals of plays and coached the actors and actresses.

From Brahmamohun Mullick, alumnus of both Hare School and Hindu College, we find the following information about the texts taught at the Hindu College *c*. 1843–53:[16]

Class	Text(s)
4th	*King John*
3rd	*Hamlet*
2nd	*Macbeth, Henry VIII*
1st	*The Merchant of Venice, Othello, The Tempest*

The use of such plays as texts in class increased exponentially with the burgeoning of new schools and colleges in far-flung corners of Bengal. There was a performance of *Hamlet* in 1857 at Keshub Chandra Sen's residence at Gouribha village in Hooghly district. Other reports tell us of a performance of *The Merchant of Venice* at Krishnanagar in 1870. The year 1870 also witnessed the first production in Bengali adaptation of a Shakespearean play, when a group from Bantra in Howrah District performed *Prabhabati*, an adaptation of *The Merchant of Venice*. A vibrant tradition of performances in Bengali translation or adaptation proceeded to develop in the next sixty-odd years in colonial Bengal. A list (not exhaustive) of the best-known adaptations is given below:

Year	Bengali title	English original
1874	*Kusumkumari*	*Cymbeline*
1874	*Rudrapal*	*Macbeth*
1875	*Bhimsinha*	*Othello*
1893	*Macbeth*	*Macbeth*
1896	*Hariraj*	*Hamlet*

Putting together a connected account becomes extremely difficult, as we have to fit together various accounts or pieces of evidence into a larger picture of how bardolatry emerged in Bengal. D. L. Richardson's *Literary Leaves or*

Prose and Verse has come down to us as a text which is perhaps close to the class lectures he delivered at Hindu College.[17] In these essays, Richardson underlines Shakespeare's sympathies for the underdog and the marginalized, which perhaps gives us clues as to not only how the students interpreted these texts but also the reasons for their abiding popularity. We can assume, for instance, that Richardson's students were inspired to sympathize with Shylock from the tone of the eponymous essay in *Literary Leaves*.

> *Shylock* is supposed to have lived in a time and country in which his tribe were bitterly persecuted and kept in a state of subjection and alarm. ... Had he attempted to take the law into his own hands, he would have been crushed like some obnoxious animal.[18]

The notion that Shakespeare's sympathies lay with the Jew, and not with his Christian tormentors, had been voiced by Nicholas Rowe in 1709 and was popularized by Edmund Kean's portrayal of the Jew on stage. References to Kean's acting are found in "Othello and Iago," the next essay in the same volume, so we can assume that the young men of Hindu College had access to the latest acting trends as well as fashionable Romantic interpretations of Shakespeare, courtesy their English professor.

We need to look in greater detail at these two essays in order to see how close to post-colonial criticism are the positions displayed here. The following quotations are from "Shylock":

> A respectable Jewish audience would not regard *Shylock* with the horror that thrills a Christian audience. They would not only sympathize in his sufferings, but admire his indomitable character and his unanswerable logic.[19]

> The conclusion of the play is unsatisfactory. We are pained to see a powerful and deeply injured spirit so completely thwarted and subdued by a mere quibble, and are shocked at the absurd and unnecessary insult of insisting (as a part of his punishment too!) "that he do presently become a Christian!"... It is at all events difficult to conceive the glory or utility of making a nominal convert to Christianity by taking advantage of a legal quirk, and "convincing a man against his will" by the threatened alternative of sundry pains and penalties.[20]

It is almost unbelievable that D. L. Richardson was raising his voice against forced conversions at such a sensitive phase of colonial history. But traditionally, the professors of English at the Hindu College projected a tolerant, secular view of society. Moreover, Richardson is suspected of having been a Freemason, and author of a poem professing "social brotherhood" titled "The Final Toast."

A footnote in the essay "Othello and Iago" reveals his egalitarianism by discussing Thomas Rymer's (1641 1713) antipathy to Othello: "He [Rymer] is especially angry that Shakespeare should have given rank and reputation to '*a Negro*'."[21] Rymer's notorious attack on *Othello*, published in 1692, had in its time warranted replies by Dryden and John Dennis, and was thought to be an example of narrow dogmatism filled with objectionable words like "Blackamoor." Richardson counters Rymer's racial intolerance:

> He [Rymer] is apparently ignorant of the fact that in Morocco the Negroes were in such high repute for their warlike qualities that they constituted the most considerable part of the Emperor's army, and were generally appointed to the government of provinces and towns.[22]

In this longish footnote, Richardson further takes Rymer to task for considering Iago an insult to the military profession—that is to say, that soldiers are always honourable men: "as if a red coat must charm away all impurities, or cover, like charity, a multitude of sins; or in other words that in certain human flocks that are blessed with Rymer's approbation, there can be no black sheep."

Thus strong arguments against religious intolerance and racial discrimination were foregrounded in the two essays, which project a vision of the universal brotherhood of man. Such texts were no doubt read enthusiastically by Richardson's students. One of them, Kylash Chunder Dutt, wrote what has been identified as "the earliest extant [Indian] narrative text in English,"[23] *A Journal of Forty-eight Hours of the year 1945*, dealing with an imagined armed future uprising of Bengalis against oppressive British rule. It was published in the *Calcutta Literary Gazette*, edited by Richardson, in 1835.

How far revolutionary ideas were implanted in youthful minds by the teaching of Shakespearean texts we do not know. But records testify at least to feeble attempts at fostering harmony between the dominant and the subjugated culture, for instance the rare appearance of the Bengali Baishnav Churn Addy in the role of Othello at the Sans Souci Theatre in 1848.[24] A letter in *The Calcutta Star*, quoted by Kironmoy Raha in his *Bengali Theatre*, offers clues to the vitiated atmosphere in which the landmark performance (was it prompted by experimentation or economic considerations?) took place. The letter talks of the "debut of a real unpainted nigger Othello" which set "the whole world of Calcutta agog." Newspaper reports present conflicting accounts. The *Englishman* commented: "In the delivery the effects of imperfect pronunciation were but too manifest." The *Bengal Hurkara*, on the other hand, was sympathetic: "but under all circumstances his pronunciation of English was for a native remarkably good. ... The performer had substantial demonstration that the feelings of the audience were fairly enlisted on his side."

Although this performance of *Othello* is widely accepted as the first appearance of an Indian in the title role, there is an intriguing mention of an "Indian Amateur" playing the role of Othello in Richardson's essay "Othello and Iago" referred to above. Richardson begins with a discussion of a recent performance at the Chowringhee Theatre (date not mentioned, but has to be prior to 1836, the year of publication of *Literary Leaves*):

> The tragedy of *Othello* has lately been acted with very considerable success at the Chowringhee Theatre in Calcutta. The gentleman who undertook the principal character is an imitator of Kean; though one of the Calcutta critics insists that he is an imitator of Kemble. If the Indian Amateur really takes the latter for his model, he imitates him "most abominably," and falls by an odd fatality into the directly opposite style of a greater though less perfect actor.[25]

The "gentleman well known in Calcutta as an excellent amateur actor" who played Iago received praise for a "firm and spirited" execution, except for making the character at times too villainous:

> The appellation of *Honest Iago* sounded oddly when applied to a man sneaking into the room with a slow cautious gait and a sinister expression of blended fear and malice. It interfered with our respect for *Othello*, who began to look too much like a *gull*.[26]

We may infer that Richardson's method of expounding the general sentiments of the plays with reference to the actual experience of watching them as theatre was influential in moulding the tastes of his young students. A villain named Dhanadas in the play *Krishnakumari* by his student Michael Madhusudan Dutt was created on the model of Iago. As Richardson put it in that essay, Dhanadas too, like Iago, "did not himself see his own way with perfect clearness and precision. His plans were at first confused and undefined, and the course of events became more fearful than he had expected."[27]

The individual tastes of professors of English often played a disproportionate role in determining the popularity of the plays as well as their interpretation. Thus young Bengalis did not discover Caliban, although *The Tempest* was also a text for study. By expounding the beauties of Shakespearean sonnets, and by including extracts from plays alongside poetry in the *Selections*, Richardson also fostered the belief in Shakespeare as the world's greatest poet. Teachers at rival establishments like Duff's General Assembly's Institution realized this to their consternation, as an anecdote related by the Reverend Lal Behari Dey indicates. Upon being informed by Dey, as a student, that he had been reading a play by Shakespeare, John Macdonald, professor of Theology, had reacted as follows:

> "Shakespeare!" he repeated. He then told me that he, when a young man, had a copy of Shakespeare's works in his library, and that instead of burning it he very foolishly exchanged it in the shops for another book—*foolishly*, because another might have bought the book and injured his soul.[28]

There were more "injured" souls in Calcutta at this juncture than professors of theology would have cared to believe. Thus Bankimchandra Chattopadhyay could safely assume the presence of the complete works in every home (though he takes for granted that almost all homesteads where his journal would reach had received Western education), as also the familiarity of the texts to every college-goer.

In a writer as influential in Bengali society as Bankim the novelist and essayist, the impact of institutionalized training in reading literary works may be discerned as late as the revised *Krishnacharitra* (1892). Here he set out to analyse one of India's most celebrated mythological characters, Sri Krishna of the epic *Mahabharata*, in a daringly Positivist light. He aroused controversy by separating the heroic "good" Krishna from the "bad" Krishna of amorous exploits. Moreover, in this long essay he attempted to project Krishna as an ideal human figure possessing leadership skills, but cast doubt on his supernatural powers. The framework of the essay, however, recalls the familiar methods of dating, location of sources, and realistic character-analysis, that he was taught to apply to Shakespearean plays. The subtext of Shakespearean criticism that lies submerged in *Krishnacharitra* was instinctively grasped by Rabindranath Tagore in his essay entitled *Bankimchandra*.[29] While discussing Bankim's notable attempt to establish the *Mahabharata* as history, Tagore brings in the analogy of Shakespeare's history plays to point out that we cannot rely upon these plays to recover history. Later, while arguing that the greatness of a character does not lie in its consistency (thereby casting doubt on Bankim's separation of the good and the bad Krishna), Tagore refers to the failure of the critics to establish Hamlet's consistency. He stresses that this does not reduce our faith in Hamlet as a realistic creation.

Thus Shakespeare had the honour of arbitrating in knotty points of creative distinction between two of colonial Bengal's literary giants. The empire of the mind had been established on a solid foundation for future generations, secure in the knowledge of the virtual indestructibility of the English playwright.

NOTES

1. Following common Bengali practice, the author has been referred to as 'Bankimchandra' or 'Bankim' throughout this essay.
2. D. L. Richardson, *Selections from the British Poets: From the Time of Chaucer to the Present Day* (Calcutta: Baptist Mission Press, 1840).
3. Partha Chatterjee, "Whose Imagined Community?" in *Empire & Nation: Essential Writings 1985–2005* (Ranikhet: Permanent Black, 2010) 23–36.
4. *The Calcutta University Calendar 1860–61*(Kolkata: Baptist Mission Press, 1860). See also *The Calcutta University Calendar 1858–59* (Kolkata: Bishop's College Press, 1858); *The Calcutta University Calendar 1862–63* (Kolkata: Thacker, Spink & Co., 1862); *The Calcutta University Calendar 1863–64* (Kolkata: Thacker, Spink & Co., 1863).
5. William Shakespeare, *The Complete Works*, ed. Stanley Wells and Gary Taylor (New York: Oxford University Press, 1988), 670. All Shakespeare references to this edition.
6. Bankimchandra Chattopadhyay, "Shakuntala, Miranda ebang Desdemona," in *Bankimchandra's Bangadarshan: Selected Essays in Translation*, ed. Tapati Gupta (Kolkata: Das Gupta & Co. Pvt. Ltd., 2007), 232.
7. *Coleridge's Poetry and Prose*, ed. Nicholas Halmi, Paul Magnuson, and Raimonda Modiano (New York: W. W. Norton & Co., 2004), 321.
8. Chattopadhyay, 227.
9. Ibid., 227.
10. Ibid., 227.
11. Ibid., 232.
12. Brajendranath Bandyopadhyay, *Bangiya Natyashalar Itihasa 1795–1876* (Kolkata: Bangiya-Sahitya-Parishat, 1933), 38 (in my translation).
13. Ibid., 51 (in my translation).
14. Ananda Lal and Sukanta Chaudhuri, eds, *Shakespeare on the Calcutta Stage: A Checklist* (Kolkata: Papyrus, 2001), 23ff.
15. *Rajnarain Bose's Atma-charit* (Kolkata: Kuntaline Press, 1909), 20.
16. Bipinbehari Gupta, *Puratan Prasanga* (1913; Kolkata: Pustak Biponi, 1989), 174–8.
17. D. L. Richardson, *Literary Leaves or Prose and Verse* (Kolkata: Samuel Smith and Co.; 1836), 451ff.
18. Ibid., 451.
19. Ibid., 457.
20. Ibid., 457.
21. Ibid., 462.
22. Ibid., 462.

23. Meenakshi Mukherjee, "The Beginnings of the English Novel," in *An Illustrated History of Indian Literature in English*, ed. Arvind Krishna Mehrotra (Delhi: Permanent Black, 2003), 94.
24. *Shakespeare on the Calcutta Stage*, 22.
25. Richardson, 464.
26. Ibid., 465.
27. Ibid., 467.
28. Lalbehari Dey, *Recollections of Alexander Duff* (London: T. Nelson & Sons, 1879), 195.
29. Rabindranath Tagore, *Rabindra Rachanabali*, vol. 13 (Kolkata: West Bengal Government, 1961), 925–38.

4 Shakespeare in Maharashtra, 1892–1927: A Note on a Trend in Marathi Theatre and Theatre Criticism

Aniket Jaaware and Urmila Bhirdikar

Mahadevshastri Kolhatkar's translation of *Othello* (as *Othello*, 1867)[1] is considered to be the first translation of a Shakespeare play into Marathi. Over the next fifty years, almost all of Shakespeare's plays were translated into Marathi. Nine of them—*Hamlet, Macbeth, King Lear, Othello, Romeo and Juliet, The Merchant of Venice, A Midsummer Night's Dream, The Tempest,* and *The Taming of the Shrew*—appeared in more than one translation. These works were important not only as translations, but as occasions for beginning a new trend in drama criticism and theory of translation. Words like *bhashantar* (exact translation, as opposed to the more familiar type of annotated translation known as *tika* or *vyakhya*) and *adaptation* (the English word taken over in Marathi, though later replaced by *rupantar*) came to be used frequently to evaluate translations.

The two forms of translation suggested by these words often lead to a debate on the possible functions of translation: its use to readers, as against its suitability for performance. Vishnushastri Chiplunkar,[2] arguably the foremost Marathi commentator on translation practice, distinguished between translations for monolingual readers and those for bilingual readers. He argued that the former could be called adaptations, and needed to capture the "essence" (*sara*) of the original work without having to render literally all the allusions in the original, and still less the actions pertaining to forms of sociality. Translations meant for bilingual readers, however, had to be exact, so that readers could evaluate them against the original text, and also educate new entrants to the study of English language and culture.[3] In Chiplunkar's opinion, as well as some others', "adaptations" were best suited for stage performance, as a theatre audience was generally monolingual and would not appreciate unfamiliar forms of sociality. Thus Chiplunkar could approve of the transformation of Cymbeline's family into a Maratha royal clan, and of Cloten (the queen's son by an earlier marriage in the original) into the Maratha queen's brother in *Tara Natak*;[4] but he did not condone the scene in which Iachimo/ Khanduji tests Imogen/Tara's fidelity, arguing that a stranger's entry into a princess's bedchamber was impossible in a Maratha household. *Tara Natak*, according to Chiplunkar, was a failed adaptation:[5] that it was very popular with the audience showed the gap between the critic's views and public taste.

The gap persisted even while some plays grew in popularity. Tragedies were especially popular, even though critics pointed out that Sanskrit theatre (alternatively "Indian" or "our" theatre) did not have a tradition of tragedy. However, tragedy was perceived to be a welcome addition to the dramatic forms. The attraction of tragedy for Marathi theatre cannot be mapped onto the reception of Sheakespeare's tragedies alone: we must consider the way Shakesperean tragedy was received in the context of classical Greek tragic theory, combined with the theory of rasa.

The discussion of tragedy in Marathi seems to have started with the publication of *Thorale Madhavarao Peshve* (*The Elder Madhavarao Peshava*, 1864) by Janardan Vinayak Kirtane.[6] This was the first recorded "bookish" play (so called in Marathi: *bookish natak*, that is, a formally composed play in printed book format, as against the manuscript records of mostly improvised mythological drama). The play depicts the death of the Peshva ruler and the death by *sati* of his devoted wife Ramabai. The last scene, where Ramabai sacrifices herself on her husband's pyre, was reported by several commentators as being exceptionally tragic and effective owing to the acting skills of the female impersonator-actor Vishnu Watve.[7] In an early discussion of this play, an anonymous commentator welcomes the new practice of writing tragedies because it "imitates life, which is a mixture of happiness and sorrow," clarifying that tragedy is most effective when it portrays a virtuous hero: "the dramatist must remember that the hero, whose tragic end is portrayed in the play, must not commit a despicable act."[8] In later years, more "tragedies" were written on themes from the history of Maharashtra. Of these *Narayanravancha Mrutyu* (The Death of Narayanrao Peshva) became very popular. Interestingly, this play was also known as *Narayanravanchya Vadhacha Farce* (Farce on the Assassination of Narayanrao).[9]

Kolhatkar's *Othello* was both published and staged in 1867, inaugurating the practice of stage performance of Shakespeare's tragedies. Among the ensuing offerings by various companies, the Shahunagarvasi drama company's productions of *Zunzararao* (*Othello*), three versions of *Hamlet,* and *Manajirao* (*Macbeth*) have been noted as some of the most effective productions.[10] The lead actors Ganapatrao Joshi, who played the heroes, and Balvantrao Jog, the male actor playing the heroines, were especially popular in key scenes in the tragedies.

Two important points are to be noted about the production of tragedies. First, they drew specifically on the acting styles of well-known English actors. David Garrick and Sir Henry Irving were the most widely invoked names in this context, Garrick being the more prominent presence. Theatre journals like *Rangabhumi* and *Natyakala* published various informative articles about him, and also discussed his acting and plays. Shankararao Mujumdar, the editor of *Rangabhumi,* published a biography of Garrick.[11] The aforementioned Ganapatrao Joshi is supposed to have successfully introduced the model of realistic acting, so that he was called the "Indian Garrick," praised in *The Times of India* and by the English officers who saw his Marathi plays.[12]

Sir Henry Irving, likewise, was a model for Ganapatrao Bhagwat of the theatre group Maharashtra Natak Mandali. Bhagawat was an English-educated actor, who studied English literature and Irving's acting style. In his short career, Bhagwat played only one Shakespearean role, that of Iago; but his villains in other plays on Indian mythological themes like Krishnaji Prabhakar Khadilkar's *Kichakvadh* (The Assassination of Kichak, 1907)[13] and *Bhaubandaki* (1909), based on the theme of political rivalry in the Peshava family of warriors and rulers, were said to testify his studious acting, modelled on Irving's style. More importantly, Bhagawat also played the role of Keshavshastri in Khadilkar's *Sawai Madhavaravancha Mrutyu* (The Death of Madhavarao Peshava, 1906), in which he modelled the villain's portrait on Iago.[14] (This play is discussed below.)

The second point about these plays relates to evil and villainous acts in the context of tragedy. This particular concern seems to have developed gradually from the 1870s. In a pioneering essay "Natak Ani Naval" (Drama and the Novel, 1872), K. B. Marathe initiated a discussion of the structure of plays based on the idea of the three unities, stressing the importance of the unity of action and explaining it in terms of the classical Indian doctrine of the nine *rasas* in the Sanskrit treatise *Natyashastra.*[15] Tragedy, thus, concerns the *rasas raudra* (ferocity), *bhayanaka* (terror or horror), *karuna* (pathos), *krodha* (rage), and *bibhatsa* (disgust). Further, Marathe specifies that the heroic action in tragedy, specifically that of Shakespeare, consists of "serious idea, serious demeanour, uncommon strength, valour and generosity."[16] Clearly, for Marathe the main function of drama is to set an ideal example that the audience can imitate. The idea of the virtuous hero, proposed in this version of what may be called didactic realism, commanded importance for some time.

Similarly, the definition of the tragic genre in terms of a combination of the nine *rasas* also gained ground. Throughout the 1880s and '90s, the proliferation and popularity of the anti-social-reform farces (plays that satirized such "social evils" as English education, remarriage of widows, and advancing the age of consent) led critics to debate the aims of drama. The "stark realism" upheld by the dramatists was countered by a bid for "didactic realism": even though the dramatists portrayed the "tragic end" of social reforms, the critics considered these efforts as harmful because of their "realistic" portrayal of social ills. Instead, they argued that drama must aim to valorize virtue and exemplary characters.[17]

The 1890s, especially with the publication of plays like *Sawai Madhavrao Peshve Yancha Mrutyu* (1896) by Khadilkar and *Sangit Sharada* (1899) by G. B. Deval, saw a change in the way the function of drama was understood. *Sangit Sharada* introduced a virtuous pair of hero and heroine adversely affected by social practices like marrying girls to older men, and portrayed a "reformist" religious head who sanctioned reform of this practice. Additionally, the old man eager to marry a young girl was caught out in deceitful practices. Virtue was upheld through the portrayal of an innocent young girl and a selfless young hero. The play ended in the marriage of the young pair, so that it became a romantic comedy". Some critics did not approve of this ending. In their opinion, the play would have been more effective as a tragedy, for virtue is not easily rewarded, and if it is shown to be so, it is less effective.[18]

It need not be supposed that this was the only understanding of tragedy. Krishnaji Prabhakar Khadilkar's *Sawai Madhavrao Peshve Yancha Mrutyu* evinces a more complex understanding of tragedy, both from the author and from his reviewer Govind Ramachandra Oak.[19] The gap between the publication (and performance) of the play in the late 1890s and the appearance of the anonymous review in 1906 is also important for understanding the changes in the notion of tragedy as well as the way in which "history" is understood. Khadilkar, better known for other plays, had published his *Savai Madhavarao Peshve Yancha Mrytu* in the journal *Vividhadnyanvistar* in 1892–93.[20] Later, at the insistence of the Maharashtra Natak Mandali, he revised the script for publication in book form. At this time, Oak brought out a longish critical article, where he quotes from Khadilkar's preface describing how the latter came to write the play, and what changes he later made:

> When I saw Shakespeare's *Hamlet* and *Othello* on the Marathi stage, my attention was especially drawn to them. And I was engrossed by the idea that a good play will emerge if characters like Hamlet and Iago were brought together in one play ... I then read Mr Khare's biography of Nana Phadanwis, and found in it the character of the *mantrik* (shaman) that Bajirav sent to Madhavarav ...[21]

It is clear that Khadilkar had read about the historical Savai Madhavarav Peshva,[22] and found in him a Hamlet-like figure ("thoughtful" but "melancholy"). Also, Khadilkar "put Iago's dress" onto the character of Keshavashastri the *mantrik* (minister or adviser) from Khare's biography of Nana Phadanwis.[23] Oak goes on to discuss the merits and demerits of the attempt, having recourse to historical writing about Savai Madhavarav, alongside a discussion of the characters of Iago and Hamlet. He finally concludes that, in the case of Madhavarav (Hamlet), the attempt is both historically inaccurate and psychologically inappropriate. It is historically inaccurate and unconvincing because the playwright depends mainly upon Grant Duff's account of the characters involved,[24] and this account is baseless. Moreover, according to Oak, Grant Duff himself seems to doubt the veracity of his statements, since he makes them in a footnote, in a "very small typeface."[25] Oak argues further that there is no mention of an illicit relationship between Gangabai and Nana Phadanwis in any other historical source. Moreover, the attempt is psychologically inappropriate and unconvincing because Shakespeare's Hamlet only pretends to be mad, whereas Madhavarav is held to have truly gone mad (though Oak says there is little proof of this). Thus in either case, the Madhavarav/Hamlet in the play is like neither Madhavarav nor Hamlet. Oak does not compare Keshavashastri and Iago, because neither of them is a historical character.[26]

What is interesting about both play and review is not merely the idea that one can do what one wants with Shakespeare's plays, but also the assumption that it is possible to isolate a character in a play and transplant him or her into another play like a detachable unit, not organically embedded in the original context. It seems to us that this is a significant moment in the history of Marathi theatre and of Maharashtra in general, because here we find a shift in the notion of character. Marathi theatre often claimed its descent from classical Sanskrit theatre, drawing on Bharata's treatise *Natyashastra* with its *rasa* theory, typology of heroes, and so on; but this new notion of character as sovereign to itself (as if Hamlet's character does not become what it is because of other characters with whom he relates) seems to function on the unexamined notion that characters in plays have an individuality that makes them what they are. Such theories move away from the type-casting of characters.

This notion of an unchangeable individual character with a consistent psychological profile slowly crystallizes as more and more plays are written, translated, and performed, shaping a fully formed notion of "character" as a sovereign being with stable physical and psychological attributes. As already indicated in Khadilkar's attempt, the character remains "stable" across plays: it can be discussed independently of the plot and, even more remarkably, of other characters. What, for instance, would the character of Iago be like if there were no Othello, Desdemona, or Cassius in the play? What would the character of Hamlet be if there were no Claudius, Polonius, Laertes, Ophelia, or Horatio?

The strangeness of this attempt to write a single play featuring Hamlet alongside Iago becomes clear if we ask the above questions. This is not to suggest that Shakespeare's characters have not been discussed, in Shakespeare studies generally, precisely as such independent stable units. Such ventures call for a much more detailed analysis, which we cannot undertake here. There are other issues involved as well. It is remarkable that while authors, reviewers and critics continue to use the traditional Marathi word for character, *patra*,[27] the word now means individual character rather than simply a dramatic persona. Clearly, if we have a typology of heroes as in the *Natyashastra*, the conception of character is very different. Marathi theatre and writings on it continually struggle and juggle with these varying concepts. If in the earlier mythological musicals there was much fighting, swordplay, and other boisterous action, and characters might even be demons (*rakshasa*), they cannot be individuated: the actors only have to play out the type, without projecting any significant interiority. The newer plays seem to move towards a notion of character with some interiority. There is reason to believe that Shakespeare's tragedies played at least a small role in this transition.

Another monograph on the theory of drama showcases the transformations noted above. This work, entitled *Natak Vishayak Vyapak Vichar* (A Detailed Consideration of the Subject of Drama) and written by G. V. Bapat, was first serialized in the journal *Rangabhumi* in 1908–9.[28] Bapat follows the established pattern of contextualizing tragedy in the light of the three unities and the virtuous hero, but he also initiates a few changes. In his work, the theory of *rasa* is definitively related to the unity of action. He refines the idea of the main and subsidiary *rasas*, and explains it in terms of dramatic action and the relation of main plot to subplot. Further, he defines a dramatic persona (*patra*) as one who has an intention or agency (*vasana*) guiding his "actions" (*kruti*), which in turn are consistent or inconsistent with his inner or mental "character" (*sheel*). Still more importantly, Bapat initiates the idea of the individuation of characters by combining "Moulton Saheb's" understanding of man's character as "the grand resultant [*sic*] of all the forces from within and from without that have been acting upon him since he became a conscious agent"[29] with the idea of the three *gunas* or tendencies of human nature (*rajas*, *tamas*, and *satva*: passion, indifference, and purity) from the *Bhagavadgita*.[30]

The same transition also gives rise, by 1927, to a discussion of the villains in Ram Ganesh Gadkari's plays[31] by Narayan Seetaram Phadke, in an article called "Gadkaryanche Durjan" ("Gadkari's Villains").[32] Phadke begins by offering a psychological typology of villains. One type allows one of the "six enemies" or basic vices (lust, anger, greed, jealousy, delusion, and pride) to overcome oneself. Claudius and Macbeth are cited as examples of this type. Another type is exemplified by Iago: he is compared to Hamlet as both are intent on revenge, but the motive and means of Iago's revenge is base whereas Hamlet's is noble. The third type of villains are base by their very nature. An original disposition of this sort is rarely to be found, but those who allow baser passions to rule over them ultimately degenerate into this type. Phadke also argue that tragedies are more effective when they have strong and cunning villains.

Having offered such a typology at the outset, Phadke begins his discussion of villains in Gadkari's plays. This discussion is entirely in terms of psychological motivation and consistency. The three villains Kamalakar (from *Premsanyas*), Vrindavan (from *Punyaprabhav*), and Ghanashyam (from *Bhavabandhan*) are found to be inadequately portrayed. The motives or occasions for their villainous acts are often trivial: at times Gadkari seems to randomly add one villainous act to another, without asking himself if there was a solid psychological foundation for such behaviour. One villain, Vrindavan in *Punyaprabhav*, has a change of heart at the end of the play, which is held to be psychologically inconsistent; another's actions are disproportionate to the injustice he faces. Phadke observes that, in *Bhavbandhan*, Ghanashyam's villainy begins in the third scene of the first act, though in the earlier scenes, he seems pleasant enough. He then starts to plot against others, almost to the point of getting someone killed, but then has a complete change of heart in the end. The origin of his villainy is never really explained in the play. It is hinted that it is because the world has ill-treated him, but no evidence is offered to bear this out. In *Premsanyas*, Phadke argues, such tragic moments arise more from other characters' guilelessness and stupidity than from the villain's cunning. Citing the example of Iago, Phadke observes that villains have to be extremely cunning, otherwise they will be ineffective as villains. He concludes by suggesting that, if Gadkari was taken up with an image or an idea while writing a play, he simply incorporated it without caring much for detail, balance, and psychological probability.

In short, then, Phadke's discussion is couched entirely in terms of motivation, intentions, and, in one case, actions disproportionate to their cause: all matters of interiority. It seems to us that, in some way, Phadke's essay completes the movement commencing in Khadilkar's creative idea of putting the characters of Hamlet and Iago in the same play, and transforming Shakespearean action and dramatis personae in terms of the history of a Marathi royal family. Once this process is complete, an older typology of characters disappears forever from Marathi theatre, persisting only in middle-order comedies of the slapstick variety. From this moment, the Marathi stage begins to look towards "modernity" and a different kind of theatre altogether, though it would take another two decades to arrive.

NOTES

1. This translation was probably never performed on stage. However, Govind Ballal Deval prepared a playscript on its basis, and staged it as *Zunzararao* in the early 1890s. Govind Ballal Deval (1855–1916) wrote seven plays, of which six were adaptations: three from the Sanskrit (*Mrichhakatik, Vikramorvashiya,* and *Shapasambhram*) and the others—*Durga Natak, Zunzararao,* and *Saunshaykallol*—of, respectively, *Isabella* (David Garrick's adaptation of Thomas Southern's *A Fatal Marriage or The Innocent Adultery*), *Othello,* and Arthur Murphey's *All in the Wrong.* Deval's original play *Sangit Sharada* will be considered later in this essay.
2. Vishnushastri Chiplunkar (1850–82) was a prominent essayist, journalist and biographer. He edited the well-known periodical *Nibandhamala* (Garland of Essays) from 1874 till his death, and wrote most of the essays published there. Closely associated with the patriots Bal Gangadhar Tilak and Gopal Ganesh Agarkar, he was a founder member of the newspapers *Kesari* and *Marhata.* His literary essays are known for their studious research and fundamental ideas, although his attacks against the social reformist Gopal Hari Deshmukh (who wrote under the name Lokahitavadi) and the radical thinker Jotiba Phule identify him as a staunchly orthodox thinker.
3. See Vishnushastri Chiplunkar, "Bhashantar" ("Translation"), in *Nibandhamaletil Vangmay Vishayak Nivadak Nibandha* (Selected Essays from the Journal *Nibandhamala*) (Pune: Chitrashal Prakashan, n.d.), 116–46.
4. Vishnu Moreshwar Mahajani, *Tara Natak: Mahakavi Shakespearekrut Cymbeline Yachyavar Adharit* (Pune: Marathi Granthottejak Mandali, 1879).
5. See Vishnushastri Chiplunkar, "Tara Natak," *Nibandhamala,* 22 (1879): 525–50.
6. R. S. Walimbe, *Marathi Natyasamiksha: 1860–1935* (Marathi Theatre Criticism: 1860–1935) (Pune: Pune Vidyapeeth Prakashan, 1966), 12–14.

7. A detailed report is found in the seminal essay "Natakachi Sthityantate" ("Transitions in Theatre") by Krishnaji Abaji Guruji, published serially in the journal *Rangabhumi* in 1911. Guruji effectively describes the last scene as enacted most "realistically" by Watve, so that not only did the audience shed tears, but the women would be moved to perform the ritual worship of the "nataki" (fake or false) *sati* and seek her blessings.
8. Quoted in Walimbe, 14.
9. The word "farce" (pronounced "phars") was adapted in Marathi for a short prose play perfomed at the end of the main *pauranik akhyan* (mythological musical play). In the 1860s. most "farces" were comic and based on "social" themes. Soon, however, the name was used for any short prose play, whether comic or serious, social or historical.
10. Among the earlier performances, *Tara Natak* (= *Cymbeline*) and *Brantikrut Chamatkar* (=*The Comedy of Errors*) were perfomed by other drama companies from the mid-1870s. Similarly, Guruji in his aforementioned essay mentions that some drama companies used *Othello* to make a transition from the manuscript (and largely extempore) mythological plays to "bookish" plays, perhaps in the late 1870s. The Shahunagarvasi drama company too performed *Tara Natak*, but after Ganapatrao Joshi's entry in the company around 1890, it also produced three versions of *Hamlet, Tratika* (=*The Taming of the Shrew), Zunzararao* (=*Othello*), *Kantipurche Don Gruhastha* (= *The Two Gentlemen of Verona*), *Veermani ani Shringarasundari* (=*Antony of Cleopatra*), *Manajirao* (=*Macbeth*), *Kapidhwaj* (=*King John*), and *Vishwamitra* (=*Timon of Athens*). Aryoddharak Natak Mandali is credited with "intellectual" productions of some of Shakespeare's plays, notably of *Othello* between 1880 and 1884. The group Natyakala Pravartak Natak Mandali produced Shakespeare in the *sangit natak* (musical drama) form from 1896 onwards. Their noted productions include *Vikalpavimochan* (=*The Winter's Tale), Samanshasan* (=*Measure for Measure*), *Premagumpha* (=*As You Like It*), and *Priyaradhan* (=*All's Well That Ends Well*). Most of the above information is based on the brief biographies of actors in Sumant Joshi, *Naman Natawara: Arthat Kahi Divangat Natyasevakanche Parichay* (Mumbai: Sahitya Sahakar Sangha Prakashan, 1971).
11. Shankar Bapuji Mujumdar, *Jagaprasiddha nat Garrick Yache Charita* (Pune: Vijay, 1930).
12. Joshi, *Naman Natawara*, 165.
13. Krishnaji Prabhakar Khadilkar (1872–1948), a close associate of the social and political leader Bal Gangadhar Tilak, was editor of both *Kesari* (1897–1904 and 1905–20) and *Navakal* (1923–27), and a well-known political writer). He wrote twelve plays, of which *Kichakvadh* (1907) was banned because of allegorizing and criticizing Lord Curzon's regime. All his musicals, including *Sangit Manapaman* (1911), *Sangit Swayamvar* (1916), and *Sangit Draupadi* (1923), had the star actor Balgandharva as heroine.
14. Keshavrao Bhole, *Antara* (Essays on theatre and music) (Mumbai: Mauj Prakashan Griha, 1996), 2212.
15. K. B. Marathe, *Naval va Natak Hyanvishayi Nibandha*, read in the Dnyanaprasarak Sabha, Mumbai, on 16 February 1872 (Pune: Modern Prakashan, 1962).
16. Ibid., 29.
17. This information is based on articles published in newspapers like *Induprakash, Kesari* and *Native Opinion* in the 1880s and '90s.

18. For example, "If Sharada was to be given an elevated status, would it not have been appropriate to let her commit suicide? Or shouldn't she have remained unmarried ...and served the nation?" Anonymous book review, "Sangit Sharada Natak: Pustakpariksha," *Vividhdnyanvistar* 9 (1899): 279.
19. Govind Ramachandra Oak, "*Sawai Madhavrao Peshave Yancha Mrutyu*: Pustakpariksha" (book review), *Vividhadnyanavistar* 37 (1906): 464–72.
20. Ibid., 464.
21. Ibid., 465.
22. Savai Madhavarav Peshva (1774–95) was too young to assume power, and this led to the increasing importance in the Maratha court and empire of Nana Phadanwis (1742–1800). The plot of the play revolves around Madhavarav (Hamlet), his mother Gangabai, Nana Phadanwis, and the *mantrik* character Keshavshastri (Iago). Legend has it that Madhavarav went mad and jumped from a high wall of his palace, Shaniwar Wada.
23. Oak, "Pustakpariksha," 465.
24. James Grant Duff (1789–1858), soldier, statesman, author of *History of the Mahrattas*, 3 vols (London: Longmans, Rees, Orme, Brown, and Green, 1826). For a very long time, this was taken as an authoritative account.
25. He quotes from Duff: "Gangabai was the cause of her own death, by having taken medicine for the purpose of concealing the consequence of her illicit intercourse with Nana Furnawees." Ibid., 469.
26. Ibid., 472.
27. The word literally means a vessel, implying a completely different notion of character and histrionics.
28. Gopal Vaman Bapat, *Natak Vishayak Vyapak Vichar* (Pune: Shankar Bapuji Mujumdar for *Rangabhumi*, 1910).
29. Ibid., 84. "Moulton Saheb" is perhaps Richard Green Moulton, the author of *Shakespeare as a Dramatic Artist: A Popular Illustration of Scientific Criticism* (Oxford: Clarendon Press, 1885) and *The Ancient Classical Drama: A Study in Literary Evolution Intended for Readers in English and in the Original* (Oxford: Clarendon Press, 1890). See http://en.wikipedia.org/wiki/Richard_Green_Moulton (accessed on May 20, 2011).
30. Bapat, 857.
31. Ram Ganesh Gadkari (1885–1919) was a prominent playwright, poet, essayist, and critic. Among his plays, *Premsanyas* (1910), *Punyaprabhav* (1917), and *Bhavbandhan* (1919) are known as serious comedies, while *Vedyancha Bajar* (incomplete) is considered as an exemplary light comedy. Finally, his *Ekach Pyala* (1919) is considered as a milestone in Marathi tragic drama.
32. Narayan Seetaram Phadke, "Gadakaryanche Durjan," *Ratnakar* (June 1927): 435–43.

5 Story-teller, Poet, Playwright: Three Oriya Translations of Shakespeare (1908–1959)

Jatindra K. Nayak

It has already been pointed out that, unlike in other parts of India such as Bengal or the Hindi-speaking region, "the reverence for Shakespeare in Orissa is matched paradoxically by disinclination to translation his works into Oriya."[1] A bibliography of translated texts in Oriya lists only seventeen published works, and most of these are not easily available.

The reasons are not far to seek. The English-educated middleclass in Orissa was a late entrant on the cultural scene. Its counterpart in Bengal had at least a hundred years' head start. The first institution of higher education was established in Orissa as late as 1869, and post-graduate classes in the humanities came to be opened much later, in the early twentieth century. The Bengali officials and *zemindars* (tax-collectors and de facto "landlords") who had settled in Orissa brought with them their reverence for Shakespeare, and it is not surprising that four out of the seventeen Oriya translations of Shakespeare have been done by Bengalis. The number of British officials in the state was also quite small, and they seemed more interested in horses and bands than in staging Shakespeare's plays. The memoirs written by British officials such as John Beames, Andrew Fraser, and John Austen Hubback do not mention any theatrical activities carried out by the British residents in stations like Cuttack, Puri, or Balasore. As far as the British or the whites were concerned, Orissa was primarily a site of revenue administration, missionary activities, and bison-hunting or other diversions.

Even among the early recipients of Western education in Orissa, Shakespeare does not figure as a major influence. Radhanath Ray borrowed extensively from Greek myths and the British Romantics, but he rarely if ever turned to Shakespeare as a source of themes or plots. Nilakantha Das suggests in his introduction to the collected works of Fakir Mohan Senapati that the latter's novel *Prayaschita* (The Expiation) was influenced by *Romeo and Juliet*; but this is an inspired conjecture not supported by any statement from Fakir Mohan himself.[2] However, in a poem written by Fakir Mohan on the impact of Western education on Oriyas, "Mu Hatabahuda" ("I am on my way back from the market"), there occurs a reference to Shakespeare, who is placed alongside Byron.

Nonetheless, it would be wrong to look upon these few Shakespeare translations in Oriya as culturally insignificant or unworthy of critical attention. True, most of them have been undertaken by rather obscure translators or authors, and they do not seem to have attracted a large readership. But, they should not be dismissed as marginal: viewed from an appropriate perspective, they assume a significance not hitherto attributed to them. An insightful observation by Sisir Kumar Das on the reception of Shakespeare in India may open up a useful and illuminating perspective on these translations:

> It is extremely difficult to try to present a picture of a uniform reception of Shakespeare in India. Here deep and pervasive, there scanty and sparing—it is as complex and problematic as the story of western impact on Indian literature itself.… The potentiality of Shakespeare translations was defined by the nature of Indian understanding and perception of Shakespeare as a dramatist, a poet, a narrator, and a storyteller. These translations, therefore, should be considered as part of experimentations of new literary genres that were emerging in various Indian languages in the nineteenth century. In other words, Indian encounter with Shakespeare is an essential part of the history of Indian literary transformations in the last century.[3]

In this essay I will make an attempt, taking into account three Oriya translations of Shakespeare produced over fifty years from 1908 to 1959, to illuminate aspects of the Western impact on Oriya literature, and to show how historical and political forces conditioned responses to Shakespeare in Orissa. The translators, it will be seen, did not simply try to project a "dehistoricised, universal eternal author,"[4] but used him subtly to intervene in the cultural-political contexts of their own times and implement their own cultural and political agenda.

The earliest Oriya translation of Shakespeare can hardly be called a translation in the usual sense of the term. Available evidence indicates that it was made by Jagannath Ballav Ghose in 1908. It was published under the title *Premika-Premika* (A Lover and His Beloved). The decision not to use the foreign-sounding names in the title is significant, as it foregrounds the love element in the play. The title page makes it clear that the translation is "based" on *Romeo and Juliet*, written by the "world-famous poet" Shakespeare. It expresses unbounded admiration for Shakespeare's genius and emphasizes the translator's inadequacy in rather exaggerated terms:

> I am not very well educated. Equipped with so little learning, undertaking a translation of a play by the great poet Shakespeare, which is rich in such profound meaning, would belike trying to cross the seas on a mere raft.[5]

The translation, "in token of deep respect is, with kind permission, most respectfully dedicated by his most obedient and humble servant" to The Hon'ble John Joseph Platel, Esq., I.C.S., Sessions Judge at Cuttack District. It is thus clearly indicated that the translation has been undertaken by a loyal subject of the British Empire, and the blessing of the colonial authorities is duly invoked. In the short two-page introduction, the translator informs the readers that the translation has been serialized in the literary magazine *Mukur* (The Mirror) before being brought out as a book. The reader is further informed that most of the text is based on Charles Lamb's version of the play in his *Tales from Shakespeare*, although a part of the translation corresponds to the text of the original play. Ghose states, "My story is not a faithful rendering of Lamb's narrative, but is based on it to a large extent. The rest I have translated from the original play" (i). It is possible that Ghose might have been inspired by Haranchandra Rakshit, who translated Shakespeare's plays into Bengali prose intwelve volumes (1896–1903). The attempt seems to aim at popularizing Shakespeare's plots in Orissa. No wonder the translator repeatedly refers to his work as a "story" in the introduction. The book is divided into ten chapters, each of them bearing a title in Oriya and a quotation from the English play. The titles are as follows: "Prema Kalika" (The Bud of Love), "Bibaha" (The Wedding), "Shoka Sambad" (Sad Tidings), "Tattvopadesh" (Good Advice), "Biday" (Farewell), "Satira Sahas" (The Courage of a Chaste Woman), "Harsha Bishada" (Joy and Grief), "Bishabriksha" (The Poison Tree), "Parinam" (The Outcome), "Shanti" (Peace). Such titles indicate that the play has been presented as a moral tale involving human actions and their consequences. The first chapter begins with these lines from the English play:

> This bud of love, by summer's ripening breath,
> May prove a beauteous flower when next we meet.
>
> *(Romeo and Juliet,* 2.2.121–2)

Similarly, the next chapter bears the title "Bibaha" (Marriage), accompanied by this quotation:

> Young men's love then lies
> Not truly in their heart but in their eyes.
>
> *(Romeo and Juliet,* 2.3.63–4)

Each chapter provides a brief prose account of the events, into which, in two of the ten chapters, is interpolated a short exchange of dialogue between two characters. But elsewhere too, the prose summary is interspersed with exchanges among characters, presented in direct speech. In the chapter titled "Shoka Sambad" (Sad Tidings), for instance, a simple straightforward account of events leading up to the murder of Tybalt and the expulsion of Romeo from the city of Verona ends with a dialogue between the Nurse and the grief-stricken Juliet. Nearly a whole page is devoted to Juliet lamenting bitterly her separation from Romeo (18). Similarly, the chapter titled "Satira Sahas" (The Courage of a Sati or Chaste Woman) contains a lively exchange of words between Friar Lawrence and Juliet (28).

However, reducing Shakespeare to a story-teller and the play to a narrative does not simplify the translator's task; rather, it leaves him burdened with residual difficulties. A particular character and the context he inhabits in the play may at first sight resist successful assimilation into the framework of the play, as with the character of the friar and the ambience of the monastery or church. By presenting Friar Lawrence as a "tapasvi" or a Hindu hermit, and the church as an "ashram" or (primarily Hindu) retreat, Ghosemay have chosen to ignore or erase the Christian underpinnings of the play. The decisions to present the cemetery as "samadhi mandir" or the temple of graves, and Juliet as a "sati," also appear somewhat problematic. However, the translator's negotiation of these difficulties may be seen as ways of Indianizing or indigenizing Shakespeare.

Placed alongside *Premika-Premika*, the Oriya translation of *Hamlet* made by Akshaya Kumar Bandyopadhyay in 1934[6] marks an ostensibly more ambitious attempt to render a Shakespearian play into Oriya. It radiates a confidence that is conspicuously missing in the translation of *Romeo and Juliet*. Although produced during British rule, it is not dedicated to any colonial official. It does not seek to summarize or paraphrase the play: it presents the full text in Oriya translation. The cover of the book simply has *Hamlet* at the top (the subtitle, "The Prince of Denmark," is left untranslated), and the name of the translator and his educational qualifications at the bottom of the page. The title-page verso gives information about the play and its author in Oriya. *Hamlet* is presented as a play "full of mystery or suspense" (*rahasyamay*) written by the "world-famous renowned poet and playwright, Shakespeare." The reader is further informed that the play has been translated in *amitrakshar chhanda* (blank verse). The name of the translator, his profession (a school teacher at Sambalpur Zilla School) and his educational qualifications (MA, BEd) are given on the title page. The omissions in the English are significant: the references to Shakespeare's world fame and to the element of mystery in the play are left out. An English-knowing readership is supposed to be familiar with Shakespeare's fame.

The way information about the author and the translator is presented reveals several interesting things: the emphasis on the iconic status of Shakespeare, his identity as a poet (no less than as dramatist), and the translator's role as a mediator between Western culture and the vernacular. In Oriya literary journals from the early decades of the twentieth century, it was customary to mention the degrees obtained by the contributors. In fact, in an advertisement in an Oriya almanac published in the 1920s one comes across at an initiative to prepare avillage directory of educated Oriyas.[7] It indicates a self-conscious attempt by the English-educated middleclass to distinguish itself from the recipients of traditional education and to view itself as a distinct community. The translator seeks to serve as a representative of this class, offering a classic of Western culture to the "natives."

The decision to translate the play in *amitrakshara chhanda* (blank verse) assumes special significance in this context. In the nineteenth century, English blank verse was naturalized as *amitrakshar chhanda* in Oriya and other Indian languages, especially Bengali. Certain new literary forms and techniques were introduced through translation from English literature into Oriya literature. Sonnets and elegies made their appearance in Oriya literature, and blank verse in Oriya was popularized by Radhanath Ray in his long poem *Mahayatra*. Bandyopadhyaya's translation thus takes advantage of formal elements already introduced through earlier translations from English. It reflects the suppleness and flexibility that the Oriya language had achieved as a result of the sustained movement, in the latter half of the nineteenth century, to strengthen the language and confer stability on it, by standardizing it and bringing it closer to Sanskrit.[8]

Hence a striking feature of the translation is the translator's choice of a heavily Sanskritized Oriya. The effect aimed at is sonority, which is achieved partly through liberal use of alliteration and partly through a deliberate choice of more difficult *tatsama* words (that is, derived directly from Sanskrit) where simpler alternatives might have served. The flexibility and suppleness of Shakespeare's blank verse in *Hamlet* gives way to an oppressively majestic tone, impressively consistent but ultimately monotonous. One cannot rule out the possibility of the translator having come heavily under the influence of mythological plays in Oriya and Bengali which used *amitrakshar chhanda* to achieve the rhetorical effect of sublimity.

Another distinguishing feature of this translation is the extensive, almost obtrusive, use of footnotes. There are about 130 footnotes in the text. They occur on almost every page of the translation, and indicate that the translator intended his work to be read rather than staged. These notes can be grouped under the following broad categories, according to the functions they serve in the text:

(a) *To supply information on places, mythical figures alluded to in the text, customs and rituals*: The reader is informed that Elsinore is a harbour located to the north-west of Copenhagen. In Act IV scene 8, Normandy is described as a region lying in the northern part of France and founded as a province by the Normans. Caesar is introduced as the Roman dictator who ruled from 100 BCE to 44 BCE. Wittenberg is identified as a university in Germany. A longish footnote appended to Act I scene 2 tells us that Niobe was the wife of the King of Thebes, that she prayed to the gods to be turned into stone after losing her sons, and that the statue sheds tears in summer. Similarly, information on mythical figures such as Hercules, Dido, Hecuba, Priam and Aeneas, and biblical characters like Herod, are provided in footnotes. As far as customs are concerned, a footnote in Act I scene 2 informs the reader that all the subjects of the kingdom should mourn at the same time. In scene IV of the same Act, we are told that pilgrims to Jerusalem used to wear sea-shells in their caps, and that grass and stone plaques were used on the graves of poor people.

(b) *To explain culture-specific terms*: In Act IV scene 5, Valentine's Day is referred to as a *Mahotsav Divas* (great festival), and a footnote tells us it is celebrated on 14 February. It goes on to inform us that in ancient times, lovers used to meet on this day. In Act I scene 2, the reader is informed of the Western practice of drinking someone's health. It is interesting that in Act I Scene 4, the Day of Judgement is not glossed in a footnote, but simply rendered literally as *bichara dibasa*.

(c) *To provide simpler equivalents of difficult words used in the text*: *arbhaka* for *ajna* (ignorant), *chamikar* for *swarna* (gold), *ambar* for *basana* (clothes), *madar* for *sukar* (pig), *kunapa* for *saba* (corpse), *jambal* for *siabala* (green moss), *chala dala* for *aswattha* (peepul tree), *abaskanda* for *sibir* (army camp), *askandana* for *akramana* (attack), *deshakarsa* for *pradeepa* (lamp), *khamanigabhasti* for *surya kiran* (sunshine), *tamrasamputa* for *shabadhar* (coffin). One can go on multiplying such instances. The effect aimed at through such deliberate insertion of heavy Sanskritic words in the original is an impression of greater solemnity and majesty.

(d) *To explain English words retained in the text of the translation*: There are only three instances of such retention of English words. In Act V scene 1 a footnote explains that a coroner is an official who enquires into the cause of unnatural death. In the same scene, parchment is described as the skin of a goat or sheep used to write on. The word *sponge* used in Act IV scene 2, however, is left untranslated.

Although nowhere does the translator make a conscious attempt to domesticate the text of the play, here and there he suddenly makes himself visible by bringing in expressions not clearly warranted by the context. Take, for instance, the translation of "Latin" into *debabhasa* or "the language of the gods" (Act I scene 1). At many other points, Bandyopadhyay unobtrusively brings in references to Hindu gods and goddesses or echoes well-known Sanskrit literary texts. In Act I scene 2, he refers to *Astadashadhyayi Bruhat Sanhita*, a Sanskrit text. In Act I scene 5, the King of Denmark is described as *bishakumbha payomukham* (a pot full of poison with milk at the top). In Act III scene 1, music is said to be as bewitching as the sound of Murari or Lord Krishna's flute. Scene II of the same Act carries references to the divine bird Garuda genuflecting before Lord Vishnu, and to Ugra Chandi (the goddess Durga assuming a terrifying expression), while a king is compared to Indra, the king of the gods. In Act III scene 3, Hamlet refers to Chitragupta, the record-keeper of the god of death. A gratuitous reference to Malllinath, the famous commentator on the poetry of Kalidasa, at another point in the play indicates an irrepressible desire to introduce cultural references from home.

Despite this heavy load of footnotes, the translator does not always successfully negotiate the cultural problems of rendering Shakespeare into Oriya. He omits, almost as a matter of routine, inconvenient words like "nunnery," expressions like "drinking one's health," and terms referring to duelling conventions. The translation of "cuckold" as *srungi prani* ("creature with horns") also shows the translator's ineptness. But all these do not take away from the extraordinary achievement of Bandyopadhyay's rendering of *Hamlet*, which displays a consistency of idiom and a virtuosity born of triumphant linguistic nationalism.

The 1959 Oriya translation of *Othello*[9] (here too the subtitle has been left untranslated) contrasts strikingly with early translations of Shakespeare in Orissa. A new context of political and social realities endows this rendering with a very different character, illustrating the subtle and significant changes that distinguish this work from pre-Independence translations. Those earlier translators were not important literary figures; but the Oriya *Othello* was undertaken by a famous poet and Shakespeare scholar, Dr Mayadhar Mansinha. Another significant fact about this translation should not be overlooked: although published by Das Brothers, a local publisher, it was brought out under the aegis of the Sahitya Akademi or National Academy of Letters. It was part of a national initiative to introduce the four great tragedies of Shakespeare to the Indian readership through translations into all major Indian languages. The book's cover carries a picture of Shakespeare, and does not even mention the translator's name. The importance of Shakespeare as a cultural icon no longer needs to be emphasized: it istaken as self-evident. The blurb on the back cover piles up the superlatives in presenting Shakespeare as a playwright without an equal in the world.

Like Bandyopadhyay's translation of *Hamlet*, Mansinha's translation of *Othello* is clearly not meant to be staged. We may assume that Shakespeare is presented to Oriya readers primarily as a reading experience. In fact, the blurb mentions the "opportunity available to Oriya readers to read Shakespeare in their own language."

Two aspects of Mansinha's translation of *Othello* deserve attention. One is his decision to render the play in prose, a prose which generously accommodated Sanskritized Oriya words as well as Oriya words of Perso-Arabic provenance and colloquialisms. The other is inclusion of the Oriya version of an introduction by John Dover Wilson, commissioned by the Sahitya Akademi for its entire Shakespearean venture in all languages. These features assume significance in view of Mansinha's own distinction as a poet. His prose rendering often rises effortlessly to lyrical heights. Sachidananda Mohanty's observations on Mansinha's choice of prose deserve to be quoted at some length:

> Mansinha's grasp of the nuances of both English and Oriya, especially the disparate cultural context through which the original as well as the translated text come through,

is uniformly sound. He employs unfailingly the correct register of the "high" and the "low," alternating with the precise Oriya equivalents. However, while Shakespeare's lines are for the most part in blank verse, Mansinha prefers a literal prose style. This is probably guided by the fact that verse plays in Oriya are comparatively rare and would not make for easy acceptance by the modern Oriya audience. Mansinha's attention in this translation endeavour is always riveted to the small, and it is the smaller details and frames that receive the greatest treatment in his hands.[10]

However, a closer look at the text of the translation makes us discover the real reason behind Mansinha's decision to render the play in prose. The blurb articulates a political concern which shaped his response to the play and his decisions as a translator. Unlike Ghose and Bandyopadhyay, who viewed Shakespeare as a story-teller and poet respectively, Mansinha regards Shakespeare primarily as a playwright, whose preoccupation is not with poetry but with the portrayal of characters. Mansinha believes that Shakespeare admired aristocratic characters and treated characters belonging to the common strata of society with contemptuous disdain.

The new Indian names bestowed on the characters have a distinct aristocratic ring about them, owing to their Sanskritic bent. Othello becomes Atala or the Unshakeable One; Desdemona, Diptibarna or the Radiant One: Brabantio, Birabanshi or one who belongs to a clan of warriors; and so on. The introduction by Dover Wilson also focuses on Shakespeare's art of characterization, and goes on to psychoanalyse characters such as Othello and Iago. Mansinha's focus on Shakespeare's characters has a political dimension, emerging from the following comment in the blurb. Now the emphasis is not on Shakespeare as a storyteller, nor on his extraordinary achievement as a poet, but on the distinctiveness of the way he portrayed his characters:

Today Shakespeare is universally recognized as the greatest playwright of the world. Although his plays focus on the lives of characters belonging to the aristocracy, and although they clearly regard ordinary people with contempt, he is counted among the most popular authors even in all communist nations. (Translation mine.)

The shadow of the Cold War evidently falls across Mansinha's translation of *Othello* as one can see him going out of his way to establish Shakespeare as transcending political divides.

The three Oriya translations of Shakespeare discussed above thus represent three key moments in the history of the Western impact on Oriya literature. The first embodies an attempt to introduce Shakespeare primarily as a story-teller, concentrating chiefly on the plot of *Romeo and Juliet*. This is part of a wider attempt in the later nineteenth century to borrow plots and themes from Western sources and give them a local habitation and a name, and establishing possibilities of innovation in the process.

More notable were the experiments made by Radhanath Ray, who borrowed plots from classic Western sources and assimilated them into the Oriya literary tradition. His preference for stories with unhappy ending created a space for a new sensibility in Oriya literature[11] and the retelling of *Romeo and Juliet* in chaste Oriya prose contributes to and strengthens this initiative. This Shakespeare translation coincides with the triumph of the movement whereby Orissa was acknowledged as a separate province on the basis of language. Its technical virtuosity exudes a linguistic confidence, seeking to demonstrate the ability of standard Oriya to convey vividly the power, and richness and intricacy of Shakespeare's blank verse.

Mayadhar Mansinha's Oriya *Othello* locates itself in the yet larger cultural and political universe of the 1950s, reflecting the anxieties and concerns of a Western world split into two blocs by their professed political ideologies. The Shakespeare the translator seeks to project is not a story-teller or a poet but a playwright with an aristocratic bias, who is nonetheless adored in the pro-proletariat communist countries. The focus shifts from Shakespeare's poetry to his nuanced portrayal of human characters. Translating Shakespeare is now a part of a wider strategy to counter aggressively egalitarian tendencies by celebrating the uniqueness and greatness of individuals. The decision to render the play in prose needs to be seen as part of Mansinha's attempt to divert attention from lyricism and plot-construction, instead bringing it to bear on his art of characterization.

In the course of half a century, the image of Shakespeare thus changed in Orissa from a renowned story-teller to a great poet, to a playwright without parallel who offered rich insights into the irreducible uniqueness of human beings as individuals. These changing responses to Shakespeare have been defined by the shifting political and cultural context, by the transition from a search for Western models, to an assertion of linguistic identity, to the exigencies of Cold War cultural politics.

ORIYA TRANSLATIONS OF SHAKESPEARE

Premika Premika (*Romeo and Juliet*). Translated by Jagannath Ballava Ghose. Cuttack: The Union Printing Works, 1908.
The Merchant of Venice. Translated by Bimal Chandra Ray Chowdhury. Cuttack: H. M. Dutta, 1923.
The Tempest. Translated by Bimal Charana Ray Chowdhury. Cuttack: B. S. Das, Mukur Press, 1924.
Hamlet. Translated by Akshaya Kumar Bandopadhyay. Cuttack: Cuttack Trading Company, 1934.
Macbeth. Translated by Chandramai Das. New Delhi: Sahitya Akademi, 1958.
Othello. Translated by Mayadhar Mansinha. Cuttack: Das Brothers, and Delhi: Sahitya Akademi, 1959.
Shakespeare Kahani (containing *Twelfth Night*, *Much Ado About Nothing*, *As You Like It*, *Cymbeline*). Translated by Shridhara Das. Cuttack: Grantha Mandir, 1970.
Bibhranti (*The Comedy of Errors*). Translated by Nabaghana Panda. Cuttack: Orissa Book Store, 1978.
Tofan (*The Tempest*). Translated by Samaresha Roy. Cuttack: Orissa Kishore Sahitya Akademi, 1978.
Othello. Anonymous translation. Sambalpur: Shaha Publishers, 1979.
Julius Caesar. Translated by Udaya Natha Panda. Sambalpur: Aranpoona Sahu, 1982.
Shakespeare Kavyamala (containing *Macbeth*, *Romeo and Juliet*, *The Merchant of Venice*). Translated by Samaresha Roy. Cuttack: Orissa Kishore Sahitya Akademi, 1984.

NOTES

1. Mohanty Sachidanada, "Shakespeare in Orissa: Culture, Ideology and Translation Practice," in *Gender and Cultural Identity in Colonial Orissa* (Hyderabad: Orient Longman, 2008), 163.
2. Nilakantha Das, "Fakir Mohan O Odia Shaitya" ("Fakir Mohan and Oriya Literature"), in *Odia Bhasha O Shaitya* (Oriya Language and Literature) (Berhampur: New Student's Store, 1958), 191.
3. Sisir Kumar Das, "Shakespeare in Indian Languages," *Jadavpur Journal of Comparative Literature* 36 (1998–99): 111.
4. Harish Trivedi, *Colonial Transactions: English Literature and India* (Kolkata: Papyrus, 1993), 32.

5. *Premika Premika (Romeo and Juliet)*, trans. Jagannath Ballava Ghose (Cuttack: The Union Printing Works, 1908), i (translation mine). All subsequent citations from this translation are given in the text.
6. *Hamlet*, trans. Akshaya Kumar Bandopadhyay (Cuttack: Cuttack Trading Company, 1934).
7. Jatindra K. Nayak, "Sacred Time Secular Space: The Printed Oriya Almanac," in *Science, Literature and Aesthetics*, ed. Amiya Dev (New Delhi: Centre for Studies in Civilisations, 2009), 787.
8. Narendra Nath Mishra, *Adhunika Odia Kavyadhara: Adiyuga* (The Development of Modern Oriya Poetry: The Early Phase), (Santiniketan: Visva-Bharati Gabeshana Prakashan Samiti, 1964), 312–18.
9. *Othello,* trans. Mayadhar Mansinha (Cuttack: Das Brothers, and Delhi: Sahitya Akademi, 1959).
10. Mohanty, 161–2.
11. D. P. Pattanaik, "Introduction," in *Kabilipi* (Letters of Poets) (Kolkata: Visva-Bharati, 1957), 11–12.

6 "We the globe can compass soon": Tim Supple's *Dream*

Ananda Lal

A Midsummer Night's Dream has endured so well in all languages of South Asia as to become perhaps the most-performed Shakespearean comedy there, according to one Indian scholar.[1] The preferred medium of transference for Shakespearean drama in India has always been the adaptation, to which the *Dream* lends itself quite easily. The commercial Parsi theatres mounted it in their typically free and lavish extravaganzas during the nineteenth century. Early literary translators also indigenized it, such as Srikanthesh Gowda's *Pramilarjuniya* in Kannada, using Hindu mythical characters. An intriguing experiment took place in Calcutta when Satishchandra Chatterjee transformed it into a Bengali opera, *Jahanara* (1904), set exclusively among the Muslim community. After India's independence in 1947, two versions by famous socialist directors gained considerable attention: Utpal Dutt's relatively faithful *Chaitali Rater Swapna* (1964) in Bengali with his own comic genius enacting the part of Bottom, and Habib Tanvir's *Kam Devka Apna, Basant Rituka Swapna* (1993) in Hindustani and Chhattisgarhi, which omitted Hermia and Helena completely and relegated Theseus and Hippolyta to the background, concentrating on the forest spirits and mechanicals—the groups that Tanvir's rural cast understood perfectly.

Meanwhile in England, the original in the hands of Peter Brook had revolutionized Shakespearean staging in 1970, as he stripped the conventional pictorial approach for what one critic called the play's Platonic essence. The internationalization of theatre over the next three decades led to intercultural *Dreams* as well as novel settings. Brazil recurs in its recent history. The American director A. J. Antoon placed it amidst the Brazilian carnival at the

New York Shakespeare Festival (1988); the Brazilian arch-anarchist Caca Rosset produced a charactcristically Rabelaisian version (1990); and the illustrious German film auteur, Werner Herzog, located it in the Amazonian rain forests (Rio de Janeiro, 1992). Some reviewers thought well of the eminent French Canadian director Robert Lepage's dark, grimy, nightmarish multicultural edition (1992) that consciously opposed Brook's *joie de vivre*, citing Jung and Freud in the accompanying brochure. Japan's much-lionized interpreter of Shakespeare, Ninagawa Yukio, staged the *Dream* in a rock garden (Tokyo, 1994) as his first attempt at comedy. The young German regisseur Karin Beier employed nine European languages in her most lauded production to date (Dusseldorf, 1995), to show that Shakespeare was a pan-European author.

In this continuum arrived Tim Supple, already a director of world repute, still a disciple of Brook in many ways. Like Brook, he regards Jan Kott highly, and strives to make "Shakespeare our contemporary"—the title of Kott's book, influential since the 1960s. Like most directors today, he has assimilated much from Brook, even such a simple matter as the doubling of Theseus and Hippolyta with Oberon and Titania, first introduced by Brook, now a stage staple in Britain. Supple had travelled to India with the Royal Shakespeare Company's *Comedy of Errors* under his own direction in 1997, and worked on several other productions with Asian performers: notably, dramatizing Salman Rushdie's fiction. Invited by the British Council to direct an intercultural production in South Asia, he came on a recce in 2005, chose the *Dream*, and the rest, as they say, is history. After its India tour, Stratford run, and Verona gig in 2006, Supple's *Dream* played the UK in 2007, returned to South Asia in 2008 and then embarked on an international tour, flooring audiences everywhere and drawing comparisons with Brook's masterpiece. From *The Toronto Star* across the globe to *The Australian*, its triumphal progress, stretching over 300 performances, is well documented: I need not repeat it here.[2] My purpose is to record the production as an insider—the dramaturge on the project—and discuss it as an Indian academic who specializes in theatre, neither of these perspectives having received much exposure so far.[3]

PROCESS

Very few intercultural projects in India have permitted the director to invest as much time (not to mention money) as the British Council bountifully allowed Supple. He travelled all over India twice in early 2005, first on a reconnaissance trip during which he also took in several traditional performing arts, and then to conduct workshop auditions with nearly 300 prospects in separate sessions spanning over a month in April and May. For the first time in Indian theatre, auditions were held on a nationwide level without linguistic discrimination in cities across the country and in Sri Lanka: Delhi, Kolkata (not "in the jungle outside Calcutta" as misreported twice by the London *Times*[4]), Chennai, Bangalore, Thiruvananthapuram, Colombo, Mumbai, and Ahmadabad. The implementation of such a non-discriminatory policy involved elaborate logistics, which Indian theatre cannot even dream of owing to the costs involved. Because a visit to Imphal fell through owing to security regulations, the Manipuri candidates were even flown to Kolkata.

Eventually, Supple realized he had far too many gifted artists to choose from: his shortlist of sixty-odd candidates called for another round of sifting. So he called them for workshops in July at the National Centre for the Performing Arts in Mumbai. Originally not on the cards, this intensive week-long recall session resulted in a strange, inspiring thing that I witnessed at first hand. The sixty performers from diverse Indian backgrounds—many of them barely able to communicate with one another, at best through a pidgin Hindi or English—bonded together to form close ties that I am sure nobody expected. All knew that two out of three among them might never meet again because they would not make the final cut, but making the grade did not seem as important as forging new friendships. It was national integration at the microcosmic level, and the multiple promises that networking would continue even after this production was over generated very positive vibes about Indian theatre in the future.

It is important for non-Indians to understand the difficulties in communication that arose even at this preliminary stage. Supple's production ultimately utilized seven languages—English, Tamil, Malayalam, Sinhalese, Hindi, Bengali, Marathi, to which Rajasthani was added later—plus a smattering of Sanskrit. But in 2005 he had to assess performers speaking nearly twenty languages. The query could naturally arise very early on: how did he comprehend and communicate in these multilingual circumstances? Interpreters did translate regularly, but as he put it:

> Often we did not need translation as the expression and tone of what I said got across. The main point about the different languages is that they forced us all to pay heightened and careful attention to each other, a quality one would wish of all actors, directors and audiences. Communication with the actors demanded exceptional clarity, brevity and focus. In this way I feel we were blessed in the language differences.[5]

Design and production plans continued after Supple returned to London. He weighed all the permutations for a month before deciding on his cast and crew. The twenty chosen, plus three musicians, three designers, a choreographer and the production unit (all Indians except for one Sri Lankan actor, the Australian-Indian composer Devissaro, and Supple himself) reassembled for seven weeks of rehearsals in January–February 2006. Their home for this period was the idyllic performance centre of Adishakti, built over the preceding few years by director-choreographer Veenapani Chawla outside Pondicherry in southern India. It is hard to imagine a more ideal place for such work. Located on a quiet, secluded, wooded plot of land surrounded by cashew-nut groves, Adishakti has a fully functional and elegant auditorium modelled after the indigenous *kuttampalam* theatre architecture of Kerala. With walls constructed of local red-laterite bricks and a pinewood stage floor, it provided the actors with a perfectly rooted, Indian ambience in place of the nondescript generic halls in urban India. The fact that everyone, following traditional custom, had to leave their footwear outside before entering heightened the earthy feel.

In this beautiful space, the daily schedule left the whole unit blissfully exhausted. Over the entire period, setting aside Sundays as the weekly holiday, Supple rehearsed intensively from 9 a.m. to 9 p.m. every day. Warm-up exercises, dance and music sessions occupied the mornings. After lunch came preparation of individual scenes, with just a tea break in the middle until dinner was served. Supple spared Saturday and Sunday nights for letting hair down in much-deserved party time. I mention the routine because it is so rare in South Asian theatre, long divorced from its professional system barring a handful of exceptional companies. But even in England, Supple commonly rehearses only between 10 a.m. and 6 p.m. The India experience was a luxury even by his standards. Yet I noticed that his intensity never flagged. Everyone else could manage an hour's respite or more during the course of the day, but he stayed in charge for twelve hours at a stretch, save for meals: an object lesson for directors.

Most directors are dictators, and aloof, even superior. Not Supple. He did not distance himself from the ensemble, but considered himself one of them and, after hours, shook a leg with the best of them. He dealt with each individual on equal, personal terms (I was amazed that he knew everybody's names in Mumbai before I, an Indian, did) and had a separate relationship with each one. He never said no to requests at odd hours for textual explanation or insights into improving the translated passages. His hands-on approach to dance (coaching difficult movements himself), music (frequently breaking into percussive sounds to guide the accompanists: lest we forget, Supple has a parallel career in opera) and sets (exhaustive one-on-one discussions with the designer) inspired those who led their own groups.

Should anyone think that the portraits in the interpretation were Supple's impositions, perish the thought. The cast will verify that no characterization was fixed beforehand: everyone underwent a continuous search and exploration of his or her part that perhaps has still not ended. Constantly challenged and pushed to look within, all agreed that, without the dangerous edge to which Supple led them, the new possibilities that ultimately appeared on stage could not have emerged. Not forcibly, but subtly, he got what he wanted *out of* them, not just *from* them. Much of this extra dimension involved depths of nonverbal communication; and to counter those who believe in the sanctity of one language, the actors (in reply to my questioning) never felt that their communication suffered on account of linguistic barriers.

An entire gamut of Indian performance forms was on display, since those selected had training in particular skills. Kalarippayattu martial arts from Kerala jostled with Chhau dance steps from West Bengal; classical Bharatanatyam from the south with popular acrobatics from the north; urban Western-style realistic acting with rural and traditional stylization; rope climbing with stick fighting; sacred wedding hymns with coarse street songs; lyrical Manipuri string instruments with pounding Tamil percussion. Gradually, the play took shape in its pan-Indian avatar. My contribution involved occasionally offering solicited advice to Supple. He needed no advice, really, but in these contentious times of globalization, everyone is rightly sensitive to the troublesome aspects of intercultural theatre. Peter Brook's *Mahabharata* had proved it to Indians. Supple understood the problem.

The immediate inclination of a Western intercultural director who views the stunning traditional abilities of an Asian cast member is to showcase that talent, interpolating its exotic colour out of context for the sake of novelty. Here, however, Supple treated the unit just like any group of theatre workers, not as *Asian* theatricians, as one of the actresses told me of her own accord. As corroborated by the other performers, no appropriation occurred. Wherever these skills did get manifested on stage, they emerged finally out of numerous options offered in rehearsal after internalizing the meaning of the text. The same approach characterized Supple's management of delicate cultural differences. Whereas multiculturalism has become official policy in several "developed" countries, and to that degree fashionable, intercultural theatre has not had unqualified success, being confronted with numerous accusations of neocolonial exploitation from the "less developed" partners in the exchange. Inevitably, Supple's activity came up for scrutiny under those vigilant magnifying glasses. Knowing the debates, and having observed him direct at close range and questioned members of the team, I can vouch for his sensitivity to the issue and to its dangers. Individual talents converged in a rigorous process strictly governed by the demands of the text, with no eye to exotic effects, but with every sense of what Peter Brook always insisted on: "theatre lives by surprise."

All reassembled for a fortnight of technical fine-tuning in Delhi, preceding the opening night on 1 April 2006.

PRODUCT

If one word can possibly sum up Supple's production in all its senses, it is translation. The transformative threat in all of us, uncovering latent bestial urges but hopefully exorcising them, is what Supple inherited from the psychoanalytical legacy and delved into further in his *Dream*. It is not insignificant that he directed Ovid's *Metamorphoses* in 1999—incidentally, one of Shakespeare's sources. The *Dream* is all about translation, in the old meaning of metamorphosis. Helena is prepared to give the world to be "translated" into Hermia; Puck declares that he has "translated" Pyramus; and, in the most familiar line in this vein, Bottom's colleagues tell him, aghast, "thou art translated." But Supple sought to go beyond Brook, believing the *Dream* "to be a great drama of discord and reconciliation that takes place in the social, sexual and spiritual arenas," as he put it in correspondence with me, and looking to see "what happens if each episode is given absolute seriousness and dignity."[6] This intent was recognized by perceptive critics like Michael Dobson:

> all [the characters], faced with real opportunity, are liable to find their adherence to monogamy faltering. ... The reunion and reintegration of not just the couples but all the disparate elements of this production ... within the wedding celebrations of Act 5 is both a relief and a miracle, complete with acres of red silk, semi-modern wedding clothes, and thousands of falling petals.[7]

One Shakespearean scholar remarked that it was "filled with moments of grace and tenderness (as in Hermia's reconciliation with Egeus),"[8] which clearly served to sublimate the tense scenes or bravura spectacle that may have hogged the media limelight.

But I anticipate. The translation in fact began with the locales, each one of them transformed. As the production flew anticlockwise round India in April 2006, spectators walked into some very uncommon and striking open-air venues picked specifically for their suitability to the play. Delhi offered the classical lawns of the showpiece Indira Gandhi National Centre for the Arts. The Mumbai Metropolitan Road Development Authority reclamation grounds, of late the site of big-time rock concerts, evoked a different atmosphere altogether. In Chennai, the readymade amphitheatre of Buck's Theatre presented another charming outdoor location. The tour concluded in Kolkata on the sylvan, magical, sloping landscape of Tollygunge Club, home to jackals that howled appreciatively and fireflies that flitted in the dark. In each case, the entire performance space was created from scratch and then returned to its pristine condition. Titania's words "in the spiced Indian air, by night," invoked later by several critics responding to the British shows inside regular halls, carried a breathtakingly naturalistic association on the Indian tour.

The *Dream*'s trajectory occurred within India, not merely in the facile sense of travelling geographically. Within minutes of the opening scene, Indian audiences became conscious of Supple's innovative use of multiple tongues. How appropriate that translations—this time in the modern sense—into so many Indian languages should have jostled side by side in this production, for Indians are after all a multilingual people. The last act also alluded to the sensitive politics of the English language in India: the aristocrats talked in English, somewhat condescendingly at first, while watching the sincere theatrics of the mechanicals. This seemed like what Shakespeare himself had in mind, for his mechanicals mispronounced and malapropized the Queen's English, but ultimately impressed the elite viewers with their unmistakably genuine passion. Too often we treat the artisans patronizingly as uneducated and unsophisticated, at best unintentional farceurs.

Another aspect of Shakespeare's play struck home unexpectedly in India. As reported by the representative of the London *Times* in Delhi, the father arranging for his daughter to marry a man of his choice and the divisions between social classes resonate more with audiences in India than in the West. She quoted Supple: "All those things are alive in India. I have actors whose families have not spoken to them for 20 years because they married the wrong person; actors whose experiences come closer to the play than those of British actors."[9]

Translation as metamorphosis is an idea not too far removed from reincarnation. Indeed, the *Dream* belongs to the subgenre of classic philosophical dream dramas like Calderon's *Life Is a Dream* and Strindberg's

Dream Play. The concept of dreaming should have drawn Indians, since the concept of maya, which sees life as a dream, deeply embeds the Hindu-Buddhist consciousness. There is something metaphysically and metatheatrically Indian about Puck stepping out of character and addressing the audience in the coda: "you have but slumbered here/While these visions did appear." The many occurrences of the word "dream" are complemented by Shakespeare's ambivalent use of "vision": just as in Indian tradition, a dream can seem a revelatory vision upon awakening,[10] while a vision can carry connotations of deception because it relies on the sense of sight. Hence Oberon says the lovers' nightmare in the forest both "Shall seem a dream and fruitless vision." After Titania and Bottom wake up separately, she exclaims "what visions have I seen!" while he states matter-of-factly, "I have had a most rare vision." What is the nature of each of these "visions"? Visuals create the most immediately appealing dimension of any *Dream* production. But if presented too literally, for instance in the spectacular nineteenth-century manner, they detract from visionary insight. Supple's art attempted to slice through superficial artifice into deeper visual reality, the kind we see in dreams, in the dance of the forests and in the realm of the spirit, and—to continue the play of words on vision—appeared to have succeeded.

Much of this formed the stuff of pure coincidence, since Supple told me that he did not choose the play for its Indian links, if any. But an artistic product takes on its own life that the creator can never foresee, and the choice seemed to me delightfully serendipitous nonetheless.

To bring us back to ground reality, I overheard some cynics voicing their disapproval of the enormous funding (translated quite visibly into the stagecraft) that the British Council lavished on the production. I found the scepticism misplaced, because the same people never criticize art films that typically have even bigger budgets. They assume that cinema has every right to such finances, whereas theatre must remain idealistically poor. They also did not consider that nobody stood to gain a single rupee, except for the deserving artists, technical support, and ancillary units directly engaged in providing services to the production. This is because the British Council, under Indo-British bilateral agreements on arts and culture, does not charge admission to such shows. Tickets were not sold: free passes were distributed—first come, first served.

As I indicated briefly above, the project did not terminate there. It went in June 2006 to the Swan Theatre in Stratford-upon-Avon, for twelve shows at the first-ever "Complete Works of Shakespeare Festival" organized by the Royal Shakespeare Company. The acrobatics on display, reported Michael Dobson, included "feats so excitingly risky that the show was nearly forbidden by health and safety officers before it even opened."[11] It had three performances later that month in a huge ancient Roman amphitheatre in Verona, Italy. Subsequently, it ran indoors at the Roundhouse, London, followed by a UK itinerary in 2007, and returned to proscenium stages in India and Sri Lanka in 2008, concluding with a world tour stretching from Australia to Canada.

Reception

Keval Arora, a professor of English and arguably Delhi's most caustic critic, raised multilingualism as a bogey:

[The languages]operate indiscriminately in performance, cropping up and dropping out without evident purpose or necessity. With some characters speaking primarily in one language and others switching between languages for no apparent cause; with no patterns being discernible in the connections drawn between situation, character and the language/s used, Supple's multilingualism add [sic] up to little more than a noble-hearted linguistic egalitarianism. ... The idea that languages are grounded in socio-cultural spaces and are imbricated in personal identity, that they shape memories of shared pasts and imagined futures, that they are as much bones of contention as means of contestations—none of these, on the evidence of the performance, seems part of Supple's plan. ... It's ironical that Supple's inclusivist gesture towards the individual actor ends up as an exclusionary experience for his spectators.[12]

Vasanthi Sankaranarayanan in Chennai repeated the charges, specifically targeting the awkward Malayalam translation, which in her view resulted in inferior acting from the speakers.[13]

Let us address the language issue before continuing to other matters. Christopher Conway, professor of modern languages at the University of Texas, Arlington, saw the *Dream* in London and wrote in his blog:

The potential objections are obvious: *The whole point of Shakespeare IS the English language. How can we appreciate what we don't understand?* ... Is a Shakespeare play primarily to be understood as the sum of the poet's words in English or the sum of his invention as a creator of scenes and plots and themes that transcend language? Supple's version may estrange English speakers from Shakespeare at first, but then we discover that we are able to experience the play on new, different levels. We see it chromatically, musically, in terms of choreography, stage design and acting. Freed from English, we discover a new Shakespeare, one that is constructed out of visual metaphor and action. And surprise, it is wonderful and hypnotic, it is entertaining and moving.[14]

Susanne Greenhalgh, of Roehampton University, London, reviewed the Stratford show for Shakespeare Bulletin:

> If English-only speakers missed out on the raunchy humor of some of the Hindi lines (translated by the actor who played Puck), the poetic cadences of Lysander's words in Bengali, or the archaic style of Malayalam spoken by Oberon, the production's soundscape was both dreamlike and teasingly meaningful: in Supple's words, like "a voice that is made up of different sounds." Rhythms—both aural and visual—were created that were equivalent in power, if different in form, to Shakespeare's poetry. With no one common verbal language, body language became a kind of lingua franca, especially the martial art Kalarippayattu, in which the entire cast trained during their seven weeks of rehearsals. It was this shared high-energy physical expertise, together with the cast's commitment to transparent storytelling, that both created a strong a sense of ensemble playing, and enabled unimpeded communication between the performers, and, crucially, with the audience.[15]

David Green, Director General of the British Council, present at the premiere in Delhi, made an unusual observation:

> What was created in that production of A Midsummer Night's Dream was a third space between the players and the audience—a place where real communication and connection happens. Musicians talk about such a space, the interactive space where the performance meets the audience. ... That interactivity, that suspension of disbelief by both partners in the communication, that willingness of both parts to make an effort to bridge a gap, that is the art of communicating, and communicating internationally, across borders and other less easily identified boundaries between people.[16]

Returning to Kolkata in 2008, Supple, in an interview to a student of English at Jadavpur University (which has a faculty reputed for teaching Shakespeare), countered the attack on multilingualism tartly:

> "Everybody asks that question as if it is a problem, but why? Why in life are we so stuck with language?" he retorts. "Language is important and I'd find it very hard to have a close friendship or love affair with someone who spoke a different language, but you never know. Why should we restrict our communication to only languages we know? Of course it helps, but it's not necessary. Theatre is the magic, it's the magic of communication."[17]

I wish to add one more provocative point to the defence, that the original English itself may have become an alien medium in our times, that Shakespeare's own language is in such grave danger of unintelligibility to even Anglophone lay audiences today that it has turned into an exclusionary experience (in Arora's terminology): many passages of his unedited text may just as well be in Malayalam or Hindi, for all that the ordinary theatregoer may understand. Modern directors know only too well that it needs translation through various art forms.

Going back to the economic/exploitative debate, we find Dobson summing up the positions:

> An uncharitable account of this production, putting the least generous construction on its explanatory programme notes, would say that Tim Supple had been given a budget to travel around the Indian subcontinent cherry-picking the best talents in a range of local types of performance and had then simply gone through the script of *A Midsummer Night's Dream* deciding where they could each show off their respective acts to best effect, thereby assembling a show masquerading as a Shakespeare revival but really offering a composite, exoticized vision of India for audiences of *de facto* tourists. ...It is difficult to sustain this critique, however, in the face of Supple's *Dream* itself which ... ground[s] itself in an intelligent, original and cogent reading of the play. (It is also so consistently enjoyable—not least, frankly, because its cast are all unnaturally good-looking and wear few clothes, and those beautiful—that criticism is largely in abeyance for its duration.)[18]

That parenthetical throwaway, however tongue-in-cheek, opens another front, of the generic Western critic's inherently problematic gaze, relishing exotica and erotica while periodically tut-tutting at their incorrectness. Some of their words that recur tell a revealing tale: "fantastical" (not fantastic), "sexy," "sensuality," "ravishing," "savage," "strangeness"—innocuous by themselves, but tricky when applied to non-Western performances because of their associations with otherness. Despite Supple's rejection of exoticization, despite the media's acceptance of his disclaimers, despite politically-correct sensibilities, despite twenty-first-century sensitivity, the West's fascination for difference and novelty continued to raise an off-key voice amid the chorus of encomia. Old Orientalist habits die hard.

Squarely in my sights is Michael Billington of the *Guardian*, so respected a critic that the *Oxford Encyclopedia of Theatre and Performance* even has an entry on him. He called Ajay Kumar (Puck) "raccoon-haired" and Archana Ramaswamy (Hippolyta/Titania) "raven-haired," echoed in 2007 as "raven-black hair" by Charles Spencer in the *Daily Telegraph*.[19] Many reviewers were fixated by her "cascade of black hair falling below her waist" (*Observer*).[20] The *Independent*'s critic, an obvious devotee of Billington, even lifted some of his vocabulary, describing Puck with "a raccoon haircut ... lustrating a phallic symbol."[21] The raccoon, a much-maligned American animal, does not normally occur in British writing, and "lustrating" is a rare term, accurately used by Billington for Puck's actions. Plagiarism is the best form of flattery. But, besides the fact that Kumar's Mohawk hair-style hardly resembled a raccoon, I wondered whether an Indian would ever describe Kenneth Branagh as "fox-haired" or Gwyneth Paltrow as "jute-tressed." The epithets are irrelevant; based on looks, they do not illuminate character. And Billington noticed "an audible gear change when actors switched from their first language into English."[22] I wondered what he thinks of Scot-inflected or Irish-accented English, let alone West Indian or African English.

Amusingly, the reviews attempted to display some familiarity with Hindi films. According to the *Daily Telegraph*, "The lovers are Indian rich kids, gorgeous in their silks, like the stars of Bollywood movies."[23] *The Times* considered Bottom (appreciated by all the newspapers) "as vain as a Bollywood heart-throb."[24] I doubt Supple ever had such ideas, nor did I see any similarities between the actor, Joy Fernandes, and any of the Khans. At the other extreme of popular entertainment, the *Daily Telegraph* referred to "fire-eaters" in the show:[25] they certainly were not present. India's artistic image seems caught between fire-eating and "filmy" gyrating. At least Billington pointed out, "But if this production brings out the play's sexiness and savagery, it is not because it is Indian: it is because those qualities are there in the first place."[26]

By all accounts, however, most spectators were emotionally overwhelmed. David Green said of the Indian tour, "By the end audiences were spell-bound, gave standing ovations and, when it came to the wedding song at the end, performed in Sanskrit, were often, myself included, in tears."[27]

The production received unanimous accolades from the mainstream British press. The *Daily Telegraph* predicted that it "will be remembered, and talked about, for decades to come, just like Peter Brook's landmark staging for the RSC in 1970."[28] Others repeated the same thought. Dobson documented a rare sight: "When did I last see an audience standing to applaud at the end of a show in the Swan? At the end of Suzman's *Hamlet*, come to think of it, and I don't think that this just represents a hospitable impulse to be indiscriminately nice to all this season's foreign visitors."[29] A friend who lives outside Stratford and sees a lot of plays confirmed this: "At the end all the audience stood up to applaud immediately! I have never seen that before."[30] Supple himself told his cast not to expect a standing ovation in Stratford, and was astonished that every performance there elicited one.[31]

Susanne Greenhalgh considered it a "celebration of a Shakespeare no longer owned by any one language or culture: a Shakespeare, in Helena's words, 'Mine own and not mine own'."[32] Christopher Hart of the *Sunday Times* redoubled the praise after the Roundhouse rerun in London: "This troupe has taken our national poet, transmuted him into something rich and strange and almost unrecognisable, then given him back to us. What a gift. What a dream of a Dream."[33]

INFLUENCE

As we have seen, for the Indian audiences to whom Supple's *Dream* first played, the most resistant element may have been its polyglot script. Their unreasonable expectation of monolingual drama arises not only from habituation to that mode in theatre but also from the tyranny of literary studies dependent on the reading of books printed necessarily in one, "pure" language. This is all the more so when that language is the revered Bard's very own English, which Indians may indeed regard as more sacrosanct than the English themselves do. A hangover of the British Raj, this attitude forgets, ironically enough, that a vast body of South Asians in their daily routine speak at the very least bilingually. It conveniently ignores as well the hallowed precedent of Indian classical theatre, for which "Sanskrit drama" is a misnomer, since the manuscripts are not exclusively in Sanskrit, but frequently utilize various ancient Prakrits (commoners' regional languages) in the same play according to the situation.

By contrast, in the West, thanks to globalization and the increasing frequency of cross-cultural exchange, multilingual theatre has become fairly common, particularly in international projects. Not too many playgoers there raise their cyebrows any more at the fact that they cannot understand every word of such productions. One logic is that good actors convey the meaning of their speeches nonverbally anyway. Supple did not feel handicapped by the multiplicity of languages, and expressed his views to me unambiguously: "Of course the original text has a special quality, whether Shakespeare or Schiller ... on the other hand, I can't accept the superiority of any language."[34] So, in arguably the first-ever Indian production of this nature—at least to my knowledge—he brought together actors speaking eight different South Asian tongues on stage.

This had happened so far only on a much limited scale (a maximum of three languages) in specific cities under guest directors, never at a national, leave alone subcontinental, level. In this historic event, a foreign director achieved some kind of linguistic national integration for Indian theatre before any Indian did. Keval Arora dismissed my opinion "as an instance of our Indian habit of being hospitable to the point of embarrassing everybody around,"[35] but I hold my ground. Indian theatre had never featured so many languages in a single performance before, and many could not accept it precisely because of this; world theatre history tells us how often revolutionary steps have been initially rejected. Usually, whether on screen or stage, Indian films, plays and television programmes are delivered in one language, though cinema and television increasingly adopt Hinglish (a Hindi-English melange). We might have some other bilingualism, for instance a Hindi movie that contains some dialogue in a language like Marathi. Conversely, a regional drama, film or serial may have a smattering of Hindi or English, since these are India's linguae francae. Multilingual theatre lives in the West, even if as something of a fad; but in India where it has barely entered, it has every empirical reason not only to exist, but to unite the diverse country and thrive.

Supple applied one principle of great significance in his casting. He refused to reject talented Indian actors merely because they might not talk well enough in English. Thus he gave everybody a fair chance at auditions whereas, in the normal process, speakers of only one language would have been considered. Already I notice the impact of viewing Supple's *Dream* in the work of some younger Indian troupes. Although I would not go so far as to say that they audition language-blind, yet they have opened up significantly to performers in other mother tongues who previously would never have entered their ken. Dramatists, too, have written some multilingual scripts; or, to put it more accurately, a certain trend towards bilingual drama that existed before Supple accelerated after the *Dream*. One of my students, a Tamilian in Bengal studying English, incorporated several languages (including Spanish) into a play he offered me in 2009, which I directed. My current production of a Tagore classic has upset purists because I use four Indian languages in it—the first time Tagore has received more than monolingual treatment. I cite these examples only because I know of their debt to Supple; I have seen many others over the last five years, but never asked the directors if Supple influenced them, though I suspect he did.

Secondarily, Supple's direction taught most of his cast techniques that they had only read in theory. One actor told me that this was the first time he had encountered the grammar of Shakespearean performance. Others must have registered that Supple's psychological archaeology of characterization, his emphasis on what a character *does* in a scene, crystallized the Stanislavskian tenets of the through line, units, and objectives. Supple was not the first foreign director of his stature to interact with Indian actors, but it helps for them to refresh their praxis given such an opportunity. Yet, much as he relies on the introspective realistic school of acting, he has a sharp eye for the openly extroverted, presentational, and theatrical; and this combination creates his original stamp. Additionally, his emphasis on stripping the performers of superfluous emotions and getting to the truth, paring from excess to essence, made them aware of the overblown style of mainstream proscenium and screen acting in Asia. A few confided to me that they would try to adopt his directorial methods. If so, his influence on Indian theatre seems assured. One actor raised an unexpected point in praise of the ready accessibility to various *Indian* forms in the process of this production: it allowed for long-term exposure to many traditions that would have been impossible to gain elsewhere, because this kind of experience, even in India, generally takes place only in short-term, single-form workshops.

Supple's practice also offered a model code for one ordinarily neglected aspect of the arts: payments to performers. He insisted on equality in emoluments to all, regardless of seniority or contribution, thereby removing the major stumbling block that has tainted intercultural theatre. Naturally this principle increased the budget, but Supple stayed firm. Highlighting his democratic method of working, the *Times* interviewed Dharminder Pawar, one of the fairies:

> Raised in a Delhi slum, he is from a traditional acrobat family who worked as street entertainers across north India. ... "In the beginning I was nervous because there were all these people from good backgrounds and I am from the slums. But Tim has been a unifying force for everybody," he says in Hindi. "Wherever he has stayed, we have stayed. Whatever he eats, we eat."[36]

Simple sentiments in our sceptical times; nevertheless, one hopes that this ideal percolates into many more theatre groups, not just in India but everywhere.

And to conclude, the influence did not operate only one way, upon Indians. The *Sunday Times* quoted Supple in 2007:

> the way I work here is the way I want to work with actors from now on. ...Text, characterisation, realism: those things aren't there [in Indian theatre] in the same way. But there's a wealth of skill and artistry, coupled with this bursting, vibrant ability to connect that is so hard to find in the West. I discovered I'm much happier working this way around.[37]

NOTES

1. Poonam Trivedi, "Introduction," in *India's Shakespeare: Translation, Interpretation, and Performance*, ed. Poonam Trivedi and Dennis Bartholomeusz (Newark: University of Delaware Press, 2005), 36.
2. An excellent analysis of the production is to be found in Sofía Muñoz Valdivieso, "'Mine ear is much enamour'd of thy note': Shakespeare's Intercultural Dream in the Indian Subcontinent," *SEDERI* 19 (2009): 99–119. Valdivieso saw the play in San Francisco in 2008.
3. In this essay I have used material from my programme notes for the British Council (India) and Royal Shakespeare Company (Stratford) playbills, and my articles in *The Telegraph* (Kolkata) and *Connecting* (New Delhi).
4. Raekha Prasad, "All the world's on stage," *The Times*, 15 April 2006; Lucy Powell, "In his wildest dream," *Sunday Times*, 4 March 2007. Supple, in "Making The Dream—a director's story," British Council playbill for *A Midsummer Night's Dream* ([April 2006]), had mentioned seeing vibrant theatre at various places in India, including an unspecified "jungle outside Kolkata," on the first trip. The journalists took that phrase and applied it to his auditions. See my section on "Reception," below, for an examination of such exoticized responses to the production.
5. Tim Supple, quoted in Ananda Lal, "Language and the Dream," Royal Shakespeare Company playbill for *A Midsummer Night's Dream* ([June 2006]). Edited from his email to me, 6 May 2006.
6. Tim Supple, email to me, 6 March 2006.
7. Michael Dobson, "Shakespeare Performances in England, 2006: 15 June 2006," *Shakespeare Survey* 60 (2007): 302.
8. Michael Shapiro on the Chicago performance: email to me, 9 December 2008.
9. Prasad.
10. In many Indian folkloric or traditional stories, a sleeper wakes up to find that the dream he has seen actually holds a deep spiritual significance, like the dream that inquisitive Narada had when Vishnu induced him to sleep: he dreamt his entire life up to his own death, and woke up to find himself with Vishnu exactly where he had last left him. Sanskrit drama plays with the idea too, most famously in Bhasa's *Svapnavasavadatta* (literally "Vasavadatta in the Dream," or in the usual rendering "The Dream of Vasavadatta").
11. Dobson, 301.
12. Keval Arora, "Dabbling in Babble," at http://www.stagebuzz.info/PAGES/Columnists/Keval%20Dabbling%20in%20Babble.htm.
13. Vasanthi Sankaranarayanan, "A Midsummer Night's Dream," 28 April 2006, at http://www.narthaki.com/info/reviews/rev344.html.
14. Christopher Conway, "Tim Supple's A Midsummer Night's Dream at the Roundhouse Theatre, London," 22 March 2007, at http://drconway.wordpress.com/2007/03/22/tim-supples-a-midsummer-nights-dream-at-the-roundhouse-theatre-london/.
15. Susanne Greenhalgh, "Theatre Reviews: A Midsummer Night's Dream," *Shakespeare Bulletin* 24 (Winter 2006): 66–7.
16. David Green, "The Role of the Third Space in Inter-cultural Dialogue," printed paper delivered at a conference on "Multilingualism and Intercultural Dialogue in Globalisation," University of Delhi, 11–12 December 2008, 2.

17. Monidipa Mondal, "Creating a Dream: An Interview with Tim Supple," 1 February 2008, http://exnihilomagazine.wordpress.com/2008/02/01/creating-a-dream-an-interview-with-tim-supple/.
18. Dobson, 301–2.
19. Michael Billington, "Indian Summer," *Guardian*, 31 May 2006, at http://www.guardian.co.uk/stage/2006/may/31/theatre.india; Michael Billington, "A Midsummer Night's Dream," 9 June 2006, http://www.guardian.co.uk/stage/2006/jun/09/theatre.rsc; Charles Spencer, "A delirious Dream of India," *Daily Telegraph*, 15 March 2007.
20. Kate Kellaway, "Indian summer of heat and lust," *Observer*, 18 March 2007.
21. Paul Taylor, "A Midsummer Night's Dream," *Independent*, 12 June 2006.
22. Billington, "Indian Summer."
23. Charles Spencer, "A fantastical, unforgettable Dream," *Daily Telegraph*, 12 June 2006.
24. Sam Marlowe, "A Midsummer Night's Dream," *The Times*, 10 June 2006.
25. Spencer, "A fantastical, unforgettable Dream."
26. Billington, "Indian Summer."
27. Green, 1.
28. Spencer, "A fantastical, unforgettable Dream."
29. Dobson, 302.
30. Lady Christabel Watson, email to me, 19 June 2006.
31. Muñoz Valdivieso, 103.
32. Greenhalgh, 69.
33. Christopher Hart, "Oh, what a night," *Sunday Times*, 18 March 2007.
34. Tim Supple, quoted in Lal, "The Dream—a journey through time."
35. Arora.
36. Prasad.
37. Powell.

7 Shakespeare in Indian Cinema: Appropriation, Assimilation, and Engagement

Rajiva Verma

The broad lines of development in the history of film adaptations of Shakespeare in India are by now well delineated. The earliest period, or the appropriative phase, which stretches from the silent era to around the middle of the 1950s, was dominated by adaptations in the Parsi theatre mode, with the 1930s being the most prolific decade. The term Parsi theatre refers to professional theatrical companies that flourished in the period 1850–1940 and constituted the first commercial theatre in modern India. Owned mainly by Parsi businessmen from Gujarat and Mumbai, these companies had playhouses in several cities across the country that staged popular melodramas in Gujarati, Urdu, and Hindi. Like the earliest Shakespearean films in the West, which were based on stage performances, the early Indian films, including silent versions of *Hamlet* and *The Merchant of Venice*, were probably shot from staged versions of Parsi theatre adaptations of the plays. That certainly was the case with Sohrab Modi's film *Hamlet* (1935), based on his own theatre company's version of one of the most popular Urdu plays in the Parsi theatre repertoire, *Khoon-e-Nahak*. As the hero of the film, Modi brought to his role his experience of acting in his own stage productions of the play.

The major difference between the Western and Indian adaptation seems to have been that while the reference point for the former was the Shakespearean text, for the latter is was the very loose Parsi theatre adaptation or appropriation of the original play; and it was only through such adaptation, if at all, that the Shakespearean original became a point of reference for a select few among the audience. Though it is undoubtedly important, the Shakespearean connection of the Parsi theatre should not be exaggerated. In the majority of the Parsi theatre plays, as well as in their film versions, there was no real engagement with the Shakespearean play, no attempt to construct a parallel structure of action. What we have here is not adaptation but appropriation of some striking individual scenes or episodes. Thus in Agha Hashr Kashmiri's play *Khwab-e-Hasti* (1908), a close adaptation, almost a literal translation, of the sleep-walking scene from *Macbeth* has been fitted into a sequence of very different events. The only other parallel is a scene which echoes Lady Macbeth's chastisement of Macbeth with the "valour of her tongue," including the taunt about his manhood, the sexual nature of which is even more emphatic in the Urdu than in the original.[1]

Similarly, Hashr's *Said-e-Havas* (1907), which was turned into a film by Sohrab Modi under the same title in 1936, contains scenes which are, but for the changed names of the characters, an almost literal translation of the scenes relating to the episode of Hubert and Arthur in *King John*; however, the two plays have little else in common.[2] The alleged connection between *Said-e-Havas* and *Richard III* is even more tenuous.

The fact that Hashr used portions of a play like *King John* is itself of considerable interest, for it is not a play that was widely known. Though excerpts from the play constituted the first ever film made anywhere on a Shakespearean play, it is unlikely that Hashr had seen it. Another possible reason for the choice of *King John* could have been an interest in the history plays for their resonances with an evolving national consciousness, but of this too there is little evidence in *Said-e-Havas* or other Parsi theatre plays. The film versions of these plays, made during the 1930s, a period of great intensification of the national movement for freedom from British colonial rule, also failed to address the issue of nationhood. This is true even of Sohrab Modi, many of whose films were deeply imbued with the spirit of nationalism and social reform, for his two Shakespearean films do not seem to have established any significant connection, however oblique, with such issues.

This is in striking contrast to films such as *Sikandar* (1941) and *Jhansi ki Rani* (1953). While the latter is about the queen who fought against the British in 1857, the former is equally nationalistic in its celebration of the heroism of King Porus in a battle against Alexander the Great in 326 BCE. Even though the film made no explicit reference to contemporary times and was passed by the censors, its popularity made the British government so apprehensive that it was thought prudent to prevent its screening in cinema halls in sensitive areas, particularly cantonments. No such apprehensions were aroused by the film adaptations of *King John* and other Parsi theatre films, since none of them reflected any historical awareness of the present. Thus the choice of *King John* probably had nothing to do with any interest in the play as a whole, or in Shakespeare's historical vision, or in the historical reality of colonial India, but depended on purely contingent factors. Similar factors were probably behind other surprising choices like Sheridan's *Pizzaro* and Addison's *Cato*, both of which were adapted for the Parsi theatre.

Kenneth Rothwell divides films based on Shakespeare's plays into two broad categories of "adaptation" and "derivative," the major difference being that "adaptations rely heavily on Shakespeare's actual words, and derivatives abandon his language altogether."[3] Rothwell then proceeds to identify seven kinds of derivatives, but excludes foreign-language Shakespeare films from this classification, though it applies equally well to Indian Shakespeare films. The majority of Parsi theatre films may be seen as derivatives of the fifth or "parasitical" type, "which exploit Shakespeare for embellishment and/or graft brief visual or verbal quotations onto an otherwise unrelated scenario," provided the "brief visual or verbal quotations" are understood as extendable to an entire scene or even several scenes.

Since these films, with a few exceptions to be discussed below, appropriate rather than adapt Shakespeare, it is not usually a profitable exercise to do a comparative study of the original and the derivative. The Shakespearean interest of these films is of a broader kind: as the first commercial theatre in India organized on the lines of professional popular theatres in the West, the Parsi theatre offers many interesting parallels with the development of Shakespeare's own theatre. Each developed in a period of newly emergent and intense national consciousness. Yet as they developed and flourished, the demand for fresh material led both theatres to draw from vast reservoirs of stories of diverse kinds in diverse settings, native and foreign, familiar and exotic, reflecting an openness to other cultures and peoples, at least in imagination if not in actual practice, that is rarely found at other times. The Parsi theatre plays and films, as well as other Bombay films of the period 1920–50, drew their stories from diverse multicultural sources, of which European drama including Shakespeare was only one. Others included the *Ramayana* and the *Mahabharata*, a variety of tales of romance and courtly intrigue, episodes from history, and the lives of saints.

We find here the same imaginative openness that characterized the Elizabethan drama. In scores of mainstream films of the 1930s and '40s, including the Shakespearean films, the protagonists were Muslims; on the other hand, several Parsi theatre plays, including many written by Agha Hashr Kashmiri, were based on episodes from the Sanskrit epics, and both kinds of films and plays could be equally popular. There has been a gradual shrinking of this imaginative space since those early days: in later mainstream popular cinema, it is difficult to find examples of films that have foreigners or members of minority groups as protagonists. The only exceptions are films made within the well-recognized parameters of the ethnic or regional film.[4]

Another common feature of the two theatres is the primacy given to language and rhetoric. They were verbal theatres, not merely because they depended on words rather than stage properties and props (the Parsi theatre indeed often exploited the popular appeal of grand sets and costumes) but because they actually revelled in the arts of language and flaunted this delight unabashedly.[5] More than any other feature, it is its striking language and peculiar rhetoric that distinguishes Parsi theatre from other theatrical traditions, and the Parsi theatre films, including the Shakespearean derivatives, made no effort to depart from this to adopt a distinctively cinematic style. This was the main reason for their appeal but also, as the art of cinema developed and moved away from its theatrical origin, the main reason for their decline.

Apart from several parasitical derivatives of the fifth type mentioned earlier, particularly in the 1930s, there were three films, all in Urdu, in the Parsi theatre mode that engaged with Shakespearean plays in a more sustained manner, and can be seen as attempts to adapt rather than merely appropriate. These were Sohrab Modi's *Hamlet* (1935), whose full title was *Hamlet alias Khoon ka Khoon*, Akhtar Hussain's *Romeo and Juliet* (1947; with Nargis and Sapru as actors), and Kishore Sahu's *Hamlet* (1954). While the Parsi type of adaptation was still a point of reference, these films presented a more complex web of intertextuality within a triangular relationship with the Shakespearean text and its Parsi theatre version. Adding to this complexity was the fact that both the film and its Parsi theatre original did not merely refer to the Shakespearean play or to a part of it as its source, but also made frequent allusions, either specific or general, to various Indian texts including, in particular, classics of Urdu poetry. There was also, as mentioned above, an earlier silent movie on *Hamlet* titled *Khoon-e-Nahak* (Unjust Assassination) *or Hamlet* (1928) by Raja Athavale, as well as a silent movie, directed by M. Udvadia, using *The Merchant of Venice* under the title of *Dil Farosh* (1927). Little is known about these films, except that both were obviously derived from Parsi theatre adaptations of the two plays.

It has been remarked that Modi's *Hamlet* was one of the earliest talkies based on a Shakesepeare play made anywhere in the world.[6] It was derived from Modi's own adaptation of the play for his brother Rustam Modi's theatre company Arya Sobodh Natya Mandali. Titled *Khoon ka Khoon* (Blood for

Blood), it had Indian names for the characters. Modi himself played the central role of Jehangir (Hamlet), and the play was a great commercial success. According to Modi's own account, the film was shot as a stage performance of the play, and the producer must have hoped to capitalize on the play's popularity. As all prints of the film seem to have been lost, and there is little specific information about the script and staging of the play, any comment on the relation of the film to the play *Khoon ka Khoon* must be purely conjectural. Still, on the basis of the film's posters, stills, and reviews, a few points can be made with a reasonable degree of certainty.

The film was not merely based on a Parsi theatre play: it highlighted this connection through its very title and assumed the audience's familiarity with the play. But, unlike the play, it seems the film gave the characters Shakespearean names, though there is no absolute certainty on this point. The film looked back to the Shakespearean original as well as its Indian adaptation, and addressed the elite as well as the masses. As brought out by the costume, sets and gestures, the film also evinces a familiarity with the Western performance tradition of *Hamlet*, and there is a witty allusion and tribute to its author in the play-within-the-play scene, where Shakespeare's portrait adorns the arch in front of the inner stage where that scene is enacted.[7] The double title of the film also points to an interesting intercultural and intertextual phenomenon: while one component, "Hamlet" is designed to attract the educated English-knowing elite and to dignify a popular art form, the other, "Khoon ka Khoon," seeks to draw the crowds by offering them the chance to experience once again the thrill and pleasure of sitting through a performance, in a different mode, of a familiar and popular play. In other words, it seeks to exploit both the cultural capital of the canonical text written in the language of the colonial rulers and the commercial possibilities of the popular Parsi theatre play.

Presumably the silent *Khoon-e-Nahak or Hamlet* also had this double appeal. What we have in each of these two instances is not a text and a subtext, or a text in the foreground and a network of analogues and allusions in the background, but two texts equally foregrounded and on the surface. This was not the case with the majority of Parsi theatre plays using plots or scenes from Shakespeare, for in them the "source" text is quite overwhelmed by an aggressive and supremely confident act of appropriation.

The more literary translations of Shakespeare in the nineteenth century present yet another and more peculiar relation to the source. Formally they would be classified as adaptations: they used Indian names for characters and places without trying, except in a few instances, to historically recontextualize the action. It seems they were thrilled by the possibility of finding similar-sounding Indian equivalents, derived from Sanskrit, for Shakespearean names. Thus in Bharatendu Harishchandra's *Durlabh Bandhu* (1880), a Hindi adaptation of *The Merchant of Venice*, Shylock became Sarlakhsh, Antonio Anant, Bassanio Basant, Portia Purashree, Venice Vanshpur, and Belmont Bilwamath. Similarly, in a Hindi translation of *Othello*, Othello is rechristened as Atal, Iago as Agya, and Desdemona as Digdamini.[8] The resemblances hinted at actual etymological derivations for which there was no sound linguistic basis, but the practice probably has its origin in the nineteenth-century discourse of comparative mythology and Indo-European philology. In a colonial situation, the idea of a common Indo-European origin upon which this discourse was premised must have been greatly attractive, and an important factor in this kind of assimilation of Shakespeare.

Bharatendu's play *Durlabh Bandhu* (Rare Friends) is perhaps the only adaptation from this period to seek a quasi-historical equivalent for the action of the original. In it, the Christian–Jew antagonism is converted into the antagonism between Hindus and Jains in an unspecified historical period; but the conversion is casual and incomplete, and in one instance Bharatendu forgets the equation already established and makes Shylock refer to his antagonists as Isai (Christians)![9] However, while the adaptation of the action was thus most perfunctory and casual, the text itself was translated here and in many other such plays in its entirety, with literal accuracy and sometimes with great verbal felicity. The purpose of such adaptations seems to have been to show how easily and naturally a Shakespearean play could be assimilated into the Indian context, though both this context and the original context of the play were presented in the most general, unlocalized manner. The most striking difference between the two traditions was in the language of the plays. These plays, which could be in either verse or prose, used Hindi, Bengali or other regional languages with varying degrees of Sanskritization, eschewing the most distinctive feature of the Parsi theatre, its highly inflated and flamboyant rhetoric.

We thus have two extremes: on the one hand, plays which are ostensibly adaptations since they include changed (though similar-sounding) names of characters and places, but which are actually accurate, almost literal translations; on the other hand, a film like Modi's *Hamlet*, which promises to be a translation but is in reality a free adaptation or appropriation in the manner of Parsi theatre plays. However, both kinds of adaptations lacked historical specificity, setting the action in some unspecified and unhistoricized period in the past: pre-Islamic in Bharatendu's play and in other adaptations of the earlier period, including Ishwar Chandra Vidyasagar's *Bhrantibilas*

(1869; a narrative version of *The Comedy of Errors* in Bengali prose), or India of the Islamic period in the Parsi theatre plays. Unlike his stage version of *Hamlet*, Modi's film does try to create an "authentic" Western setting for the action, especially with regard to costume; but some of the sets still seem to be an amalgam of Western and Islamic architecture, and in its use of songs and dances—and, presumably, its rhetorical language—it falls squarely within the tradition of the Parsi theatre.

Unlike Modi's *Hamlet*, the 1947 Urdu film of *Romeo and Juliet*, produced by the film star Nargis's own company and with her and Sapru in the lead roles, was not derived from any specific Parsi theatre play, and there was no attempt to Indianize the action. Nevertheless, there is little doubt that it retained the style and idiom of the Parsi theatre, with songs and dances and Urdu rhetoric. At least one of the songs was written by Faiz Ahmad Faiz, one of the leading Urdu poets of India and later of Pakistan. It is also quite probable that, through the very choice of a play like *Romeo and Juliet* as its base, the film sought to address obliquely the literally burning issue of the bloody partition of the country. That event was so fraught with emotion, and accompanied by such extreme and unprecedented violence, that any direct allusion to it in the film, whose making coincided almost exactly with the event, could have been risky. Both the print and the script of the film seem to have been lost, but there is the tantalizing possibility that unlike all previous Shakespeare translations and adaptations, this film boldly addressed an urgent topical issue through a straightforward, "literal" presentation that made no attempt to localize the action in an Indian setting.[10]

With Kishore Sahu's *Hamlet* (1954), the Parsi theatre tradition of Shakespearean adaptation comes to an end. By this time, an audience of young cinemagoers had emerged that had never seen a Parsi theatre play, at least not since attaining adulthood. The film makes no attempt to Indianize the action. Not only do the actors retain their Shakespearean names, but there is also an attempt at authentic costume, setting, and locale. The influence of Olivier's *Hamlet* was noted by several contemporary reviewers. There were, however, many significant departures from that film (and Shakespeare's play), especially in the plot. Moreover, the language of Sahu's film preserved the Parsi theatre heritage, while setting up the kind of complex web of intertextuality among various works and literary traditions referred to earlier: the Shakespearean text, Olivier's film, the Parsi theatre adaptations (especially *Khoon-e-Nahak*), and the Urdu literary tradition in general. But by this time, with the decline of Parsi theatre, the number of viewers who could summon their memories of the Parsi theatre adaptation while watching this movie, and thus see it merely as a filmed version of an Urdu play, had also declined. Like Modi's film, Sahu's *Hamlet* eschewed the kind of extremely free and gross appropriation of the Shakespearean text marking the typical Parsi theatre play, attempting instead a faithful and authentic depiction of the action of *Hamlet*. At the same time, both films used the characteristic language and rhetoric, songs and dances of the Parsi theatre tradition. But Sahu's film no longer had the kind of double appeal, to the elite as well as the masses, that Modi's film enjoyed, and the rhetoric of the dialogue (some of it taken verbatim from *Khoon-e-Nahak*), must have sounded rather quaint to the younger members of the audience.

The Comedy of Errors dominates the next, assimilative phase of Shakespearean adaptations, with the production of at least three films based on the play. The first of these, *Bhrantibilas* (1963), a Bengali film featuring the superstar Uttam Kumar, was based on Ishwarchandra Vidyasagar's nineteenth-century prose narrative with the same title. This is duly acknowledged in the credits, where Vidyasagar is mentioned as the author but Shakespeare's name is omitted altogether. Unlike Vidyasagar's narrative, however, the film places the action in a modern setting: and it is most likely the first Indian Shakespearean film to do so. The other two films (both in Hindi), Debu Sen's *Do Dooni Chaar* (1968; closely based on *Bhrantibilas*) and Gulzar's *Angoor* (1981), also have contemporary settings. However, none of these films sets up any creative tension between the contemporary Indian vehicle and the Shakespearean tenor. Though contemporary, the setting is unlocalized and unhistoricized in all three films, so that the only detail from the original play that none of them has been able to accommodate is the Ephesian law against the Syracusans. There is a good deal of wit and felicity in the finding of equivalents for various elements of plot and character in the original, particularly in *Angoor* in which, to cite just one example, the Syracusan Antipholus' apprehensions regarding sorcery and charlatanism in Ephesus is transformed into a paranoia fed by an addiction to detective novels; but the focus is on the similarity rather than the difference between the contemporary setting and the Shakespearean text. The setting itself is never foregrounded, but merely taken for granted and kept firmly in the background. Had the films kept to the original setting of Vidyasagar's narrative in some undefined period in the past, it would have made little difference except, perhaps, at the box-office.

The Shakespeare film renaissance of the 1990s in Hollywood and in England ushered in the third phase of Shakespearean films in India, in which there is an active, conscious and sustained engagement with the original text and its context, and a constant back-and-forth movement between the two texts. So far, there have been three important direct adaptations, besides a couple of films that could be placed in Rothwell's category of "mirror" movies.[11] These films include Vishal Bhardwaj's *Maqbool* (2003), a Hindi adaptation of *Macbeth* set in the underworld of Mumbai, and Rituparno Ghosh's English film *The Last Lear (*2007), which, with some stretching, can be seen as a mirror film, since it deals with the making of a film for which a famous old retired stage actor is persuaded to play the main role. Steeped in Shakespearean verse, the actor is deeply regretful of the fact that he never got a chance to play King Lear, the one role that he had aspired for all his life. In the relation between the old stage actor and the young, ambitious auteur-film-maker there is some reflection of the generational conflict of the Shakespearean original.

But the period has been dominated by *Othello*, which has now caught up with *Hamlet* with three screen versions in less than ten years: Jayaraj's *Kaliyattam* (1997), a Malayalam adaptation in a village setting where the low-caste hero is a *theyyam* artist who dances as a god or goddess in this ritual and folk art form of Kerala; Royston Abel's *In Othello* (2003), a mirror film in English about a theatre group in Delhi; and Vishal Bhardwaj's Hindi *Omkara* (2006), set in a violent world of crime and politics in western Uttar Pradesh.

It has been remarked that *Othello* has been Shakespeare's most popular tragedy in India, where it is regarded as a "tragedy of caste."[12] While this statement may broadly be true with respect to translations, adaptations and performances of the play, the film adaptations call for a more nuanced generalization. Contrary to the general expectation and impression, the issue of caste is conspicuous by its absence from mainstream Indian cinema. Just as the government of India decided to exclude caste from the national census from 1931 onwards, the popular cinema too banished caste from its stories. It is true that, right from the early days of Indian cinema, the exploitation of Dalits, or the caste-oppressed, has been an important subject in films made by socially conscious and ideologically progressive film-makers. There have also been many films satirizing the chicanery of the priestly class, though never of *brahmins* as a caste. But if we exclude this special category of films, the subject of caste is totally absent from popular Indian cinema. The caste of the characters is never ever mentioned, let alone foregrounded, as subject. The characters are not even given surnames that might reveal their caste. In the rare instance where that is done, usually as a gesture towards verisimilitude, the surname is not a marker of caste but of regional identity. Most of the time, caste is slid under and subsumed within class. In the daily life of urban India, caste remains submerged and surfaces only on occasions like the search for a suitable bride or groom; but it is an astonishing fact that in the hundreds of popular films depicting familial opposition to the union of young lovers, the opposition is always on the ground of class or regional origin, never caste. There is probably not even a single film that shows the family opposition as based on the boy's being, say, a *brahmin* or a *kayastha* and the girl a *rajput* or a *yadav*, though such situations are depressingly common in actual life.

In view of the above, the popularity of *Othello* would be surprising, but for the fact that the caste factor as such is underplayed in the films. It is most manifest in *Kaliyattam*, whose hero would now be called a Dalit; but class seems an equally important factor in the tragedy, since the Desdemona figure is the daughter of the village head. In *In Othello*, class and region rather than caste is the crucial factor. In a theatre group engaged on an English production of *Othello*, the Assamese actor selected to play the hero is perceived as an oustsider because of his regional accent and weak command over English grammar and diction, reflecting his class status. In *Omkara* too, though the half-caste status of Omi the hero is mentioned, not much is made of it: the father of Dolly (Desdemona) objects to the match not because Omi is only half a Brahmin, though that is something to abuse him with, but because he is a gangster.

As argued above, in the earlier Indian film adaptations of Shakespeare, there is a relatively seamless transposition from the original play to the adaptation. To change and mix the metaphor: in the absence of specific historical recontextualization, the distance between the vehicle and the tenor remains small and negotiable, so that the sense of similarity is greater than that of difference. Precisely the opposite is the case with Vishal Bhardwaj's two films, where the actions of the original plays are transposed to the world of organized crime and criminalized politics in two different locations in contemporary India. Each is presented with such wonderful specificity of detail with regard to action, setting, and language that, at one level, they can be taken as two of the most distinguished among a spate of such films to emerge from Bollywood in recent years. But the films also work at another level, where the yoking together of the heterogeneous worlds of Shakespearean drama and Indian gangster movies makes the audience move back and forth between the two worlds and the two texts, evoking both surprise and recognition as they work out witty and ingenious equations: for instance, the transformation of the witches of *Macbeth* into two astrologically-minded policemen who are both actors and observers of the action.

Though apparently similar, this is quite different from Elizabethan burlesque of classical myths such as the Danaë myth, where the shower of gold into which Zeus transforms himself to enter Danaë's chamber is presented as, in reality, a bribe given to the jailors. The astrological cops do not debunk the idea of the witches; and though they provide "comic relief," such episodes, as in a Shakespearean tragedy, are integral to the thematic concerns of the film, and to some extent to its plot as well. The equations are worked out not only at the level of plot and character but also, quite minutely, at the imagistic level. In *Maqbool,* for example, the cops, who combine the role of the witches with that of the Porter, rework, while urinating, the Porter's "streamy" Freudian association of wine, fire, water, and urine into their philosophy of the equilibrium of power, in which water balances fire just as one gang balances another. The naked newborn babe, on the other hand, acquires a literal instead of a merely metaphorical existence at the end of the play, though transformed into a neatly swaddled infant held in the protective arms of Guddu (Fleance/Malcolm).

The scripts of the two films show familiarity not only with the minutest details of the plays but also with current critical approaches and interpretations. For example, *Omkara* hints at sexual insecurity as one of the motivating forces behind Langda Tyagi's (Iago's) actions in a little scene where Indu (Emilia) shows him Dolly's (Desdemona's) stolen girdle, after which they make love. Later, while they are still lying in bed, Indu says that he has a ravenous beast inside him. What beast, he asks, obviously pleased: a cheetah? a wolf? a snake? a chameleon? You are my little rabbit, she replies, and a cloud passes over his face. She then gets up and asks what he would like to eat: upon which he says, the joviality gone, that he would like to drink some blood.

The main critical issues raised by these two adaptations have to do with the aesthetic and ideological implications of placing the action in the Mumbai underworld, or amidst the nexus of crime and politics in Uttar Pradesh or elsewhere, as against the world of "legitimate" heroism in the original plays. To a large extent, of course, the choice is the purely logical consequence of the nature of the plays' action, and the decision to adapt them to a modern setting, for where else could the violence of the action be accommodated with any degree of plausibility? The absoluteness of the demand for loyalty and allegiance, the patriarchal authoritarianism in the family, and the social conservatism (with a strong emphasis on traditional values, including the ties of family and kinship) are the other factors that relate the underworld to the world of the plays. The one crucial difference is the apparent absence of a heroic individual as the "hero."

However, there is greater complexity to the issue, as illustrated by an example from *Omkara*. Very near the beginning of the film, Bhai Ji, the local political leader, deputes Omkara to negotiate a deal with Indore Singh, his political rival, through a man called Kaptan (Captain), relating to the forthcoming elections. When Omkara asks what he should do if the negotiation fails, Bhai Ji tells him, in English, that he can then "go ahead." The negotiations have not quite ended when Kaptan makes an insulting remark about Omkara's affair with Dolly (Desdemona), to the effect that he has bet a hundred rupees that Omkara, being a sensible chap, will enjoy Dolly and then discard her. Though Keshu and Langda try to restrain him, Omkara pushes them aside and walks slowly, with measured steps, to a handpump where an old lady has just filled a pitcher to carry home. Omkara lifts the pitcher, puts it on her head, and says: "Mother, go and tell the people of the village that Kaptan has lost his bet." He then walks back slowly towards Kaptan: as he does so, a song begins to be heard in the background. It is the title song of the film, celebrating in the manner of a folk song (with verbal and musical allusion to the heroic songs of Aalha and Udal) the martial prowess of Omkara, building him up as a great warrior of myth and legend, the greatest of fighters, on whose brow, when he frowns, three furrows appear in the shape of the god Shiva's trident. When he gets near enough to Kaptan, Omkara suddenly whips out a dagger and stabs him savagely. His team now joins in and everyone in Kaptan's team is killed, to the background accompaniment of the martial song about Omkara. Only one member of Kaptan's team is spared: Omkara tells him to go and tell his people that bets are placed on horses, not lions.

What is this juxtaposition of visuals of brutal criminal violence with a sound track of heroic song meant to convey? Is the scene a build-up of Omkara or an ironic send-up? Is the stabbing of Kaptan really a consequence of Omkara's heroic rage or was it pre-planned at Bhai Ji's prompting? Or is the scene an interrogation of the heroic ideal itself, of Othello's heroism as well as Omkara's? Is there any difference between this action of Omkara's, and Othello's smiting of the circumcised dog or Macbeth's unseaming of the merciless Macdonwald? The interrogation or erasure of difference between legitimate and illegitimate violence is common in recent critical commentary and interpretation; but, whatever its theoretical justification, dramaturgically or cinematically there is a world of difference between the reported violence of Othello or Macbeth and the violence shown in these films. Clearly "heroism" cannot be the redeeming feature of the heroes of these films, which engage with these issues raised by the source-plays but keep them in animated suspension, as it were, with no attempt at a simple moralistic conclusion.

It should not be concluded from the above that the two films reflect merely a postmodernist playing with possibilities made possible by a new, assertive post-colonial appropriation of the master texts, for they engage deeply and seriously with the social and moral issues raised by the Shakespearean originals.[13] The endings of the two films have nothing of the cynicism of, say, Polanski's *Macbeth*, where, in the last shot, Donalbain is shown fleeing from the court as his brother Malcolm is crowned, implying that the cycle of violence will continue. The spirit of Bhardwaj's films is also different from, to take another example, the dark vision of Peter Brook's *Lear*. The latter sedulously suppresses any hint of humanity or goodness in the original, such as the brief episode where one of Cornwall's servants, "thrilled with remorse," takes up his sword to prevent him from gouging out Gloucester's other eye. At the end of *Omkara* there is no hope that the nexus between crime and politics will come to an end, but at the domestic level at least, in a radical "feminist" reworking of the text, Langda Tyagi (Iago) gets justice at the hands of his own wife (the Emilia figure), who resembles the goddess Durga as she slashes him to death with a sickle. As for Omkara, the wonder is not that a girl like Dolly should fall in love with such a violent, murderous man, who does not have even the eloquence of Othello to redeem him, but that he should love her as intensely and single-mindedly as he does. In the violent and corrupt world presented in the film, this comes across as a rare thing. As in traditional humanistic readings of this most painful of the tragedies, Omkara's love and his remorse entitle him to some sympathy, and make the ending truly moving.

The ending of *Maqbool* is more complex: there is no certainty that with the death of Maqbool, the cycle of violence will end, though there is some hope of (in current bureaucratic jargon) an improvement in the law and order situation. Inspector Devsare, who was transferred to some other department at Abbaji's instance, has come back and succeeded in destroying most of the gang. The corrupt cops fail in their attempt to keep the "balance of forces" by arranging for Maqbool's escape to Dubai, so that the balance seems to shift decisively towards the forces of law and order. Most importantly, Guddu (Fleance/Malcolm), who would now take over leadership of the gang, has shown a reluctance to kill; moreover, his interreligious marriage with Sameera is symbolic of communal harmony. But unlike the condition of Scotland in *Macbeth*, the condition of the underworld is not a cause for concern in the film: it is part of its datum. It is not the hope of external restoration, but the image of human care and nurture in the shot of the baby in Guddu's arms, as he and Sameera walk out of the hospital, that gives the film its positive ending. And as in *Omkara* and Shakespeare's own *Macbeth*, Maqbool and Nimmi rise above the world around them because of their mutual love and their consciousness of guilt: their deaths are profoundly moving. At the end of the film, the voice of Nimmi as she repeats her dying question to Maqbool: "Speak, my Lord, our love was pure, wasn't it?" resonates with a power that matches the visual impact of the image of the babe in arms and of the look in Maqbool's eyes as he dies. What makes *Maqbool* one of the greatest Shakespearean films is that, with all the aesthetic and ideological complexities, and the complications that transposing the action to the Mumbai underworld entails, it succeeds in reaffirming, surprising though that might be in a postmodernist context, the universal and humane core of Shakespeare's *Macbeth* through a deep and sustained engagement with it.

NOTES

1. Agha Hashra [Hashr] Kashmiri, *Khwab-e-Hasti*, ed. Krishnadev Jhari (New Delhi: Sharada Prakashan, 1986), 47, 76–80.
2. Agha Hashra [Hashr] Kashmiri, *Havas ka Putla (Said-e-Havas)*, ed. Krishnadev Jhari (New Delhi: Sharada Prakashan, 1984), 73–7, 95–7.
3. Kenneth S. Rothwell, *A History of Shakespeare on Screen: A Century of Film and Television* (Cambridge: Cambridge University Press, 1999), 219.
4. Rajiva Verma, "*Hamlet* on the Hindi Screen," *Hamlet Studies* 24 (2002): 82–3.
5. Ibid., 87–88; Rajiva Verma, "Shakespeare in Hindi Cinema," in *India's Shakespeare: Translation, Interpretation, and Performance*, ed. Poonam Trivedi and Dennis Bartholomeusz (Newark: University of Delaware Press, 2005), 272–4.
6. Rothwell, 169.
7. Verma, "*Hamlet* on the Hindi Screen," 85; see also Esha Niyogi De, "Modern Shakespeares in Popular Bombay Cinema: Translation, Subjectivity and Community," *Screen* 43, no. 1 (Spring 2002): 19–40, for a detailed study of the films by Modi and Sahu.
8. Bharatendu Harishchandra, *Bharatendu Granthavali*, vol. 1, ed. Shivprasad Mishra (Varanasi: Nagari Pracharini Sabha, 1970); Maheshchandra Prasad, *Daah ka Phal* (Arrah: the author, 1939).
9. Harishchandra, 570.
10. Verma, " Shakespeare in Hindi Cinema," 280–81.
11. Rothwell, 219.
12. Oscar James Campbell, ed., *The Reader's Encyclopedia of Shakespeare* (New York: Thomas Y. Crowell Company, 1966), 382.
13. For a contrary view, see Poonam Trivedi, "'Mak[ing] ... Strange / Even to the disposition that I owe': Vishal Bharadwaj's *Maqbool*," *Borrowers and Lenders: The Journal of Shakespeare and Appropriation* 4, no. 2 (Spring/Summer 2009), Special issue: *Asian Shakespeares on Screen: Two Films in Perspective*, ed., Alexander C. Y. Huang. Available online at http://www.borrowers.uga.edu/. See also the essays by Amrita Sen and Suddhaseel Sen in the same volume.

8 "What bloody man is that?" *Macbeth*, *Maqbool*, and Shakespeare in India

Supriya Chaudhuri

Aristotle regarded the *mythos*, usually translated for the *Poetics* as "plot," as central to tragedy, but it has received less attention, I would suggest, than other elements in the tragic structure. Few comment on the fact that the very same term, usually translated for the Socratic dialogues as "myth," is crucial to Plato's rejection of the way in which poets treat the gods and heroes, and attention is generally deflected towards Plato's celebrated diatribe against the actor's induction of his audience into the tragic *pathos*, the hypocritical passion and shedding of tears that run counter to the Heraclitean maxim "A dry soul is wisest."[1] The commentary tradition has to some extent instituted a false distinction between Aristotelian *plot* and Platonic *myth*, as though the fabular structures on which Aristotle places so much importance in the *Poetics* were in some vital way different from the stories of incest, rape, and murder that Plato views with such disfavour in the *Republic* and elsewhere. For both philosophers, however, it is by their treatment of the *mythos* that poets must stand or fall, and neither thinks of such fables as entirely invented, or as entirely derived. Because the *mythos* provides the ground, the dynamic logic, of the work, the poet must take responsibility (and blame, so Plato thinks) for it: yet in an important sense it precedes the work, and exists beyond it.

The possibility of adaptation, especially across cultures, genres, and media, is founded on this primacy of *mythos* or fable, even if we acknowledge that it too is subject to alteration, and that the totality of the literary or cultural object being adapted is made up of many other elements as well. It is the persistence of the fable, lending itself to *narrative* recognition, that enables us to speak of adaptation at all, while the repetition of other features might simply be classed as intertextual echo or allusion. But obviously, plots do not exist as pure structures: they are housed in the density of a textually realized, physically imagined universe that demands a name: *Macbeth*, *King Lear*, *Hamlet*. This naming—the principle of thrift in the economy of the text, as Michel Foucault said of the author—allows us to speak of, even to speak to, the fables that haunt our cultural memory.[2] Linda Hutcheon, describing adaptation as "repetition without replication," suggests that what is adapted is a heterocosm, or other world; and Rabindranath Tagore (whom Hutcheon quotes, rather surprisingly, in the epigraph to her first chapter) wrote of Shakespeare's *Othello* that it was neither a character nor a subject of treatment (say, jealousy) but a totality of settings, characters, objects, and situations which then assumes a kind of existence, almost a persona, so that it can become a subject of address -- so that we can speak to it.[3] It is this *speaking to*—to the past, to a literary text, to Shakespeare's ghost—that I would like in turn to address in this essay.

Tagore himself, as a boy of thirteen, was set by his tutor the exercise of translating *Macbeth*, scene by scene, into Bengali verse, and was shut up in the schoolroom until he had completed that day's exercise. He records with relief that the full text of his translation has not survived, but he was taken by his Sanskrit pundit to show his version to the greatest scholar of the time, Ishvar Chandra Vidyasagar, and received some praise, as well as advice from the essayist Rajkrishna Mukhopadhyay, who was present, to vary the metre and verse of the witch scenes from those involving human characters.[4] He appears to have taken this advice to heart: a spirited rendering of the witch scenes was published very early in the journal *Bharati*, all that survives of this adolescent exercise.[5] In 1874, Tagore may have been among the earliest to attempt a version of *Macbeth* in an Indian language, though translation of other Shakespearean plays, and adaptations for the Parsi theatre, had commenced some twenty years earlier, with Harachandra Ghosh's *Bhanumati Chittabilas* (*The Merchant of Venice*, 1853) in Bengali, and the staging of *Nathari Firangiz Thekani Avi* (*The Taming of the Shrew*: literally *A Bad European Woman Brought to her Senses*) in Gujarati at Surat in 1852. Haralal Ray's translation of *Macbeth* as *Rudrapal Natak* was published in 1874, the same year as Tagore's schoolroom labours, and Taraknath Mukhopadhyay's *Macbeth* in 1875, from Nath Suburban Press. A decade later came Nagendranath Basu's *Karmabir* (Calcutta, 1885/86), and the greatest playwright and theatre-manager of the time, Girishchandra Ghosh, brought his version to the stage of the Minerva Theatre in Calcutta on 28 January 1893, though the text only survives in a printed edition from

1900. Ghosh's *Macbeth*, described by the playwright and actor Utpal Dutt as "a translation so brilliant that it has not been equalled yet," was a triumph of painstaking research and masterly versification. It was staged in "authentic" Scots costumes and settings through the hired services of an English stage-designer, and a contemporary reviewer hailed its "astounding reproduction of the standard conventions of the English stage."[6] But it was unequivocally rejected by its Calcutta audience, and played night after night to a near-empty auditorium; reportedly, some indignant viewers demanded their money back. Ghosh, a theatre man to his fingertips, never repeated the mistake of staging Shakespeare.

The devastating failure of Ghosh's *Macbeth* points to a crucial rift in the history of Shakespearean stagings in India: a rift, if we may so call it, between translation and adaptation. By contrast with Ghosh's faithful recreation, Shakespeare had been Indianized for the stage from the mid-nineteenth century, in versions that retained only the bare bones of the fable, altering settings, characters, and language. The most notable adaptations were for the Parsi theatre, the first commercial stage for the entertainment of the urban masses, largely funded—as the name suggests—by the practical and philanthropic ventures of the Parsi business community on India's western coast, but bringing together a highly eclectic mix of stage techniques, acting styles, and dramatic material, and spreading rapidly all over northern India. Parsi companies even went on tour to other parts of South Asia and to Africa. The Parsi stage adopted the proscenium arch from European theatre, placed the orchestra in a pit in front of the stage, and used pictorial backdrops providing illusionary perspective. These painted settings often embedded the characters in a dense mythological context, a *mise-en-scène* created by the visual regimes of the painter Raja Ravi Verma. The actors drew upon Victorian melodrama and other elements in the repertoire of European touring companies, as well as the musical performance styles of nineteenth-century courtesans, the techniques of folk theatre, and the *abhinaya*, or expressive gestures, of classical Sanskrit drama. The flamboyant popular idiom that resulted was employed to render a similarly mixed repertory of plots, from the *Arabian Nights*, the Persian *Shahnama*, the Hindu *Puranas*, and the Sanskrit epic *Mahabharata*, to Shakespeare's plays and social drama with a strong moral content. It is this hybrid theatre, increasingly vilified in its time as vulgar and reductive, that gave birth both to the Marathi *sangitnatak* or musical drama, and—through the transformation of Parsi theatres into movie studios in the 1920s, and the flow of Parsi capital into the talkies thereafter—to the Bombay film.

Shakespeare was a staple of the Parsi stage, and its greatest playwright-producer, Agha Hashr Kashmiri, achieved notable success with his versions of *King Lear* (*Safed Khoon*, 1907) and *Macbeth* (*Khwab-e-hasti*, 1909). He interpolated musical and comic interludes into his Shakespearean adaptations, which appear to have drawn audiences principally by their representations of passion and violence, and their powerfully articulated plots. As a commodity for the popular stage, in altered settings and free translations, Shakespeare then becomes recognizable through a combination of fable (*mythos*) and the rhetorical "colour" associated with a new, sensational register of emotions. Yet, as most historians of the colonial encounter have emphasized, for British administrators and for the educated bourgeoisie, Shakespeare also attracted an extraordinary investment of symbolic capital, enshrined by his place in the academic curriculum, by a limited but significant record of performance in the original, and by the labours of literary translation.

The earliest translation of Shakespeare into an Indian language was a Bengali version of *The Tempest* produced as an academic exercise at Fort William College, set up in 1809 for training colonial officers. In 1964 the National Library of India recorded 670 different translations of Shakespearean plays into Indian languages, the greatest number being into Bengali, followed by Marathi, Tamil, Hindi, and Kannada: this is likely to be only a fraction of the actual number.[7] Many of these translations Indianized the settings and proper names, while attempting to render the verse with some fidelity. Some achieved a life on the stage, like the nineteenth-century Marathi *Macbeth* (*Manajirao*, 1896), and the Bengali Shakespeares carried to villages and small towns by the Marxist Utpal Dutt's Little Theatre Group in the 1960s.

Given this double and divided history, post-colonial Shakespeare in India performs, I would suggest, not just the tiresome duty of "writing back" but the more interesting possibilities of "speaking to." The figure thus addressed is intimately associated with the formation of a modern theatre in India, with the affective and social registers of colonial modernity, and with the creation of a vernacular literary and dramatic idiom. Neither the public theatre nor the circulation of literary texts exists independent of each other, whatever their differences. One of the greatest theatrical adaptations of *Macbeth* was produced in 1979 by the actor-director H. V. Karanth at Delhi's National School of Drama, using a fine literary translation into Hindi by the poet Raghuvir Sahay. The play, acted in the *yakshagana* dance-drama style of Karnataka, was renamed *Barnam Vana* (Birnam Wood) and Karanth put a great spreading tree at the centre of his stage, making the tangled wood the play's chief symbol, while deliberately delocalizing and mythicizing settings and costumes. Twenty years on, Manipuri theatre and dance, *thang-ta* martial arts, and a stage that used the symbolism of the Meitei philosophy of nature were employed for Lokendra Arambam's *Macbeth, Stage of Blood* (1997), reflecting the political conflicts of India's turbulent north-east, and staged on the waters of the Loktak lake in Manipur. The director's father, Dorendrajit Arambam, had adapted *Macbeth* into Manipuri in 1935 as a tribute to a legendary king, a figure of the good ruler, and named it after him as *Bhagyachandra*. Lokendra Arambam saw his own later version as destructive of the mythical unities of the nation-state in a climate of state corruption and radical insurgency."It is *Macbeth* wrenched, twisted and subverted into a metaphor of the anarchy in Manipur."[8]

Arambam's verbs—"wrenched, twisted and subverted"—offer an image of the violence implicit in every act of adaptation: the violence of forced labour, or of a new birth. It is a violence, I would suggest, that overrides the persistence of textual memory, or translates it forcibly to a new context. What survives the change, the elementary structures of plot, motive, character, and feeling, inhabit the new text as residents who are also, in some sense, ghosts. They render the text uncanny, or "unhomely" (*unheimlich*, to use Freud's word)— an echo-chamber in which voices resonate and mingle, speaking to, speaking past, each other.[9] And, as every postmodern viewer knows, the voices we hear belong not to one master-text of the past, but to the innumerable shades who haunt the space of cultural re-enactment: to summon one is to summon all. "Summoning" may indeed be the best term for a transaction with spirits which, even today, places the ideas of property, propriety, legitimacy—that is, everything that surrounds the author-function—in doubt, as all adaptations do. It is worth recalling that Shakespeare himself, the most notorious author-function in literature, was alive to the possibilities of such spectral summoning: other voices, other presences, other authors, inhabit his texts.

Vishal Bhardwaj's Bombay film version of *Macbeth*, renamed *Maqbool* (2003), was inspired by Akira Kurosawa's *Throne of Blood* (1957), which had transferred the events to sixteenth-century Japan, the Sengoku period (1477–1573) of bloody internecine strife when samurai commanders fought for, and sometimes betrayed, their feudal warlords. It is a commentary on that history, but also on the dynastic hopes in Shakespeare's play, and, in the brilliant treatment of the fog-shrouded, stunted vegetation on the slopes of Mount Fuji, on post-Hiroshima Japan. Kurosawa's film, belonging to the great period of *auteur* cinema that included the work of his friend Satyajit Ray, has cult status in art cinema circles in India, a world apparently removed from that of the commercialized Bombay film. Bhardwaj, professionally a music composer, was, so he said in an interview, drawn to direction by a Krzysztof

Kieślowski retrospective at the Trivandrum Film Festival, where he was mesmerized by the "deafening silences" of the *Decalogue*.[10] That Bhardwaj discovered Shakespeare through Kurosawa is precisely the kind of postmodern coincidence that places the category of the *auteur* in *auteur* cinema, like that of the author in a literary text, itself in suspension. In an interview, Bhardwaj said:

> A very dear friend had given me Kurosawa's *Throne of Blood* to watch. That was when I got a glimpse of the power of Shakespeare's writing (and Kurosawa's cinematic interpretation, equally powerfully).[11]

Maqbool transposes Shakespeare's plot to the Bombay underworld, with its hierarchies of command held in place by patriarchal ganglords whose dynastic ambitions provide the modern parallel to the Scottish succession debate. In a brilliant but tantalizingly brief examination, Moinak Biswas has suggested that Bhardwaj's *Maqbool* depends on the "chronicle" background, the textual genealogy, established by the urban crime film, in the same way as Shakespeare's *Macbeth* draws sustenance from Holinshed's *Chronicles*. This line of films— beginning from *Ankush* (1986), *Nayakan* (1987), and *Parinda* (1989), extending through *Angaar* and *Gardish* (1993) and culminating in Ram Gopal Varma's *Satya* (1998) and *Company* (2002)—offers a set of violent, moral, melodramatic fables that are of course very far from constituting a "history," or anything resembling the royal lineages dealt with by the Tudor chroniclers. Most are generically distant from the postmodern noir of *Maqbool*.[12] Nevertheless, they do give density and depth to the criminal hinterland that throws up, from time to time, the violent upheavals so brilliantly foregrounded in Bhardwaj's film.

Moinak Biswas suggests that the task of the urban crime film is an interrupted work of mourning, that it records a loss—familial, social, or religious—which the mainstream Bombay film fails to acknowledge. This fall, this degeneration, is one that has been suffered by society as a whole, but its reflection is caught within the criminal underworld itself: it has, Biswas says, "fallen from [its] fallen state."[13] An older patriarchal order is being hollowed out by the ruthless pursuit, impelled by forces within that very same order, of money and power. The spirit of the urban crime film is, therefore, not the noble reticence of tragedy, but the *acedia* that Walter Benjamin found in the baroque *trauerspiel*, the "sorrow-play," with its hyperbolic, gestural, allegorical language, its counter-transcendence, its brutal, worldly sadness.[14]

Bhardwaj sees, as Kurosawa saw before him, that Shakespeare's principal concern in *Macbeth* is with a certain kind of violence, a law-breaking violence that claims for itself the sovereign privilege of law-making violence—the violence of the state. The terms I use are again Benjamin's, from his long essay, the *Critique of Violence* (1921): a controversial work, as Giorgio Agamben notes, because of its relation to the Nazi ideologue Carl Schmitt's *Political Theology* (1922), which Benjamin cited in *The Origins of German Tragic Drama* (1928). He wrote to Schmitt in December 1930, and Schmitt, in turn, cited Benjamin in his book *Hamlet or Hecuba* (1956), sixteen years after Benjamin's suicide.[15] The origin of law and its relation to violence is central to each of these reflections. Shakespeare's Macbeth comes very close to legitimizing his crime, that of regicide, by seizing the crown of Scotland and claiming for himself the sovereign exception (that is, that the king be not bound by his own laws). Given the climate of bloody insurrection in which the play begins, the act might appear defensible, even a logical outcome of what Benjamin calls *natural law*, in which the end justifies the means. But, as Macbeth himself notes, "humane statute" has "purged the gentle weal," and he stands condemned, not only by moral law, but also by what Benjamin describes as the *positive law* of the state, which retains its ideological hold even when it is trampled upon and defied.

At the critical juncture when *Macbeth* was written, just after James's ascent to the English throne after Elizabeth's death, the most important elements of this law would appear to concern the question of royal succession. In Holinshed's *Chronicles*, we are told that Duncan's great-grandfather Kenneth had successfully urged his nobles to abandon the custom of electing the successor to the Scottish throne, instituting, instead, succession by male primogeniture. The king "besought them that so pernicious a custome might be abolished and taken away, to the great benefite of the whole state of the realme, specially sith in all realmes commonly the order was, that the sonne should without any contradiction succeede the father in the heritage of the crowne and kingly estate."[16] Following this:

> there was a newe acte deuised and made, the olde being abrogated (by the appoyntment of the king) for the creation of the Scottish kings in time to come, many of the nobles rather consenting with silence, than greatly allowing it, either in heartes or voyces, though some currifauours among them, set forwarde the matter to the best of their powers.

The Articles of this ordinance were these:

> The eldest heire male of the deceassed king, whether the same were sonne or nephew, of what age soeuer he should be, yea though he shoulde be in the mothers womb at the time of ye fathers decease should from thenceforth succeed in the kingdome of Scotlande.[17]

This ordinance was ratified and confirmed at the coronation of Kenneth's son Malcolm II:

> Whither the Scottish nobiltie comming togither at the day and place appoynted, and consenting to crowne Malcolme king, he vtterly refused to receyue the crowne, except the law established by his father Kenneth for the fuccession therof were first confirmed & approbate, wherevpon the Lordes bounde themselues by solemne othes ... neuer to breake or violate it in any condition.[18]

Duncan followed this principle in declaring his son Malcolm (later Malcolm III), Prince of Cumberland. As Holinshed notes, the nomination "sore troubled" Macbeth, whose own hopes of succeeding his kinsman Duncan (which would have been "allowed" by the older laws of the realm, since Malcolm was a minor) were thereby hindered.[19] The validity of the new law, however, is critical to the play's politics. Succession by patrilineal inheritance lay at the root of James VI's claim to the throne of England, while Macbeth's coronation looked back to the obsolete Scottish practice of tanistry.[20] Macbeth's claim cannot be sustained in the play's own political context, and requires him to persist in a series of bloody crimes to secure the throne. That these acts, beginning from the murder of Duncan, are perceived as crimes is because (again, under the hold of *positive law*) the modern state arrogates all violence to itself, and its Christianized ethic of conscience does not permit an individual to use violence for his own benefit. Benjamin reflects on the "surprising possibility" thus thrown up: that "the law's interest in a monopoly of violence vis-à-vis individuals is not explained by the intention of preserving legal ends but rather, by that of preserving the law itself": that violence outside the law is threatening not because of the ends it might pursue, but "by its mere existence outside the law." The same, Benjamin continues,

> may be more drastically suggested if one reflects how often the figure of the "great" criminal, however repellent his ends may have been, has aroused the secret admiration of the public. This cannot result from his deed, but only from the violence to which it bears witness. In this case, therefore, the violence of which present-day law is seeking

in all areas of activity to deprive the individual appears really threatening, and arouses even in defeat the sympathy of the mass against the law.[21]

Macbeth might indeed have drawn this sympathy, were it not for his persistence, beyond the need to secure his throne, in crimes against unspecified numbers of his subjects. In his case, law-breaking violence—that is, regicide—remains unsanctioned by God or man, but it succeeds in putting a question to the constitution of the state itself, since the state is constituted by violence. The possibility that law-breaking violence might become law-making violence is the source of the play's deep, uncomfortable power. At the same time, Macbeth's persevering in acts of blood is a means of radically distancing and alienating us from him:

> Each new morn
> New widows howl, new orphans cry, new sorrows
> Strike heaven on the face, that it resounds
> As if it felt with Scotland, and yell'd out
> Like syllable of dolour.
>
> (*Macbeth*, 4.3.4–8)[22]

Macbeth's career then comes to resemble those examples of crime that Machiavelli examines in the eighth chapter of *The Prince*, coming, in the end, to the bleak conclusion that, if the prince has to obtain his kingdom by violence and treachery, it is better that he commit all his crimes at once: for otherwise he is compelled to "stand knife in hand, and can never depend upon his subjects, because they, owing to continually fresh injuries, are unable to depend upon him."[23]

No viewer of the modern urban crime film could be in any doubt about the deep attraction exercised upon a largely sedentary and pacific audience by violence "outside the law." The protagonist of Bharadwaj's gangster film thus compels, as Benjamin predicts, by his location in a lawless hinterland of violence and criminality, the "secret admiration" of his public. Unlike Macbeth, he cannot aspire to embody the law of the state itself: rather, he shows up the ineffectiveness of state law in a climate of all-pervasive corruption, moral decay, official apathy and political collusion with crime. If Scottish history and the succession debate provide Shakespeare with the ideological framework and the motives of action in his plot of regicide punished, it is an unofficial history of our times that sets the context for Bhardwaj's examination of the order that crime might itself generate to fill the space left vacant by the collapse of positive law. In a Darwinian struggle for power where individuals do not hesitate to use violence to achieve their ends, we are left at the close with a hunger for justice, rather than any assurance of law: a situation where what Benjamin calls *natural law* prevails, in so far as anything like order emerges at all. But here too—as in *Macbeth*—the individual recourse to violence puts a question to the state, a question about the origin of law, and about our interest in preserving it.

The action of *Maqbool* begins in an eerilylit, rain-drenched police van close to midnight, as two corrupt policemen interrogate a member of one of Mumbai's criminal gangs for information about the whereabouts of its leader, Mughal, and his son, Riyaz Boti. Eventually, they kill him, but not before passing on the information they have extracted to Miyan Maqbool (Irfan Khan), the principal henchman of Mughal's more powerful rival, the underworld don Jahangir. The two policemen, played by Om Puri and Naseeruddin Shah as Hindus called Pundit and Purohit (literally "sage" and "priest"), the former an obsessive caster of horoscopes, serve the function of the witches in *Macbeth*. They not only predict the rise of Miyan Maqbool, but also name his eventual successor, Guddu, the son of his Hindu associate Kaka. By turns, they aid Jahangir, Maqbool, and later his opponents Guddu, Riyaz Boti, and a politician attempting to unseat Jahangir's political patron in the government of the day, professing themselves in charge of a delicate "balance of power" (*shakti ka santulan*). Mughal, like Macdonwald, is eliminated early: Riyaz is inducted into Jahangir's gang and becomes Guddu's ally. Jahangir, known as Abbaji (father) to members of his gang and especially to Maqbool, whom he has brought up, has no son. His daughter Sameera is engaged to Guddu, who takes Fleance's place in the plot, there being no Malcolm.

What replaces the intricate genealogical plot of *Macbeth*, then, is a form of bonding that is effected across communal and kinship networks, the making of a criminal "family" ruled over by the patriarchal Jahangir. By entering into an affair with Jahangir's mistress Nimmi, Maqbool, Jahangir's adoptive son, is guilty of both incest and, ultimately, parricide, as she incites him to kill his patron and take his place. Jahangir has already transferred his sexual attentions to a younger dancer and starlet, and Nimmi fears that Sameera's marriage will produce a new line of succession. Maqbool's murder of Jahangir on the night of Sameera's engagement is placed considerably later in film time than the equivalent act of Duncan's murder in *Macbeth*—in fact the aging Jahangir, brilliantly played by Pankaj Kapoor in an award-winning performance that owes something to Francis Ford Coppola's *The Godfather* (1972), is one of the principal characters of *Maqbool*. He represents a gangland ethic of the past, an ethic of ruthlessness combined with benevolence, demanding unquestioning loyalty from his followers. This is exemplified by Jahangir's bodyguard Usman, a devout Muslim who shuns alcohol, but is forced at Maqbool's urging to drink in order to prove his devotion to him. Usman is thus made to fall into a drunken stupor on the fatal night of his master's murder, and fails to protect him. Maqbool's act violates the "family" ties which bind him, like Usman, to his patron, and his own efforts to create a substitute family with Nimmi are doomed to failure. She becomes ill and neurotic in her pregnancy, and he is compelled to order the murders of Kaka and Guddu, though the latter escapes. Increasingly, he sinks into melancholy, isolation, and suspicion, as he is assailed by visions of the dead, rising to haunt him not so much with a consciousness of his crimes as with a sense of an irrecoverable past, a past that must be both mourned and yearned for.

In a desperate attempt to recover his position in Mumbai's gangdom, Maqbool agrees to ship a load of contraband goods. These goods, which Jahangir had refused to handle, are never identified in the film. It is implied that they constitute a threat to national security, and it is through this unidentified, mysterious cargo, I would suggest, that the *nation*, a critical ingredient of the Bombay cinema, is anonymously inserted into the frame. Both Jahangir and Maqbool deal with politicians and enjoy political patronage: but the corruption of the state, its open and unashamed abandonment of law, is generally placed in a context that makes the nation irrelevant. The prolonged absence or suspension of this "idea of the nation" is compensated towards the close of the film by the unidentified shipment, presumably of arms, which is finally seized by the Coast Guard who proceed to storm Maqbool's house. By the end of the film, Nimmi has died in childbirth, and Maqbool makes a last visit to the hospital to see his son. He watches unseen as Guddu and Sameera appear to adopt his (or perhaps Jahangir's) baby. As he walks away, he is shot in the back by Riyaz Boti, a scene that reproduces almost exactly the last scene of Luc Besson's *Léon* (*The Professional*, 1994).

In numerous and extremely subtle ways, Bhardwaj's film recalls not only the principal themes of *Macbeth*, but a whole array of motifs from the Bombay film and from international cinema, establishing a logic of thick description, a densely intertextual visual field. Its conversation with the entire genre of the urban crime film is particularly rich and evocative. But with reference to the Shakespearean subtext, the most striking feature is its replacing of the dynastic thread, the line that stretches out to "the crack of doom" by new forms of kinship—not all of them ties of blood—within Mumbai's criminal clans. David Mason has emphasized that both rival gangs are Muslim, while the politicians, the policemen, and the inheritor (Guddu) are Hindu.[24] The film uses Mumbaiya Hindi and Urdu, as well as the *tapori* slang of the criminal gangs, and is filled with Muslim signifiers (like the *surma* in Jahangir's eyes), a feature that might, on Mukul Kesavan's reading of the "Islamicate roots" of the Bombay film, express nostalgia for a lost Urdu culture, or alternatively, as Mason thinks, contribute to demonizing the Muslim ganglord as the root of Mumbai's troubles.[25]

It is true, of course, that during the period when the film was being made, the reach of the ganglord Dawood Ibrahim's D-Company, with its connections to the Bombay film industry, was being newly understood, and the film repeatedly indicates such links. Indeed, the awareness of criminal investment in the very medium that produces a film like *Maqbool* allows Bhardwaj to offer a metacinematic commentary on the culture industry. But it would be wrong to think of religion or community as regulating either the criminal underworld or the world of the Bombay film. Kinship in *Maqbool* cuts across religious communities, and is cemented by adoptive rather than blood-ties. Bhardwaj cannot be accused of bias; his later film *Omkara* (2006), reworking *Othello* in rural Uttar Pradesh, is populated exclusively by Hindu gangsters. Indeed it might be argued that the urban crime film, with its combination of violence, social *anomie*, and the creating of contractual, mercenary, and adoptive communities, offers an alternative model for the construction of the new Indian nation. For this reason, it is deeply symbolic that *Maqbool* gives concrete shape to the images of newborn children that haunt the text of *Macbeth*: Lady Macbeth's missing offspring, pity like a naked newborn babe, the child untimely ripped from his mother's womb, the new orphans that cry each morning and strike heaven in the face. The film begins with a terrible scene of execution where a weeping child appears to be killed, as Macduff's children are in the play: it ends with Maqbool's son being adopted by Guddu and Sameera, as Maqbool himself was by Jahangir.

If *Maqbool* mythicizes and reinstates violence in the popular imagination, that "placing" is connected with the increasingly mythical status being assumed by the city of Mumbai, or Bombay, virtually a major character in Bhardwaj's film. This is not the Bombay of the modernist art movements of the 1940s, leading to the founding of the Progressive Artists' Group in 1947 by S. H. Raza and Francis Newton Souza, with M. F. Husain and Tyeb Mehta as early members. It is not the cosmopolitan, ghost-ridden city inhabited by refugees from Hitler's Germany like the Baumgartner of Anita Desai's *Baumgartner's Bombay* (1988), and Indian modernism's early patrons, Walter Langhammer, Rudi van Leyden, and Emmanuel Schlesinger. It is not the Bombay of the Irani cafes patronized by modernist poets like Nissim Ezekiel and Arun Kolatkar in the 1960s, the Bombay of Salman Rushdie's boyhood in the elite Cathedral School, or of Sachin Tendulkar's cricket lessons in Shivaji Park. It is not even the Bombay of a Dalit literature of protest, captured in the street and brothel scenes of Namdeo Dhasal's *Golpitha* (1973). It is a more modern, more violent, more fractured city. In the imagination of the Indian public, it is city of opportunity, of glamour and stardom, but also of terrorist outrages, gang warfare, and political collusion with crime. It is the Bombay, then, of Mani Ratnam's eponymous film (1995), focusing on the riots that followed the destruction of the Babri Masjid in December 1992, and the Stock Exchange blasts the following March. It is the Bombay reported on in Suketu Mehta's *Maximum City: Bombay Lost and Found* (2004), published shortly after the Gateway of India bomb blasts of August 2003 and the Gujarat riots of 2002, and most recently memorialized in Vikram Chandra's *Sacred Games* (2006), which is declaredly about the holing-up and capture of the gangster Arun Gawli, Hindu rival of Dawood Ibrahim, and his erstwhile lieutenants, Chhota Rajan and Chhota Shakeel. By turns dream city and nightmare town, it is a Bombay of terror and tenderness, ruled over by an underworld whose power is both visible and acknowledged, whether in politics or in the film industry.

In a sense, of course, the medium of the crime film exaggerates and mythicizes this gangland appropriation of the city space—as, for example, in the topographic detail of the city in Vikram Chandra's novel and its "placing" of the steel fortress of the ganglord Ganesh Gaitonde at the city's heart. Nevertheless, this "night vision" of the city responds to one perception of the modern metropolis: Chandra did indeed meet Arun Gawli in his fortified house, from where he was later arrested. This Mumbai/Bombay is both one space and several, inhabited simultaneously by the trivial and the terrible, a place where anything could happen, such as a notorious gangster being gunned down on the steps of a big city hospital. As I write this essay, the Mumbai police have just arrested seven members of Chhota Rajan's gang for the murder of a journalist, gunned down on his motorbike in broad daylight.[26] At the same time, of course, it is a space of love and intimacy, a space of belonging, as when Jahangir, an old-time gangster who lives by his own familial codes, refuses to smuggle an undisclosed commodity into the city, saying: *Mumbai meri mehbooba hai, main use chhorkar kahan jnau?* ("Mumbai is my beloved, where can I go leaving her behind?"). There is an implication—no more than that—that the smuggled goods are arms and explosives, and Jahangir's refusal to go and live in Dubai or Karachi probably recalls Dawood Ibrahim's ready acceptance of this option after the Mumbai riots of 1992–93, followed by the Stock Exchange blasts of early 1993.

In the film, the deal is brokered by an academic "Professor," and Jahangir's successor, Maqbool, agrees to handle the still unidentified cargo. This leads to his undoing, as the Coast Guard, having intercepted the shipment, lays siege to his house, a scene that seeks to parallel the coming of Birnam Wood to Dunsinane. This rather clumsy ending, much the weakest part of the film, is uncannily strengthened by subsequent history, a trail of events Bhardwaj could not have foreseen. As modern viewers of the film, we recall not only what is in the film's past, the smuggling in by sea of huge quantities of arms and explosives to supply the Mumbai Stock Exchange explosions on Friday, 12 March 1993, an act for which Dawood Ibrahim's D-Company and his associates Tiger Memon and Mohammad Dossa were held responsible, but a later act of terrorism. On 26 November 2008, a date popularly known as 26/11, armed terrorists landed by boat on Mumbai's sea-coast, stormed into public buildings, held the city to ransom, shot passengers in a railway station, and occupied the Taj Mahal and Trident hotels, killing guests and staff.

This urban history, as well as the near-mythical status assumed by Mumbai itself, torn apart by violence and desire, has no parallel in Shakespeare's play. It would be a mistake to equate Mumbai with Scotland, although each represents the territory ruled over by the hero. Rather, Mumbai is what Bhardwaj brings to the conversation in the echo-chamber of adaptation: aptly, in making a Bombay film that adapts and speaks to a Shakespearean play, he brings not Bombay film conventions (there are relatively few of those) but Mumbai itself, in all its terror and melancholy, its history of pain and love, its humour and grief, into the room with him. By doing this, he extends the play's history in a way that a simple gangland adaptation could not have done. *Macbeth* is, centrally, a play about violence: violence by and for the state, as a means to state power. Its central figure is a man of blood, marked out by the path he has chosen. Bhardwaj's transposition of this figure to a modern context requires him to engage, directly and unambiguously, with the life of violence, the life of the criminal, and he needs also to understand afresh the connection, not so much between violence and justice (a more primitive and naive connection), but between violence and the law.

As Bhardwaj sees it, the violence of modern urban society inhabits a space of lack—the lack of positive law, the lack of power by the state to enforce its will to legal ends. In such a condition, it is only the equivocal "balance of power" of the weird sisters, the *shakti ka santulan* preached by Pundit and Purohit, with rival gangs wiping each other out, that prevails. If

Shakespeare's *Macbeth* recalls, insistently, the unending series of murders and usurpations in Scottish history, the bloody line of criminal acts intended to secure sovereign exceptionality through exceptional violence, legal power through illegal ambition, *Macbeth* in Mumbai foresees, bleakly, the collapse of law. What is unusual about this vision is the way in which it conveys, as the mainstream Bombay film is unable to do, the modern state's loss of confidence in its capacity to uphold either its law or its power. Rather, the criminal community must generate from within itself the destructive forces that both incite and punish ambition. Both *Macbeth* and *Maqbool* are texts of mourning, as obsessed with the past as they are with a future that can never be grasped. Both are studies of kinship and community, recording a loss of familial bonds at the same time as they offer new models of social efficiency. Most of all, both texts focus uncompromisingly on violence—on its means, its ends, and its laws. Shakespeare, re-visioned as postmodern *noir*, speaks to our deepest fears and anxieties.

NOTES

1. See Aristotle, *Poetics* 50a–b, trans. Ingram Bywater (Oxford: Clarendon Press, 1920), 36–38); Plato, *Republic* Book II, 377–8, Book X, 605, in *The Dialogues of Plato*, trans. B. Jowett, 2 vols (New York, Random House, 1937), vol. 1, 640–41, 863; Heraclitus, *Fragments*, 46, cited from Heraclitus, *The Complete Fragments: Translation and Commentary and the Greek Text*, trans. and ed. William J. Harris, at http://community.middlebury.edu/~harris/Philosophy/heraclitus.pdf.
2. Michel Foucault, "What is an Author?" in *Textual Strategies: Perspectives in Post-structuralist Criticism*, ed. Josue V. Harari (Ithaca: Cornell University Press, 1979), 159.
3. See Linda Hutcheon, *A Theory of Adaptation* (New York: Routledge, 2006), 7, 1; and Rabindranath Tagore, *Introduction to Jogajog* (Kolkata: Visva-Bharati, 1929), ii, translated into English as *Jogajog/Relationships*, by Supriya Chaudhuri (Delhi: Oxford University Press, 2005), 257.
4. Rabindranath Tagore, *Jibansmriti* (My Reminiscences), in *Rabindra Rachanabali* (Rabindranath Tagore, Complete Works), vol. 17 (Kolkata: Visva-Bharati, 1954), 330.
5. *Bharati*, Ashvin 1287 (August–September 1880); reprinted in *Rabindra Rachanabali*, vol. 30 (Kolkata, Visva-Bharati, 1998), 53–6.
6. See Utpal Dutt, *Girish Chandra Ghosh* (New Delhi: Sahitya Akademi, 1992), 15; and, for a contemporary review, *The Englishman*, 8 February 1893, quoted in Sarottama Majumdar, "That Sublime Old Gentleman," in *India's Shakespeare*, ed. Poonam Trivedi and Dennis Bartholomeusz (Delhi: Pearson Education, 2006), 266.
7. See Sukanta Chaudhuri, "Shakespeare in India," 4 ("Shakespeare and Indian Literature"), in Internet Shakespeare Editions, Foyer Library Theater Annex, at http://internetshakespeare.uvic.ca/Library/Criticism/shakespearein/india4.html (accessed 18 June 2011).

8. Private comment, cited in PoonamTrivedi, "'It is the bloody business which informs thus...': Local Politics and Performative Praxis, Macbeth in India," in *World-wide Shakespeares: Local Appropriations in Film and Performance*, ed. Sonia Massai (Abingdon: Routledge, 2005), 51. Trivedi also quotes Arambam as saying that his intention was to write Macbeth as "another text": "to use its signs and symbols to transform it and place it in my culture and transform that too" (ibid.).
9. Sigmund Freud, "The Uncanny" (1919), in *The Penguin Freud Library*, vol. 14: *Art and Literature*, ed. Albert Dickson, trans. ed. James Strachey (London: Penguin, 1990), 335–76.
10. See Namrata Joshi on Vishal Bhardwaj, "Krzysztof … In Meerut," *Outlook India Magazine* (31 August 2009): at http://www.outlookindia.com/article.aspx?261415 (accessed 18 June 2011). Bhardwaj composed the score for the lyricist and film-maker Gulzar's *Maachis* in 1996.
11. Brahmanand Singh, "Interview with Vishal Bhardwaj," in *Cinema in India* (Mumbai: National Film Development Corporation, 2003), 47.
12. See *Ankush* (1986), directed by N. Chandra, at www.imdb.com/title/tt0157316/; *Nayakan* (1987), directed by Mani Ratnam, at www.imdb.com/title/tt0093603/; *Parinda* (1989), directed by VidhuVinod Chopra, at www.imdb.com/title/tt0102636/; *Angaar* (1992), directed by Shashilal K. Nair, at www.imdb.com/title/tt0103689/; *Gardish* (1993), directed by Priyadarshan, at www.imdb.com/title/tt0106986/; *Satya* (1998), directed by Ram Gopal Varma at www.imdb.com/title/tt0195231/; *Company* (2002), directed by Ram GopalVarma, at www.imdb.com/title/tt0296574/; and *Maqbool* (2003), directed by Vishal Bhardwaj, at www.imdb.com/title/tt0379370/.
13. Moinak Biswas, "Mourning and Blood-ties: Macbeth in Mumbai," *Journal of the Moving Image* 5 (December 2006), at http://www.jmionline.org/jmi5_4.htm (accessed 18 June 2011).
14. Walter Benjamin, *The Origin of German Tragic Drama*, trans. John Osborne (London: Verso, 1998), 57–76.
15. See Giorgio Agamben, *State of Exception*, trans. Kevin Attell (Stanford: Stanford University Press, 2005), 52–9; and Jennifer R. Rust and Julia Reinhardt Lupton, "Introduction: Schmitt and Shakespeare," in *Carl Schmitt's Hamlet and Hecuba*, trans. David Pan and Jennifer R. Rust (New York: Telos Press Publishing, 2009), xv–li.
16. Raphael Holinshed, *The Chronicles of England, Scotland and Ireland*, 4 vols (London: John Hunne, 1577), vol. 2 [The History of Scotland], 219.
17. Ibid. 220.
18. Ibid. 227.
19. See ibid., 244: "Makbeth sore troubled herewith, for that he sawe by this meanes his hope sore hindered, (where by the olde lawes of the realme, the ordinance was, that if he that shoulde succeede were not of able age to take the charge vpon himselfe; he that was nexte of bloud vnto him, shoulde be admitted) he beganne to take counfell howe he might vsurpe the kingdome by force, hauing a iuste quarell so to do (as he tooke the mater,) for that Duncane did what in him lay to defraude him of all maner of title and clayme, whiche hee mighte in tyme to come, pretende vnto the crowne."
20. See, for example, Michael J. C. Echeruo, "Tanistry, the 'Due of Birth', and Macbeth's Sin," *Shakespeare Quarterly* 23, no. 4 (1972): 444–50.
21. Walter Benjamin, "Critique of Violence," in *Reflections*, ed. Peter Demetz (New York: Schocken Books, 1986), 281.

22. William Shakespeare, *Macbeth*, ed. Kenneth Muir, *The Arden Shakespeare* (London: Methuen, 1964). All references to *Macbeth* are to this edition and are indicated by act, scene, and line number in the text.
23. Niccolò Machiavelli, *The Prince and the Discourses*, [trans.] with introduction by Max Lerner (New York: Random House, 1950): *The Prince*, Chapter VIII, 35.
24. See David Mason, "Dharma and Violence in Mumbai," in *Asian Shakespeares on Screen: Two Films in Perspective*. Special issue, edited by Alexander C. Y. Huang, of *Borrowers and Lenders: The Journal of Shakespeare and Appropriation* 4, no. 2 (Spring/Summer 2009), at http://www.borrowers.uga.edu (accessed 18 June 2011).
25. Mukul Kesavan, "Urdu, Awadh and the Tawaif: The Islamicate Roots of the Hindi Cinema," in *Forging Identities: Gender, Communities and the State*, ed. Zoya Hasan (New Delhi: Kali for Women, 1994), 244–58.
26. "FIR registered in journalist JD's murder case," *The Telegraph*, Kolkata, 27 June 2011, at http://www.telegraphindia.com/1110627/jsp/frontpage/story_141646690.jsp (accessed 29 June 2011).

9 Reading Intertextualities in Rituporno Ghosh's *The Last Lear*: The Politics of Recanonization

Paromita Chakravarti

Peter Donaldson characterizes Godard's quirky 1986 film, *King Lear* as a "distant and debased copy" of Shakespeare's text which like Gloucester's bastard son, Edmund, asserts "filial rights despite illegitimacy, by turns denying paternity and appropriating the riches of the paternal text."[1] In the film, "fatherhood is a metaphor for the relation between authors and texts, artists and disciples"[2] as well as cultural traditions and their complex intertextualities.

Like Godard's *King Lear*, British avant-garde films of the 1980s and early '90s such as Greenaway's *Prospero's Books* and Jarman's *The Tempest* use Shakespeare's explorations of paternity in *The Tempest* to articulate intertextual relationships between the competing authorities of the book, the play, film, and digital images of the new media to analyse the politics of canonization, insemination, and dissemination.[3]

Although set in a different context (urban, middle-class contemporary India, specifically Calcutta) and genre (realist), Rituporno Ghosh's 2007 English-language film *The Last Lear* also sets out to explore the fatherliness of Shakespearean texts and the family politics of the intertextually related arts of literature, theatre, and cinema. Compared to the films cited above, Ghosh's film is more sentimentally celebratory of the Shakespearean aura, despite its location within a post-colonial milieu in which Shakespeare is often associated with colonial hegemony.[4] It also attempts to understand cinema in the context of its complex literary legacies, allegiances, borrowings, and residues, at the same time using Lear's story to articulate a tale of thwarted paternities, surrogate fatherhood, rejected patrimonies, and competing patriarchies of literary authorship, theatrical performance, and cinematic auteurship. Its central father–son relationship between an elderly stage actor and a young film director turns into an allegorical exploration of intertextual filiations between the contested authorities of play-text, theatre, and cinema in an age of mechanical reproduction.

Mark Thornton Bennett has noted how recent Anglo-American film and televisual productions like Branagh's *In the Bleak Winter* (1995), James Callis and Nick Cohen's *Beginner's Luck* (2001), Tommy O'Haver's *Get Over It* (2001), and Roger Goldby's television drama *Indian Dream* (2003) tend to focus on "the enduring stability of Shakespearean theatre" by opening up new intermedialities between stage, screen, and new media.[5] These films posit the theatrical legacy of Shakespearean drama as a site for lost values of community, integrity and stability against the threat of the homogenizing global culture. *The Last Lear* may be read in this larger context.

Ghosh's film is based on a 1985 Bengali play, *Aajker Shahjahan* (Today's Shah Jahan) written by Utpal Dutt, one of the greatest Bengali actors, translators, and scholars of Shakespeare in the last century, also an acclaimed Marxist critic and playwright. Dutt borrows his central conceit from Dwijendralal Roy's play on the last days of the sixteenth-century Mughal emperor Shah Jahan (1592–1666), who was imprisoned by his son Aurengzeb in Agra Fort for eight years till his death. During these years, his devoted daughter Jahanara embraced imprisonment to look after her ailing father. The parallels with the Lear story are evident: Dutt does not make the connection explicit, but Ghosh points it out.[6]

For Ghosh, this complex intertextual web marks the "universality" of Shakespeare, whose characters and themes resonate with Mughal history as well as nineteenth-century Bengali historical drama and twentieth-century Marxist experimental theatre: "So, when I thought of making something with universal appeal, I arrived automatically at Shakespeare. That's how *The Last Lear* was born."[7] Interestingly, Vishal Bhardwaj, director of *Maqbool* (2003) and *Omkara* (2006), Hindi films based on *Macbeth* and *Othello* respectively, when asked why he chose Shakespeare's texts, said in an interview, "Shakespeare is a great dramatist whose works have a universal, timeless appeal." However, it is important to distinguish the deployment of Shakespeare in these films from Ghosh's evocation of Shakespearean "universality."

Bollywood Shakespeare and English Shakespeare

While *The Last Lear* continues the cultural work of earlier English-language, Shakespeare-themed "heritage" films like Merchant and Ivory's *Shakespeare Wallah* (1965), it also flirts with the marketing possibilities opened up by the phenomenon of "Bollywood Shakespeares." Unlike Vishal Bhardwaj's locally rooted Hindi films *Maqbool* and *Omkara*, *The Last Lear* is made in English with an eye towards festival circuits. In fact it opened in the Toronto Film festival to critical acclaim and did very little business in the domestic box offices, despite exploiting the star appeal, at home and abroad, of Amitabh Bachchan, one of the legendary Bollywood actors.[8] It is primarily addressed to international audiences and a small section of the English-educated urban Indian elite.

Although the title foregrounds Shakespeare's play (in a way that Bhardwaj's films do not), the film is not an adaptation of *King Lear*. It uses the text to understand the Shakespearean heritage preserved in the decaying culture of Kolkata, erstwhile capital of the British Empire in India, and its once vibrant, now obsolescent Shakespearean theatre tradition. *The Last Lear* was projected as Bachchan's first serious, English-language, Shakespearean film. Ghosh defends his decision to make the film in English:

> *The Last Lear* is about a Calcutta-based theatre actor who speaks English as he does Shakespeare. I feel English has become our language too. So it was a natural choice. Besides, the actors who have worked in the film speak English in real life… I have not tried to make an English film where the accent and diction are all very perfect. I have kept it the way that the actors speak English, their accents. I think there's a kind of charm in this heteroglossia.[9]

The indigenization of the English language in India holds true for a small section of Indians. But the unproblematized endorsement of Bachchan's elocutionary public-school accent weakens Ghosh's point about a free-flowing heteroglossia. Ghosh's insistence that "it would not have been possible (to make the film) in any other language, given the profession of the protagonist,"[10] backed by Bachchan's statement "When you talk of Shakespeare, it has to be English,"[11] is also difficult to understand, given the long tradition of Shakespeare translations and appropriations in Indian vernaculars. In recent times, Bhardwaj's two films have shown how effectively this indigenization can be achieved. Besides, Ghosh's inspiration and source-author, Utpal Dutt, was a pioneer in this regard.[12] In *Aajker Shahjahan*, Dutt inserts the murder scene from *Othello* in the original English text. This bold experiment is enabled by the essential bilinguality of most Indians, but it also demonstrates Dutt's ability to mesh Shakespeare's texts with a vernacular culture. Ghosh appears to have overlooked this inclusiveness of Dutt's Shakespearean legacy.

Ghosh, of course, refuses to accept that his film might alienate the average Indian cinema-goer. He insists that Shakespeare is deeply embedded in the culture of his city, and is an aspect of everyday Calcutta life:[13] "I grew up meeting Shakespeare on the streets of Kolkata. Theatre Road was renamed Shakespeare Sarani. Shakespeare is lodged permanently in Kolkata."[14] Although there is indeed a street named after Shakespeare in Kolkata, this is hardly indicative of the average Calcuttan's familiarity with Shakespearean texts. Even Ghosh's assumed audience, the English-educated upper-middle class, would be hard put to identify the Shakespearean lines strewn liberally in his film. But they would certainly recognize the cultural capital represented by Shakespeare. This is really the crux of *The Last Lear*, which uses Bachchan's star appeal to bolster a near-supernatural Shakespearean mystique. Ghosh has remarked that "Shakespeare almost becomes a character in the film, he acts as the divine power, and his presence in certain moments almost acts as a divine intervention."[15]

This deification of Shakespeare was a nineteenth-century colonial phenomenon, particularly in Bengal where his works became a "source of non-denominational spirituality,"[16] providing a secular space in which philosophy, metaphysics, and ethics could be discussed outside the bounds of an orthodox Hindu or Islamic framework. Ghosh appears to be resurrecting this colonial status of Shakespeare in *The Last Lear*. In a singular instance of cultural amnesia, he claims that his film is the first serious attempt in Indian cinema to indigenize Shakespeare: "*The Last Lear* is the first attempt to take Shakespeare away from the colonial context and place it in an indigenous Indian context and actually transpose it to a film unit."[17]

In fact, the film is steeped in colonial nostalgia. It pays an elegiac tribute to the dying English-language theatre of Calcutta (and its Shakespearean repertory) through the reminiscences of Harry, an ageing Shakespearean actor who lives in the past and dreams of playing Lear. Ghosh's Anglophilia sits awkwardly with his use of Dutt's *Aajker Shahjahan*, which is a tribute to vernacular Bengali theatre, particularly in its nationalist phase. Nor does it mesh with Dutt's Marxist indigenization of Shakespeare in Bengali folk-theatre modes. In his effort to trace his Shakespearean lineage from Dutt, Ghosh betrays the true spirit of this patrimony.

Archiving Theatre in Cinema: Utpal Dutt, *Aajker Shahjahan*, and Shakespeare

Utpal Dutt was one of India's greatest Shakespeareans. International audiences know him from his role as the princely patron of the touring Shakespearean actors in the film *Shakespeare Wallah* mentioned earlier.[18] Ruth Prawer Jhabwala's script of *Shakespeare Wallah* is based on the lives of the Kendals, an itinerant family drama troupe who played Shakespeare in different Indian cities in the 1940s and '50s.[19] Piquantly, the Kendals play themselves in the film. Ghosh's *The Last Lear* appears to bear the legacy of this Merchant-Ivory production. Strewn with fragments of Shakespeare performances, the film represents what Richard Burt has described as the "play within the film" genre in which Shakespeare becomes a signifier of cultural ruin, of pastness, creating a politics of lost significance by framing theatre through cinema.[20]

Nonetheless, one can question whether this reflection preserves the legacy of Utpal Dutt. Dutt belonged to the Kendals' Shakespeareana International Theatre Company before setting up his own Little Theatre Group in Calcutta in 1950, which played Shakespeare both in the original and in Bengali translations. He tried to take Shakespeare to the masses by casting his plays in the "jatra" mode, a Bengali folk-theatre form. As a Marxist, he was concerned with deploying Shakespeare for radical social transformation. In the introduction to his critical study *Shakespeare-ersamajchinta* (Shakespeare's Social Thought), dedicated to Geoffrey Kendal, Dutt deplores the tendency to regard Shakespeare as a unique genius, an individual rather than as a social entity embedded in a larger cultural and social context. Following his mentor Brecht, Dutt makes notable references to *King Lear* in his other works; but interestingly, his *Aajker Shahjahan*, the play on which Ghosh bases *The Last Lear* and which is steeped in Shakespearean references, never alludes to *King Lear* despite the obvious parallels in the plot, presenting an ageing stage actor and his tutelary, almost paternal relationship with a young film actress. For both personal and political reasons, the relationship between text, theatre, and cinema remains an abiding concern in Dutt's plays and prose writings.[21] But it is Ghosh's *Last Lear* which brings to the fore the invisible template shaping Dutt's work.

Although a dedicated theatre worker, Dutt had to find employment in films to sustain himself. Uneasy with his relationship to the film industry, which he regarded as a site of capitalist production, films come in for trenchant criticism in his plays as a commodity seducing the masses away from a critical, political theatre practice. *Aajker Shahjahan* marks this transition as unavoidably tragic. The play pays valiant tribute to Bengali theatre even while bidding it farewell.

It becomes a compendium of the great moments of the Bengali stage which an ageing actor tries to cling to against the depredations of the cinema. He passes on the legacy of the theatre to a young film actress as a patrimony that cinema should preserve rather than wipe out.

Aajker Shahjahan is a veritable archive of lost plays of the golden age of the Bengali stage and its role in nationalist history. It revolves around Kunjabehari (played by Dutt), an old theatre actor who spends his time reliving and reciting scenes from old plays, surrounded by crumbling theatre props. He is offered a role in a film in which he plays an old circus clown who kills the ringmaster, becomes a fugitive, and finally dies in a police encounter. Although at first sceptical of movies, Kunja takes up the role, primarily because he hopes to build a Bengali theatre archive with the promised remuneration. However, things go wrong during the shooting. The banality and egotism of his co-stars, their lack of talent, and the imperatives of commercial film-making depress Kunja. The only redeeming feature is his companionship with Kumkum, the marijuana-addicted heroine who confesses that she takes drugs because she is terrified of facing the camera. Kunja promises to teach her to act. They enact Desdemona's murder scene from *Othello*, a scene Dutt was famous for playing: it was his voice which was used for Uttam Kumar's performance of *Othello* in the film *Saptapadi* (*The Seven Steps of Marriage*).[22] Through the violent intimacy of the strangling act, which almost seems real, the veteran thespian and the young film star forge a close relationship of filiation. Kunja dreams of performing again the role which once built his theatre reputation—that of the dying Shah Jahan, with Kumkum playing his dutiful daughter Jahanara.

At the shooting, a quiet ego tussle begins between the film director and the senior stage actor, ending tragically. In the climactic sequence, the director challenges Kunja, so proud of his histrionic talents, to enact the fall off a hill himself rather than use a stuntman. Kunja concedes, but the neurotically perfectionist director feels that the scene did not appear realistic because Kunja hung on to some trees for support. He orders the trees to be cut down, announces falsely that the reels of the climax have been destroyed in the laboratory, and reshoots the sequence, again with Kunja. The old actor survives the fall but later suffers a stroke and loses his memory. In the closing moments of the play we see Kunja trying to remember the name of Shakespeare's play: "What is it, with the Moorish general—what is the name—*Hamilo*?" and Kumkum quietly reminds him, "*Othello*." Kunja's memory, once the storehouse of old stage anecdotes and lines from old plays, is now a ruin. Not only can he no longer build his dream project, the theatre archive for which he had ventured into films: the archive itself is now wiped out. However, Kumkum the film star has now had a taste of stage acting, and might carry Kunja's theatrical legacy forward.

Ghosh's *The Last Lear* reinvigorates the old debate of the interrelationship of theatre and cinema associated with the film theorist André Bazin. Bazin's contention that films may be used to popularize rather than threaten the existence of theatre uses the example of Shakespearean film adaptations which, he suggests, could make the plays accessible to those who would normally not go to the theatre, and prepare them for the latter experience.[23]

Films can also help in preserving lost stage traditions, acting as an archive for ephemeral stage performances.[24] The "Mounet-Sullys and the Sarah Bernhardts ... disappeared at the beginning of the century like prehistoric creatures," but "By a stroke of irony, it is the cinema that has preserved their bones, fossilized in the films d'art."[25] Bazin calls these fossils of tragic theatre "monsters," stripped of their ritual and sacral quality. In *The Last Lear*, Ghosh's protagonist Harry projects this "monstrosity." He is a prehistoric creature caught in a time warp, a magnificent theatre personality trapped within the manipulative frames of the cinema. He is constricted as much by the claustrophobic interior of his rambling mansion as by the careful and measured realism of Ghosh's art-house film genre. Ghosh heightens this mismatch between the realism of cinema and the grand, transformative illusion of theatre through dramatic lighting, transforming the room into a little stage as Harry speaks Prospero's lines on the insubstantiality of life and plays.

The cinematic attempt to archive transitory theatrical moments ends tragically in *The Last Lear*. In trying to use the old Shakespearean actor in his film, the young film director in Ghosh's film only exploits his reputation and finally kills him. Ironically, Ghosh too, in trying to memorialize Utpal Dutt, his play *Aajker Shahjahan*, Bengali theatre, and the Shakespearean theatrical tradition in Kolkata, does little more than borrow the aura and nostalgia associated with these institutions. Whereas Dutt's *Aajker Shahjahan*, with its cutting irony and self-deprecating humour, could unflinchingly revalue the history of the Bengali stage, *The Last Lear* is little more than bardolatry, both of Shakespeare and of Dutt.

The Last Lear, *King Lear*, and *Aajker Shahjahan*: Of Fathers and Sons

The plot of *The Last Lear* follows *Aajker Shahjahan* fairly closely, with some additions. However, Ghosh transforms Shah Jahan's story into that of Lear. This might resonate better with a global audience, but only by relinquishing the specificity of Bengali theatrical tradition at the heart of Dutt's play. There is an easy traffic in *Aajker Shahjahan* between the excerpts from old Bengali theatre quoted by Kunja and the *Othello* murder scene performed in Shakespearean English. They meet in Kunja's archival memory as elements of his total past repertoire.

We should not forget that, even in 1961, it was possible to have an entire Shakespearean sequence (again the murder scene from *Othello*) embedded in a popular Bengali film, *Saptapadi*, starring the legendary Uttam Kumar and Suchitra Sen. (Utpal Dutt's sonorous voice provided the English playback for Uttam Kumar in this scene.) In Tarashankar Bandyopadhyay's original novel of the same name, *Othello* acts as a leitmotif shaping and virtually enabling the romantic relationship between a Christian Anglo-Indian girl and a Hindu Bengali boy in the colonial Bengal of the 1940s.[26] The film retains this centrality of Shakespeare's play, and uses images of the *Othello* performance even in the promotionals. The hierarchies and divisions of high and low culture, popular and elite traditions disappear in this melodramatic romance produced for the commercial Bengali film industry, which became a huge box-office success.

Ghosh comments on this movement between "high" and "low" art, between popular and parallel cinema in Bengal in the 1960s, when both kinds of films were drawing upon classic literary texts in a bilingual context of use, and their audiences were not so divided as they are now.[27] Yet *The Last Lear* seems to have lost out on this legacy of *Saptapadi*. In a proclaimed cinematic tribute to a master of Bengali theatre, Ghosh subsumes the vernacular stage world of *Aajker Shahjahan* within a purely English and Shakespearean theatrical tradition.

This has obvious implications for a post-colonial society. No longer assimilated to the vernacular theatrical heritage as in Dutt, Ghosh reassigns to Shakespeare the space of privilege and power associated with class status, the English language, access to elite education, and claims to a once colonial and now global modernity. Dutt's faded thespian Kunja becomes Harry, the great Shakespearean actor who has only contempt for the philistines around him who have never heard of Robin Goodfellow or Oberon. He agrees to play a part in a film because the director knows his Shakespeare—not because, like Kunja, he needs the money. Nor does he live alone like Kunja in a theatrical wasteland, but as a gentleman of leisure in a grand house, looked after by a young and devoted partner. The grime and poverty, the stark materiality of the stage compared with the illusionism of commercial cinema, are missing in Harry's genteel surroundings. Played by the elegantly ageing Amitabh

Bachchan, Harry looks aristocratic, drinks scotch on the rocks, and speaks with a public-school English accent.

Ghosh also introduces two women in his film—the nurse who tends Harry after his fall from the cliff, and his partner who, for most of the film, reminisces about Harry's past glories. The third woman in Harry's life is a film star, the equivalent of Kumkum in *Aajker Shahjahan*. Harry seems ensconced in a cocoon of feminine care and love within a comfortable domesticity. His reclusive life is not stained by the edgy bohemianism of Kunja's down-at-heel existence. Such a Lear does not crave filial love, protected as he is by the watchful care of three young women who keep vigil for him as he lies dying. Their concern and awe for him parallels Harry's own bardolatory. Unlike Ghosh's other films which challenge patriarchal institutions, *The Last Lear* seems to be shoring up patriarchies and constructing new ones.

In every way, Ghosh depoliticizes Dutt's play, ignoring the central tenet of Dutt's ideology. In *Aajker Shahjahan*, Kunja reminds his audience that commercial Bengali theatre, like Shakespeare's, was never dissociated from social concerns:

> Shakespeare might have portrayed isolated individuals—*Hamlet*, *Timon of Athens*. But his plays are also about the rise and fall of states. Rebellion and war, a whole society.[28]

Dutt's protagonist is disappointed with bourgeois, illusionistic cinema which can never rise above individual concerns. This disillusionment has much to do with its commercial orientation. But, in *The Last Lear*, it is not the capitalist organization of the industry that is criticized: the director Siddhartha appears to be making an art-house film. Instead, Harry appears unhappy with the film medium and its methods—the long shots, the paring down of dialogue, the dependence on illusion exemplified by using stuntmen instead of actors. Here, it is Harry who insists on performing the final fall off the cliff, rather than the director demanding it as in Dutt's play. It is only when the director is unhappy with the take that he lies, saying that the original reels have been destroyed, and compels Harry to repeat the sequence. But even as Harry jumps to eventual death, he proves the moral superiority of the theatre as a site of the "real." In Dutt's play and Ghosh's film, drama is marked by authenticity, the actor's actual presence, as against the fakery and cheap tricks of the cinema.

Ironically, however, the Dover Cliff scene in *King Lear* (echoed inversely in *Aajker Shahjahan* and *The Last Lear*) tests the limits of theatrical illusion. It depends entirely on Edgar's verbal evocation of height to persuade Gloucester to jump off what is not a cliff at all. The greater challenge is to convince the audience that Gloucester actually believes that he leaps from a height. One would imagine this might be easier in cinema, which can manipulate what the audience sees much more than the theatre can. Yet in the climactic cliff scene in *Aajker Shahjahan* and *The Last Lear*, the film director refuses to give the veteran stage actor this cinematic advantage. In a reversal of the Dover Cliff scene, the old actor in Dutt's play and Ghosh's film must jump off a real cliff. This is not something that the stage, for all its "reality" (as in Shakespeare's *King Lear*), requires Gloucester to do. In fact, Gloucester's illusion of being saved after an imaginary fall from a great height is morally and spiritually therapeutic, restoring his faith in divine protection even as it marks an aesthetic tour de force, showcasing the imaginative powers of the theatre. But in *Aajker Shahjahan* and *The Last Lear*, the reworking of the Dover Cliff scene frames illusion in a negative light, associating it with the inauthenticity of cinema rather than the potency of the theatre.

While in Shakespeare's play, the good son Edgar saves Gloucester by inciting him to take a false leap, in Ghosh's film it is Harry's false son, the Edmund-like Siddhartha, who pitches him to his real death. In his fatal encounter with cinema, Harry chooses Siddhartha the illegitimate son over the devoted journalist, Edgar as much as Kent, whom he throws out of his house but who loyally follows him, truthfully and sympathetically documenting his story. In this difficult and uneasy bond of filiation, cinema appears to be an unnatural offspring of the theatre, a bastard who defiles his own lineage.

In *The Last Lear*, Lear's story is really that of Gloucester, betrayed by his false son but protected by the one he had exiled. Although Harry has the aristocracy and loneliness of Lear and is surrounded by three women, one of them clearly Cordelia-like, his persona resonates more with the play's subplot. Harry walking without his glasses, stumbling blindly, led by Siddhartha (who will later turn against him), and finally jumping off the cliff, calls up images from the Gloucester story. Does this indicate that, in these shrunken times, even the last Lear is at best a Gloucester?

Ghosh, Ray, and Shakespeare: The Politics of Nostalgia

Despite its star cast and global positioning, *The Last Lear* is a film of limited scope about the impossibility of largeness in our times. It thrives on the yearning for a lost magnanimity and heroism which it locates in Dutt's play, Shakespeare's text, and an elite theatrical culture. Very much like what Jameson has called the "nostalgia film," it attempts to access not an actual historical past but aesthetic styles of the past through ever receding frames of older texts, and is thus concerned centrally with a matrix of intertextuality:[29]

> we are now ... in "intertextuality" as a deliberate, built-in feature of the aesthetic effect and as the operator of a new connotation of "pastness" and pseudohistorical depth in which the history of aesthetic styles displaces "real" history.[30]

Despite being set in present times, *The Last Lear* lacks specific markers of contemporaneity. The darkened interiors of a cavernous house which dominate much of the film evoke a vague sense of the past. Besides, most of Ghosh's films seem to hark back to earlier modes of film-making, especially the legacy of the maestro Satyajit Ray. Deploying the basic grammar of Ray's cinema, Ghosh's films recreate the fading world of middle-class Bengali gentility, often defined by a love of literature. Even Ray's own films seems already to exude an archaic feel. His most celebrated works—*Patherpanchali* (The Song of the Road, 1955), *Charulata* (The Lonely Wife, 1964) or *Devi* (The Goddess, 1960)—thrive on cinema's loving yearning for the literary organization of the nineteenth-century novel with its dense, well-defined worlds of experience. Ghosh too has lamented the passing away of the "literariness" of mainstream Bengali cinema, snapping its "core connection to the culture" and alienating the educated middle-class audience.[31]

Ghosh's drawing-room conversations in gracious but declining surroundings, his love of the nineteenth century, and his interest in psychological realism, not only align him with Ray but make him a direct disciple. In many respects, *The Last Lear* is Ghosh's answer to Ray's *Jalsaghar* (The Music Room, 1958) and *Nayak* (The Hero, 1966), presenting respectively the decline of a once-powerful landlord and the feudal system he stood for, and an immensely successful but corrupted and disintegrating film actor.

In *The Last Lear*, the CCTV that Siddhartha, the film director, installs in Harry's room gives the latter a sense of the powerful gaze of the camera. The grainy images of the surveillance camera bring the wider world into the interiority of Harry's room, a marked, ritual space almost like the stage. The advent of these images turns this theatrically focused, centripetal space into a centrifugal and cinematic one, bringing in the streets and the city.[32] The scenes where the veteran actor and the young film director watch digitally-reproduced images of the outside world in an enclosed room ironically evoke Lear's fantasy of being imprisoned with Cordelia, playing "God's spies" to courtiers and worldly men (5.2.8–17). Siddhartha and Harry try to guess the professions of the people they watch. This is also a throwback to the opening opera-glass sequence of Ray's *Charulata*, where the protagonist's loneliness and boredom are conveyed as she moves from window to window of her mansion on a lazy summer afternoon, looking out onto the city streets and the passers-by, at a life she cannot be a part of.

The Last Lear is replete with acts of reminiscing. The action is initiated by the need to write an obituary of a dead stage actor, which is what brings the young journalist to Harry's house. That creates an occasion for the old actor to revisit his past. Harry's partner remembers his performances; Harry reconstructs his theatre career through conversations with the film director and the journalist; Ghosh remembers Utpal Dutt and Shakespeare, while *The Last Lear* recalls the legacy of the stage. Yet these acts of memorializing do not, or perhaps cannot, engage with the materiality and specificity of the past: they only create an aura, empty of content, which reinforces the authority of the classic text, the power of tradition and the patriarchy of the canon without negotiating with them. Just as Siddhartha fails to appreciate Harry's skills, experience, and hard labour—docking his lines, focusing only on his looks, choosing to exploit only his reputation—Ghosh too fails to engage seriously with the history of *Aajker Shahjahan*, Utpal Dutt's politics, and the tradition of the Shakespearean stage in Bengal. While Kunja in Dutt's play wishes to create an archive of Bengali theatre, what Ghosh is constructing is a museum of sorts, selectively showcasing hierarchized pieces of art without historicizing them.[33] While Shakespeare's plays have been subjected to this kind of nostalgia-building for centuries, it is particularly ironic to have Dutt consigned to such treatment. By nostalgizing both Dutt and Shakespeare, *The Last Lear* falls into the trap that Susan Bennet sees as unavoidable in rewritings of Shakespeare, however radical:

> To reproduce a classic text of the European imperial archive is always to risk its willing and wistfully nostalgic assent to (re)claim its own authority. Those texts are simply so heavily overcoded, value laden, that the production and reception of the "new" text necessarily becomes bound to the tradition that encompasses and promotes the old "authentic" version.[34]

Ghosh's film belongs to the genre of "heritage films" like Merchant and Ivory's *Shakespeare Wallah*, which attempt not a re-reading of Shakespeare but a re-canonization.

The nostalgia for a Shakespearean theatrical culture blends with a yearning for lost gentility and grandeur, tradition and aristocracy, linked to an imperial past. Moreover, this desire is sentimental in its inability to laugh at or question itself. While Shakespeare is unflinchingly critical of Lear and can even make him look ridiculous, Ghosh's Harry, shored up by Bachchan's charisma, is never quite allowed to make a fool of himself, except in one brief drunken moment. The values of canonicity, authority, and high culture that he represents are never scrutinized in the film. In fact, they receive not merely aesthetic but moral validation as theatre asserts its claims over cinema, "real" action replaces the illusory stunt, and the integrity and commitment of the stage actor triumphs over the crass commercialism and sly connivance of the film director.

In this respect, Ghosh's *The Last Lear* has little affinity with postmodern pastiche cinema like Godard's *King Lear*, Jarman's *Tempest* or Greenaway's *Prospero's Books*. In this latter kind of film, the classic literary text, physical theatre, even debased computer-generated images of high Renaissance art jostle for space, challenging the hierarchies of art, the politics of canon formation, and the ideology of the classic or the original. *The Last Lear* seeks instead to re-establish the central, classic status of Shakespeare within an English theatrical tradition associated with a colonial past. It is a product of modernist nostalgia for a "pure art" untouched by the plebeian, the philistine, and the corrupting influence of technology. Ghosh's film gazes longingly beyond the camera into the realm of the "real," now reduced to a simulacrum, where CCTV images mediate between the viewer and the reality outside. As such, *The Last Lear* exemplifies the paradoxical act of using cinema to denounce its own debased craft, conserving and celebrating the older and "higher" arts of theatre and literature, with Shakespeare providing the rationale for the exercise.

NOTES

1. Peter Donaldson, "Disseminating Shakespeare: Paternity and Text in Jean-Luc Godard's King Lear," in *Shakespearean Films, Shakespearean Directors* (Unwin Hyman: Boston, 1990), 189.
2. Ibid., 190.
3. See Amy Lawrence, "Daddy Dearest, Patriarchy and the Artist, *Prospero's Books*" (1991), in *The Films of Peter Greenaway* (Cambridge: Cambridge University Press, 1997), 140–64; James Tweedie, "Caliban's Books: The Hybrid Text in Peter Greenaway's *Prospero's Books,*" *Cinema Journal* 40, no. 1 (Fall 2000): 104–26; Colin MacCabe, "A Post-national European Cinema: A Consideration of Derek Jarman's *The Tempest* and *Edward II*," in *Dissolving Views: Key Writings on British Cinema*, ed. Andrew Higson (London: Cassell, 1996), 191–201.
4. See Ania Loomba, *Gender, Race, Renaissance Drama* (Manchester: Manchester University Press, 1989); Ania Loomba and Martin Orkin, eds, *Post-Colonial Shakespeares* (London: Routledge, 1998); Harish Trivedi, "Shakespeare in India: Colonial Contexts," in *Colonial Transactions* (Manchester: Manchester University

Press, 1995), 10–28; Jyotsna Singh, "Shakespeare and the Civilising Mission," in *Colonial Narratives/Cultural Dialogues* (London: Routledge, 1996), 120–52.
5. Mark Thornton Burnett, *Filming Shakespeare in the Global Marketplace* (New York: Palgrave Macmillan, 2007), 4.
6. In an interview given to Reshmi Sengupta in T2, the entertainment supplement of *The Telegraph*. For full text see http://www.telegraphindia.com/1080911/jsp/entertainment/story_9814976.jsp.
7. Rituporno Ghosh, interview, *Tehelka Magazine* 5, no. 389 (27 September 2008).
8. See Rachel Dwyer, "Amitabh Bachchan; The Angry Young Man," British Academy of Film and Television Arts, 16 November 2007; Ranjini Mazumdar, *Bombay Cinema: An Archive of a City* (Minneapolis: University of Minnesota, 2007); Susmita Dasgupta, *Amitabh: The Making of a Superstar* (Delhi: Penguin Books, 2007); and Bhawana Somaaya, *Amitabh Bachchan: The Legend* (Delhi: Macmillan, 1999).
9. Rituporno Ghosh, interviewed by Reshmi Sengupta: see http://www.telegraphindia.com/1080911/jsp/entertainment/story_9814976.jsp.
10. *Time Out*, Mumbai. Quoted in http://economictimes.indiatimes.com/News/News-By-Industry/Media--Entertainment-/Entertainment/Bollywood-talks-English-beginning-with-the-Bard/articleshow/3469908.cms).
11. See http://movies.indiatimes.com/articleshow/3470761.cms.
12. Dutt's full length translations include *Romeo and Juliet*, *The Merry Wives of Windsor* (as Phulbabu), *Macbeth* (ed. Samik Bandhyopadhyay, Kolkata: Thema, 2006), and his Bengali adaptation of *A Midsummer Night's Dream* (Chaitali Rater Swapna). He has translated numerous Shakespearean scenes, for instance from *King Lear* (5.3) *Richard II* (5.3), and *Corialanus* (1.1), all embedded in his prose dialogue *Shakespeare o Brecht* (1988), in Utpal Dutt, *Gadya Sangraha* (Collected Prose), vol. 1, *Natyachinta* (Thoughts on Theatre), ed Samik Bandyopadhyay (Kolkata: Dey's Publishing, 1988), 319–75.
13. Ghosh remarks about his own love for the city and its importance in *The Last Lear*: "I love Kolkata deeply and the city itself is one of the characters in the film, and it was important for me that Harry was played by someone who is familiar with the city. Bachchan is more than familiar with it. He has lived and worked here, and he has returned to Kolkata quite often. (http://www.rediff.com/movies/2007/sep/19ab.htm).
14. See http://www.realbollywood.com/news/2007/09/rituparno-ghosh-last-lear.html.
15. See http://www.screenindia.com/news/the-last-lear-is-a-treat-for-shakespeare-lovers/361021/.
16. Jashodhara Bagchi, "Shakespeare in Loin Cloths: English Literature and the early Nationalist Consciousness in Bengal," in *Rethinking English; Essays in Literature, Language, History*, ed. Svati Joshi (New Delhi; Trianka, 1991), 150.
17. See http://in.movies.yahoo.com/news-detail/33400/Rituparno-Ghosh-merges-theatre-cinema-in-The-Last-Lear.html.
18. A 1965 Merchant Ivory production, the film follows the fortunes of an itinerant British theatre troupe in post-colonial India as they try to keep their repertory of Shakespearean plays alive even as the taste for such drama declines and Bollywood films begin to dominate the cultural scene. The film included long excerpts from Shakespearean plays like *Richard II*, *Antony and Cleopatra*, *Twelfth Night*, and *Othello*. The cast included Bollywood star Shashi Kapoor and Madhur Jaffrey, Shakespearean theatre actors Geoffrey and Felicity Kendal and UtpalDutt, and the music for the film was scored

by Satyajit Ray. For critical work on the film, see Parmita Kapadia, "Shakespeare Transposed; The British Stage on the Post-colonial Screen," in *Almost Shakespeare: Reinventing his works for Cinema and Television*, ed. James R. Keller and Leslie Stratyner (Jefferson, NC: McFarland & Co., 2004), 42–56. Also see Robert Emmet Long, *The Films of Merchant-Ivory* (New York: Harry N. Abrams, 1991).
19. See Geoffrey Kendal, *The Shakespeare Wallah: The Autobiography of Geoffrey Kendal* (London: Sidgwick and Jackson, 1986).
20. Richard Burt, "All that remains of Shakespeare in Indian film," in *Shakespeare in Asia*, ed. Dennis Kennedy (Cambridge: Cambridge University Press, 2010).
21. See, for instance, the plays *Chhayanat* (The Shadow Player) and *Lohar Bhim* (The Iron Bhima).
22. See Paromita Chakravarti, "Modernity, Postcoloniality and Othello: the case of *Saptapadi*," in *Remaking Shakespeare:Performance across Media, Genres and Cultures*, ed. Pascale Aebischer, Edward J.Esche and Nigel Wheale (New York: Palgrave Macmillan, 2003), 39–55.
23. Andre Bazin, *What is Cinema?* vol. 1 (Berkeley: University of California Press, 1967), 120.
24. Utpal Dutt himself used film to archive theatre when he produced a serialized four-part television programme entitled *In Search of Theatre* documenting the history of the Bengali stage.
25. Bazin, 122
26. See Chakravarti, 46–50.
27. Ghosh, *Tehelka* interview.
28. *Aajker Shahjahan* in Utpal Dutt, *Natak Samagra* (Collected Plays), ed. Sova Sen, Bishnupriya Dutt, and Souvik Raychaudhuri, vol. 7 (Kolkata: Mitra and Ghosh Publishers, 1999), 217 (translation mine).
29. Jameson's own nostalgia for a "real" past and "real" history remains problematic, begging the question whether such an authentic and "pure" site can actually exist, beyond discourse and textuality.
30. Frederic Jameson, *Post Modernism or The Cultural Logic of Late Capitalism* (Verso: London, 1991), 20.
31. Ibid.
32. See Bazin, vol. 1.
33. See Andreas Huysen, *Twilight Memories: Marking Time in a Culture of Amnesia* (New York and London: Routledge, 1995), 69.
34. See Susan Bennett, *Performing Nostalgia: Shifting Shakespeare and the Contemporary Past* (Routledge; London, 1996), 145.

PART II

10 "To what base uses we may return": Deconstruction of *Hamlet* in Contemporary Drama

Aneta Mancewicz

> To what base uses we may return, Horatio! Why may not imagination trace the noble dust of Alexander till'a find it stopping a bung-hole?
>
> *Hamlet* (5.1.192–4)[1]

At the graveyard, Hamlet returns to the issues of death and afterlife, which he has been obsessively examining from the beginning of the tragedy. The prince imagines how the corpse of Alexander the Great, decayed and dissolved into earth, might be used for stopping a hole in a beer barrel (5.1.201). By analogy, he envisions the cadaver of Julius Caesar, which transformed into clay might serve to fill a crack in a building (5.1.202–205). Yet Hamlet's eschatological reflections are not limited to decomposition of bodies. As the protagonist "seems fascinated by the literal as well as spiritual 'afterlife',"[2] he expresses apprehension regarding his own *post mortem* existence and the "base uses" to which he himself might be reduced.

Hamlet's anxiety about his afterlife appears to be most appropriate when one takes into consideration the profusion of references to this tragedy. This article focuses on a specific section of *Hamlet*'s offshoots—dramatic versions written over the last five decades. Since the 1960s several plays based on *Hamlet* have exhibited an approach that bears affinities with deconstruction. In this essay, they are situated in the context of deconstructive criticism of the tragedy and the tradition of *Hamlet* adaptations. The term *dewriting* is introduced to define a set of techniques used in dramatic variations of *Hamlet* that rely on a deconstructive paradigm. So far such plays have been studied separately as manifestations of postmodern drama; here, they are analyzed collectively to reflect on transformations in the tradition of appropriating *Hamlet*.

Deconstruction and Shakespeare Studies

It may be surprising that, while the influence of deconstruction on our understanding of *Hamlet* finds its reflection in several studies of the tragedy, its impact on the play's adaptations remains open to investigation. The oversight may owe to a particular development of deconstruction from philosophical to literary theory. Shakespeare scholars not only have had to tailor philosophical ideas for the purposes of literary analysis, but also to evaluate them in the context of the Renaissance literature. Deconstruction, conceptualized by Jacques Derrida in the 1960s, was a set of ontological and epistemological propositions rather than straightforward instruments of literary analysis. As a manifestation of postmodernism, it aimed at challenging the privileged position of the logos; it subverted the "received ideas of the sign and language, the text, the context, the author, the reader, the role of history, the work of interpretation, and the forms of critical writing."[3] Adapted as a method of critical analysis by Joseph Hillis Miller and Paul de Man, deconstruction has become a way of reading which centers on paradoxes and contradictions as fundamental components of a text and instruments of interpretation.

Within Shakespeare studies, deconstruction has emerged slowly and shyly. At first, there appeared only sporadic articles, such as David J. McDonald's "'Hamlet' and the Mimesis of Absence: A Post-Structuralist Analysis" from 1978, while critics expressed reluctance towards deconstructing Shakespeare's work. James Calderwood, for instance, examining *Hamlet* in 1983, insisted that deconstructive tendencies constitute only "a part, albeit a highly significant part, of a metadramatic reading."[4] His cautious remarks reflect initial resistance of Renaissance scholars to rely on deconstruction as a method which undermines the coherence and unity of the Shakespearean canon.

In consequence, deconstruction did not make a serious impact on Shakespeare studies until 1985,[5] which saw the publication of such influential collections as *Alternative Shakespeares*, edited by John Drakakis and *Shakespeare and the Question of Theory*, edited by Patricia Parker and Geoffrey Hartman, followed in 1988 by *Shakespeare and Deconstruction*, edited by G. Douglas Atkins and David Moore Bergeron.[6] Since then, the process of appropriating Shakespeare into the deconstructive paradigm has proceeded more rapidly,[7] with a number of academic publications as well as scholarly conferences devoted to the topic.

So far several of Shakespeare's works have been analyzed from a deconstructive perspective, particularly *Hamlet*,[8] *Troilus and Cressida*,[9] *Othello*,[10] and the Sonnets.[11] Nevertheless, deconstruction has not been systematically applied to examine rewritings of *Hamlet* or any other Shakespeare's drama, although there have been individual interpretations conducted from the perspective of postmodernist poetics, which focused on Tom Stoppard's *Rosencrantz and Guildenstern are Dead* (1966)[12] or Heiner Müller's *Hamletmachine* (1977).[13]

In the case of *Hamlet*, a deconstructive approach has been justified by the very structure of the play, which has been proclaimed by several critics as postmodern *avant la lettre*. Calderwood argues that in this tragedy, "perhaps more than anywhere else in his work, Shakespeare specializes in nonbeing and inaction, in forms of verbal suicide, in interruptive modes, in junctures and caesurae, in unnamings and unspeakings."[14] Normand Berlin claims that in *Hamlet* "the questions have no answers, the doubts remain doubts, and the causes remain secret. ... we end with the question mark and silence."[15] Similarly, Andy Lavender observes, "Several resonant postmodern fancies are evident here: a refusal of closure, a taste for mindgames, a liking for play, and a penchant for metaphor rather than literalism."[16] The play's metatheatrical, ironic and elusive character has been, thus, recognized as postmodern, or deconstructive, whereas uncertainties, interruptions and inconsistencies came to be perceived not as defects but fundamental elements of the text.

When scholars like A. C. Bradley, or Harold Bloom, have been imposing on *Hamlet* the notions of universality, presence, completeness and excellence, any incoherencies or omissions in the text were either excused as shortcomings in Shakespeare's writing technique, or blamed on editors. It has led to a paradoxical situation, in which *Hamlet* functioned in mainstream criticism as "an untidy, inconsistent and badly constructed masterpiece."[17] From a deconstructive perspective, however, contradictions in the play are not to be categorized as formal flaws, resulting from Shakespeare's incapability of reworking existing sources and finding an "objective correlative" for Hamlet's emotion.[18] Nor are they to be perceived as lamentable consequences of omission, misspelling or misinterpretation of the original script by the editors. A deconstructive perspective encourages critics to see inconsistencies in the tragedy as basic components of the text, while the study of the play focuses on exposing voids and contradictions rather than imposing universal patterns.

Critics practicing deconstruction have challenged the notion of textual wholeness, "arguing that texts are always riddled by abysses, closed only by repression."[19] These claims were groundbreaking in Shakespeare studies, where the concept of the organic unity had been firmly established by Romantic poets, such as Samuel Taylor Coleridge. Undermining these unifying assumptions, deconstructive critics have rejected the idea of "an authoritative, stable, authentic original Shakespeare canon ... as the invention of eighteenth-century editors."[20] Instead, deconstruction has emphasized unexpected and often disruptive elements within Shakespeare's works.

Moreover, a deconstructive approach has undermined the tradition of Hamlet-oriented interpretations of the tragedy, which is also deeply rooted in the Romantic sensibility. Although some early critics of the play undertook the problem of character in Shakespeare's works, such as Margaret Cavendish in a letter from 1664, it was not until the late eighteenth century that Shakespearean characterization would be closely examined and widely acclaimed. As Bradley argues:

> *Hamlet* seems from the first to have been a favorite play; but until late in the eighteenth century, I believe, scarcely a critic showed that he perceived anything specially interesting in the character. ... How significant is the fact (if it be the fact) that it was only when the slowly rising sun of Romance began to flush the sky, that the wonder, beauty and pathos of this most marvelous of Shakespeare's creations began to be visible.[21]

Bradley describes the Romantic contribution to interpreting the play as an almost divine revelation, which dispersed the darkness of earlier criticism and brought into light the true value of the tragedy, its "wonder, beauty and pathos." Nevertheless, viewed from the contemporary perspective, the critic's solar imagery, which is strikingly Romantic in its form and affirmative of Romanticism in content, obscures the merit of most seventeenth- and eighteenth-century commentaries on *Hamlet*. Bradley's tribute to the Romantic interpretation of the play as a character-based piece proceeds from his own critical inclination to interpret dramatic works in a psychological manner. His position also reflects dominant tendencies in Shakespeare criticism in the early twentieth century, when Sigmund Freud's study of Hamlet in the context of the Oedipus complex encouraged interpretations focused on the hero's consciousness.

In the recently published *Hamlet without Hamlet* (2007), Margreta de Grazia questions the tradition of psychological, character-oriented interpretations of Shakespeare's tragedy. Claiming that they obscure crucial aspects of *Hamlet*, such as the themes of heritage and genealogy, she calls for a re-evaluation of the play's problems:

It was not sharper vision that brought Hamlet's complex interiority into focus. Rather, it was a blind spot. In order for Hamlet to appear modern, the premise of the play had to drop out of sight. The premise is this: at his father's death, just at the point when an only son in a patrilineal system stands to inherit, Hamlet is dispossessed—and, as far as the court is concerned, legitimately.[22]

Refusing to accept a character-based approach as a symptom of a "sharper vision," de Grazia seems to be refuting Bradley's argumentation as well as his imagery. Moreover, her reference to "a blind spot" evokes Derrida's claims about the nature of writing and the purposes of reading. Assuming that writers are determined by a textual system, Derrida encourages the readers to focus not on the author's intention, but on blind spots, those moments in the text which reveal inconsistencies and paradoxes of writing.[23] De Grazia's rhetoric as well as her critical attitude are reminiscent of Derrida's approach to criticism; there are also parallels in their approach to the past. Although de Grazia makes extensive use of historical material, in contesting the Romantically-inclined approach to the Elizabethan hero, she does not claim to be reconstructing Shakespeare's original purpose or the authentic experience of early modern viewers of the tragedy. Her reservations evoke the deconstructionist dismissal of authorial intention and objective historical reconstruction.

Deconstructive attitudes in philosophical and literary debates have revolutionized, however, not only critical evaluations of *Hamlet*. They have also inspired a new wave of dramatic adaptations since the 1960s. Although the playwrights whose works will be evoked as examples of dewriting do not directly refer to Derrida's observations in their texts, there are significant parallels between the plays and the deconstructive paradigm. Even if the affinities do not fully determine interpretations of these works, which originate from distinctive generic and cultural traditions, the theory of dewriting offers useful terms to conceptualize their approaches to *Hamlet* and to the Romantically-oriented tradition of reading this tragedy.

DEWRITING

Similarly to critics applying deconstructive theories to the study of *Hamlet*, playwrights dewriting this tragedy perceive it as an inherently paradoxical and contradictory construction. They tend to explore several possible interpretations within their works rather than offer a single, universal perspective. Such an approach is encouraged by the deconstructive emphasis on deferral, negation, absence and subversion of established meanings. Moreover, the strategies used in the process of dewriting might be conceptualized in terms of Derridean categories of supplement, *différance* and trace. All three undermine the idea of the text as a logical, referential and author-controlled entity,[24] as well as oppose semantic closure, which would entail reduction of meaning.[25]

Encouraging openness of the text and the free play of signifiers, supplement, *différance* and trace have an ambiguous ontological status, suspended between presence and absence. According to Derrida, supplement encompasses addition and replacement; it enriches as much as it substitutes.[26] Similarly, *différance* combines difference and deferral; being "neither a word nor a concept,"[27] it "has neither existence nor essence,"[28] whereas "the trace itself does not exist,"[29] but is only "the simulacrum of a presence."[30] The unique ontological status of these terms in Derrida's deconstructive philosophy owes to the fact that they challenge logocentric assumptions, questioning the privileged position of writing over speech or presence over absence.

Juxtaposing the terms which seem to mean the same, yet describe the process of signification in a slightly different manner, Derrida illustrates "the systematic play of differences, of the traces of differences, of the *spacing* by means of which elements are related to each other."[31] As G. Douglas Atkins observes, "In deconstruction, 'something' always prevents the collapse of differences into identities, as well as the possibility of 'rigid differentiation'; that 'something' may be called, if not the *supplément*, the 'trace', or *différence*."[32] The critic suggests that the three terms perform a similar function—they maintain differences without imposing the ultimate closure of meaning. In the context of dewriting, they encompass interrelated yet distinctive aspects of adapting *Hamlet* in a deconstructive manner.

Dewriting involves an extensive reorganization of the literary source by such means as omissions, reductions, reshuffling of scenes, juxtaposition of high register with low, contemporary language with old-fashioned diction, or tragedy with burlesque. The supplemented action focuses on illogical and incomprehensible incidents rather than grand endeavors. The marginal characters from the literary source are given the primary position in the process of adaptation, whilst the principal protagonists might entirely disappear from the script.

The substitution of primary protagonists with secondary figures runs parallel to the recent trends in Shakespeare criticism, which under the influence of feminism, post-colonialism or queer studies have explored hitherto neglected characters and themes. The shift of interests reflects also general tendencies in postmodern culture, which is concerned with issues of marginalization and difference. Playwrights who supplement the Shakespearean tragedy with a new perspective tend to choose as main heroes those characters from *Hamlet* whose role in the tragedy is subsidiary or enigmatic and who over the last few centuries were silenced or schematized, such as Fortinbras, Ophelia, or Gertrude. The Norwegian prince is the protagonist of Jerzy Żurek's *After Hamlet* (1981) and Janusz Głowacki's *Fortinbras Gets Drunk* (1990). Ophelia, for example, has the leading role in such plays as Saverio La Ruina's *Kitsch Hamlet. Calabro-Shakespearean Tragedy* (2004), Eduardo Quiles's *An Ophelia Without Hamlet* (1993), or Jean Betts's *Ophelia Thinks Harder* (1995); Margaret Clarke focuses on two heroines in *Gertrude and Ophelia* (1993). In *Rosencrantz and Guildenstern are Dead*, the primary importance is given to characters whose position in the Shakespearean tragedy is purely instrumental—initially, they are employed by Claudius to spy on Hamlet; finally, they are exploited by Hamlet to mislead Claudius.

Protagonists like Fortinbras, Ophelia, Gertrude, or Rosencrantz and Guildenstern have gained importance in Western drama of the last decades because of changing historical and social conditions. The popularity of the Norwegian prince coincides with such turning points in the world history as the outbreak of World War II, the fall of the Iron Curtain or the eruption of the Cold War. In postwar communist countries in Europe, Fortinbras became the key figure in interpretations of *Hamlet*, whereas Rosencrantz and Guildenstern were evoked to explore the problems of espionage and political manipulation. The expansion of feminist studies in academic circles has, in turn, led to re-evaluation of Ophelia and Gertrude. The growing significance of these protagonists also owes to a general tendency in postmodern culture, which has challenged the hierarchical division into centre and periphery, giving voice to previously under-represented social groups.[33]

The meaning of supplementation as a strategy of dewriting becomes particularly apparent in adaptations which centre around Fortinbras, such as *After Hamlet* or *Fortinbras Gets Drunk*. Fortinbras is a figure par excellence supplementary to Hamlet. While the position of the two characters in Shakespeare's scenario is strikingly similar, the Norwegian prince is capable of completing those actions which his Danish counterpart cannot perform. Fortinbras sets an alternative path of behavior for a revenging son and exemplifies those qualities which are lacking in Hamlet's conduct: self-assurance, efficiency and success. Both Żurek and Głowacki focus on Fortinbras's rise to power, and present Hamlet's downfall. The Danish prince fails either because he cannot understand the mechanisms of twentieth-century politics (in Żurek's play) or because he refuses to accept them (in Głowacki's drama).

Żurek and Głowacki supplement the Shakespearean action by means of two distinctive yet closely interrelated methods. On the one hand, the dramatists impose the Norwegian perspective on the events in Denmark, attributing external, political motivation to supernatural phenomena (the ghost of king Hamlet turns out to be an actor sent by Norwegian politicians). On the other hand, Żurek and Głowacki transpose the relations between Elsinore inhabitants onto the behavior of the Norwegian protagonists.

The replacement of Hamlet with Fortinbras in Żurek's drama, accompanied by a mocking portrayal of the Danish prince as a nineteenth-century hysteric, suggests a demise of Romantic ideals of heroism and sacrifice. As the plot develops, Fortinbras gradually loses his moral integrity, betraying his fiancée and his best friend. Nevertheless, he never becomes a grand incarnation of evil, like Macbeth or Richard III. The corruption of the modern protagonist is subtle, and, consequently, highly dangerous. The Norwegian prince is convinced that even if he is cruel, it serves the noble end. Furthermore, Fortinbras does not experience a truly tragic catastrophe; he does not represent the anguish of human strife or the bitterness of failure. The prince smoothly succeeds as a political ruler, even though his victory defies the principle of poetic justice. The Shakespearean tragedy is substituted by a political drama, whereas the tragic hero is replaced by a corrupted though efficient politician.

In a similar manner, Głowacki juxtaposes ethical idealism with political pragmatics, in order to show the impossibility of overcoming dictatorship—Hamlet has no hope for change, so he dies for his principles, whereas Fortinbras survives only to rule without autonomy. Although the play is highly humorous, the overall conclusion is most alarming, as it excludes the possibility of social and moral progress. The protagonists in Głowacki's drama lack the tragic context, as well as the noble motivation which might be attributed to some of *Hamlet* characters; functioning within a pastiche version of a political thriller, they are driven by fear, ignorance and obsessive desire of power.

Transposing the Shakespearean plot on the development of action in Norway, Głowacki modifies the original script according to the principles which are typical of a political thriller genre, with its emphasis on conspiracy theory and espionage. Nevertheless, the dramatist deconstructs not only the Shakespearean tragedy, but also the very conventions of a political thriller, turning *Fortinbras* into a witty dewriting of both high and low genres, in which viewers might find an ironic revision of political struggles and historical processes of the twentieth century. The characters portrayed by Głowacki are determined to gain and maintain power, in a disarray of unstable alliances, unpredictable incidents and illogical actions.

It is important to note that in the case of dewritings the Shakespearean characters tend to function as fragmented subjects rather than fully-developed individuals. Their behavior often lacks psychological motivation or logical explanation. Consequently, dewriting undermines the possibility of identification with dramatic protagonists, particularly with Hamlet. Identity, like the text, is no longer perceived as a stable concept, but it functions according to the principle of *différance*, becoming a shifting assembly of signs, which are simultaneously differed and deferred. The empathy with the Danish prince, which was popular among Romantic poets and critics, became debatable already in modernism, when Eliot presented Hamlet's part as too dominant and heroic to render the experience of a modern subject—an excessively self-conscious, insecure and clumsy J. Alfred Prufrock. From the postmodern perspective, the act of identification with Hamlet is even more problematic—the hero no longer represents a well-defined set of values, which can be imitated or rejected, praised or scorned. Instead, he appears as a contradictory, incoherent figure, whose identity may be only eradicated in an act of denial, as when Müller's protagonist declares in the opening line of *Hamletmachine*: "I was Hamlet," to reaffirm his non-identity with the statement "I am not Hamlet."[34]

Müller offers one of the most conspicuous manifestations of *différance* in an adaptation of *Hamlet*. The playwright explodes the dramatic structure from within, yet he maintains the remnants of plot, dialogue, characterization, and even the stage directions, in order to remind the readers of the missing markers of drama as a genre. The Müllerian scenario of destruction resembles the Derridean application of deconstructive strategies, which "do not destroy structures from the outside," but occur "necessarily from the inside, borrowing all the strategic and economic resources of subversion from the old structure, borrowing them structurally."[35] Müller's play, which constitutes a dramatic chronicle of twentieth-century European history and culture, is written as an attempt at creating a new myth that might contribute to exploding the corroded structures of the European drama as well as the bloody patterns of the European history.

Constructed from images based on Shakespeare's tragedy, postwar history, literary tradition, and popular culture, *Hamletmachine* accumulates stories, positions and identities, yet without offering unifying, comfortable solutions. The drama simultaneously subverts and confirms the importance of *Hamlet*— not as a universal story of a great hero, but as a text marked by voids and traces of absent meanings. Müller's project of destroying *Hamlet*, as well as European structures of drama and history, is inherently contradictory. While the playwright aims at overthrowing the supremacy of Hamlet as a literary and historical icon, he inevitably creates a new one, which Jonathan Kalb defines as "the Hamlet Destroyer."[36] Simultaneously, as Müller strives to disable the machines of *Hamlet* and history, he produces his own *Hamlet+machine*, which repeats the same dramatic and historical scenarios that the author attempts to destroy.

In *Hamletmachine*, as in many adaptations of *Hamlet*, allusions to the tragedy reveal something important about our understanding of the Shakespearean prince as well as our perceptions of gender, power and authority. In the case of dewritings, however, where intertextual references function as traces, we are more likely to discover the absent tragic hero, the "other" of popular culture action heroes. We are also being openly confronted with paradoxes of gender relations and power transactions.

In *Kitsch Hamlet*, for instance, the eponymous hero is absent from the stage (we are told that he is sitting silent in another room), while the Shakespearean scenario is played against the social and cultural background of Mediterranean society. La Ruina suggests striking parallels between the contemporary Italian South and Elizabethan England, portraying a patriarchal society, which is highly oppressive to Ophelia and Hamlet. Alluding to Shakespeare's tragedy, La Ruina explores the themes of violence, madness, gender, and family.

Kitsch Hamlet is a story of a family that confirms all the stereotypes of a Mediterranean household. The plot centers around four young men; they all live with their mother, who despite being in a wheelchair takes care of them and supports them financially. Three of the brothers are continually on stage, the fourth one, Hamlet, remains silent in an adjacent room and never makes an onstage appearance. We learn that Hamlet as the most promising of the brothers went to study in England, but after his return he has locked himself up in a room, refusing to communicate with anyone. His fiancée, Ophelia, desperately tries to reach him, haunting his house with a coffin. The events are presented in a burlesque convention, with the comic elements exposing atrocious prejudices and violent actions against women.

La Ruina carefully selects only those protagonists and themes from Shakespeare's plot that allow him to focus on the social problems that are the most conspicuous in the Italian South. The playwright constructs the relationships between the characters on the basis of typical domestic and economic structures present in the Mediterranean, where mothers occupy the central position in the family, sons tend to live at home long after they have come of age, and the local economy exhibits signs of stagnation if not decay. Moreover, the protagonists constantly refer to the reality show *Big Brother*, testifying to the centrality of television as a source of information and entertainment in Italian society.

There are also significant similarities between the scenario of *Big Brother* and the action of *Kitsch Hamlet*, in terms of the setting and the behavior of the characters. In La Ruina's drama, the action takes place in the living room, with three brothers sitting on a sofa, playing with their mobile phones, quarrelling about trivial issues, sharing obscene jokes, repeating pop slogans, and discussing television programs. Nevertheless, the show and the play differ with reference to the articulation of value judgments and the expectations that they have towards their audiences. Contrary to *Big Brother*, where the participants are constantly judged and evaluated by the anonymous narrator and the viewers, in *Kitsch Hamlet* there is no direct commentary. The three young men not only dominate the stage, but also the dialogue; they are the principal source of information about the events in the play. It soon becomes apparent that having grown up in front of the television set the brothers are incapable of comprehending their own actions. It becomes the most striking when at a local party they proudly present a video recording of their rape of Ophelia.

In *Kitsch Hamlet*, La Ruina dewrites the image of the tragic hero, the tragic heroine, and the concept of the tragedy itself. He questions their significance in a television-dominated society, in which the spectators are discouraged from thinking critically. The playwright reveals the appalling consequences of the expansion of the television on social and cultural practices. As Hamlet chooses to disappear from the stage, the dramatic action comes closer to the script of *Big Brother*, while the play becomes dominated by the notions of burlesque, irony, and kitsch.

The influence of television and mass media on the contemporary understanding of Shakespeare's tragedy is also a dominant theme in Igor Bauersima's *Factory* (2002). In this play, *Hamlet* functions purely as a trace in the memory of the readers. The action develops within a reality show, which is based not only on the formula of *Big Brother*, but also on Warhol's Factory. The play reflects on contemporary pop culture and media entertainment, which blur the boundaries between art and exhibitionism, truth and lie, originality and imitation, fiction and reality, tragedy and a television show. Bauersima invites the readers to identify analogies between *Factory* and *Hamlet* in a play that reveals the traps of celebrity culture and exposes the confusion between reality and the show in contemporary media.

The action of the play develops in a Factory, a video-monitored building, where nine participants of a television show compete for the attention of the viewers. The name of the place, which is also the name of the show and the title of the drama, alludes to Warhol's Factory, the artist's New York studio at 231 East 47th Street. It was there between 1963 and 1968 that Warhol produced such diverse forms of art as screen prints, paintings, or films in collaboration with a group of artists, musicians, models and porn stars; his later studios at Union Square and then Broadway have also been known as Factory.

The principles of Warhol's art find their application not only in the formula of the Factory show, but also in Bauersima's approach to *Hamlet*. His method of dewriting Shakespeare's tragedy, the status which he assigns to the source play, and the relationship which he creates between the Elizabethan tragedy and the contemporary readers bears significant affinities to Warhol's perception of art as a mechanical production of serial images. More specifically, in his dramatic treatment of *Hamlet*, Bauersima adapts the technique of silkscreen printing, which to the general public has become synonymous not only with Warhol's work, but also with the idea of Pop Art itself.

Adapting silkscreen printing to drama, Bauersima systematically transposes the Shakespearean tragedy onto the development of events in the show. Unlike the playwrights discussed earlier, he does not construct a supplementary version of the source plot, nor does he open his work to an array of meanings and allusions in the form of *différance*. Instead, Bauersima rewrites *Hamlet* in a manner that resembles Warhol's transformation of public images of pop culture icons such as Marilyn Monroe, Elvis Presley, Jacqueline Kennedy Onassis, or Elizabeth Taylor into silkscreen prints.

Bauersima employs *Hamlet* in the way in which Warhol used official photographs of famous people, selecting only the most typical and popular elements of the tragedy that might be immediately recognized by the readers. The source drama becomes subtly altered in the process of changing the context, the names of the protagonists, and the dialogues. The resulting version of *Hamlet* might be then directly reproduced as an original work with its own title, similarly to prints authored by Warhol. The consequences of Bauersima's process of rewriting *Hamlet* resemble also the effects achieved by Warhol in the process of silkscreen printing. Since the playwright repeats the Shakespearean plot without any structural modifications, it allows him to stimulate a particular response from the readers. The appeal of the play depends on their recognition of an already known, already read, or already seen scenario of Shakespeare's tragedy, which is presented in a slightly altered form.

In *Factory*, Bauersima subjects *Hamlet* to a radical act of dewriting. He reduces the Shakespearean tragedy to a series of violent events, turning the eponymous hero into an insipid figure that acts within a predetermined and predefined scenario. Bauersima's experiment may satisfy the curiosity of those readers of *Hamlet*, who have imagined the tragedy developing in a new surprising context, with slightly different events and with contemporary counterparts of the Shakespearean characters pronouncing lines in modern language. As the participants of the television show take roles of the Shakespearean characters, and the program itself follows the plot of *Hamlet*, one of the greatest European tragedies, the process of democratization and commercialization of the Shakespearean drama becomes complete. The employment of Shakespeare's plot as a scenario of a television show corresponds to a general tendency in contemporary culture, which thrives upon recycling the classics.

The casting of ordinary individuals as contestants in the show makes it clear that anybody could have been selected to become a resident of the Factory. The show producers go even further, suggesting with the decor of the house as an art studio that in television everybody can become an artist. Bauersima adds still another dimension to this egalitarian myth, demonstrating that in contemporary drama everybody can become a counterpart of Hamlet or Ophelia. Moreover, while the show participants take the roles of the Shakespearean characters, the television scenario replaces the tragic convention. Throughout the play, however, Bauersima makes no direct references to *Hamlet*, with the dialogues being contemporary and colloquial. Shakespeare's drama functions in *Factory* more subtly than in *After Hamlet* or *Kitsch Hamlet*, since it might be identified only in the memory of the readers.

The example of *Factory* suggests that deconstructive adaptations depend extensively on the involvement of the readers. The playwrights encourage them not only to trace elements of *Hamlet*, but also to identify paradox and irony in the adaptations. Many deconstructive versions of the tragedy depend on parody of lofty language and grand action, as well as on elements of metatheatre. These features make them similar to drolls and burlesques of Shakespeare's plays. There is, however, a significant difference between the comic and deconstructive traditions. Drolls and burlesques overturned and overplayed tragic components of *Hamlet* primarily to provide entertainment. Dewriting, on the other hand, emphasizes fissures and inconsistencies within *Hamlet* to reveal paradoxical, contradictory aspects of signification; it results in the phenomenon that Linda Hutcheon defined with reference to postmodern fiction as "seriously ironic parody."[37]

Similarly, dewritings distinguish themselves from the mainstream tradition of Shakespeare adaptations that originated in Restoration. When playwrights in the late seventeenth century rewrote Shakespeare's works, they were most likely to gloss over coarse elements in the language and simplify the plot. The title of Sandra Clark's anthology of adaptations from the Restoration period, *Shakespeare Made Fit*, perfectly recapitulates these practices.[38] Even in the nineteenth century it was still common to stage Shakespeare's tragedies with polished diction and a happy ending. What distinguishes deconstructive rewritings from these earlier adaptations is that contemporary playwrights suggest new interpretations not as much to clarify or censor the source play, as to expose its paradoxes and inconsistencies.

Finally, dewriting constitutes a type of adaptation that is distinctive from other postmodern forms of writing. While Elinor Fuchs and Lavender offer an insightful approach to adaptations in postmodern theatre, they examine performances rather than scripts,[39] whereas Hutcheon, Patricia Waugh and Brian McHale formulate a theory of postmodern literature with reference to fiction, offering critical terminology that only partly resonates with strategies exhibited by contemporary playwrights.[40] Dewriting differs from other forms of postmodern adaptation principally because it employs techniques that are unique to drama as a medium, which is suspended between theatre and literature, or, as William B. Worthen puts it, between poetry and performance.[41]

Implications of Dewriting

The notion of dewriting confirms Jan Kott's remark that "*Hamlet* is like a sponge" which "immediately absorbs all the problems of our time,"[42] with deconstruction being another problem incorporated into the process of interpreting the play. If so, what are the implications of absorbing this particular paradigm for the "uses" of Shakespeare's tragedy? Since dewriting is openly subversive, a disconcerting question might arise as to what happens to *Hamlet* in contemporary drama. If the tragedy continues to be disrupted, and the hero tends to disappear, does it mean that they have lost their importance for contemporary playwrights and their readers? If the coherence and universality of *Hamlet* are systematically challenged in the practices of dewriting, can we conclude that Shakespeare's contribution to postwar drama is fragmentary or partial? Moreover, if supplement, *différance*, and trace all depend on suspending and deferring the presence of an object and its ultimate meaning, does it suggest that in contemporary adaptations *Hamlet* can only be retrieved from substitutes, such as supplementary representations, differences, or traces?

Contrary to these concerns, deconstructive instruments indicate that it is the pervasiveness of the Shakespearean tragedy in Western culture which makes the process of dewriting possible. Supplement, *différance*, and trace in a deconstructive adaptation depend as much on substitution as on duplication or even multiplication of meanings, as they stimulate the readers to form chains of signs. Encouraged to supplement, differ, and defer, or trace references to *Hamlet* in modern texts, the readers are expected to have some level of familiarity with the Shakespearean tragedy. The phenomenon of dewriting is, thus, directly dependent on the importance of *Hamlet* for contemporary culture. The absence of Hamlet from the plays of Żurek, La Ruina or Bauersima does not mean that these playwrights seek to erase the Shakespearean hero. On the contrary, the hero's disappearance from the stage is supplemented by his presence in the memory of the readers. The protagonist himself becomes a trace, and he continues to influence the interpretation of the tragedy.

The importance of *Hamlet* for contemporary drama is also reflected in the thematic and formal diversity of the plays that exemplify dewriting. Stoppard refers to *Hamlet*, in order to reflect on fundamental ontological and epistemological issues, such as identity, knowledge or memory. In *Rosencrantz and Guildenstern are Dead*, the Shakespearean tragedy functions as a supreme scenario, an equivalent of fate that predetermines the behavior of the protagonists and leads them to death. Żurek, Głowacki, and Müller turn to *Hamlet*, because it allows them to create alternative versions of politics and history that correspond to the experiences of twentieth century readers. The dramatists more or less openly refer to the postwar conflicts in Europe: the division into the East and West, and the atmosphere of suspicion and espionage during the Cold War. Żurek explores the dilemmas of governance, subverting the Romantic tradition of *Hamlet*'s appropriations; Głowacki portrays power struggles in a parody version of a political thriller, whereas Müller perceives history as an indifferent machine of death and destruction. Although these playwrights deconstruct or even destroy the ideas attributed to the Shakespearean interpretations of history, power or revenge, they simultaneously express their deep fascination with the Elizabethan playwright.

La Ruina turns to *Hamlet*, when he bitterly portrays contemporary Mediterranean society. The playwright shows the disintegration of a traditional family model and conventional gender roles, as well as exposing the hypocrisy of a small town community. Feminist issues become even more prominent in the adaptations by Quiles, Betts, and Clarke, who subvert the tradition of representing Ophelia and Gertrude as secondary characters. Finally, Bauersima situates the Shakespearean tragedy in the context of television entertainment and consumerist society. Inspired by Warhol's philosophy of art and his provocative artistic projects, the playwright reflects on the crisis of signification in the popular culture.

As *Hamlet* is evoked in a diversity of contexts, it becomes clear that some of the ideas or modes of behavior that are associated with Shakespeare's drama might appear as old-fashioned and outdated to contemporary playwrights and readers. The early modern constructions of madness, femininity, or poetic justice have given way to modern ways of conceptualizing the issues of mental illness, gender, or human fate. Our experience of science, religion and history does differ from that of Shakespeare and his generation. And yet, he remains our contemporary in the sense that his *oeuvre* constitutes the very basis of our culture and his influence on postwar drama cannot be denied, dislocated or erased.

Moreover, such plays as *Hamletmachine* or *Factory* show that the Shakespearean tragedy participates in ground-breaking experiments and transformations within contemporary drama. Müller's work has revolutionized postwar playwriting practices as a bold attempt at revising post-Enlightenment strategies of writing and reading drama. Bauersima's play, on the other hand has adapted Warhol's technique of silkscreen printing within a dramatic text.

New approaches to playwriting are also inextricably related to innovations in performance practice. This relationship is conspicuous not only in postmodern stagings of dramatic adaptations of *Hamlet* (Robert Wilson's production of *Hamletmachine* from 1986 is a notable case), but also in performances that result in new stage scripts. Shakespeare's tragedy has inspired some of the most cutting-edge theatre experiments in the recent decades, such as Socìetas Raffaello Sanzio's *Hamlet. The Vehement Exteriority of the Death of a Lazybones* (1992), Wilson's *Hamlet, a monologue* (1995), The Wooster Group's *Hamlet* (2006) or dreamthinkspeak's *The Rest is Silence* (2012). The exploration of innovative stage devices in these performances has led to radical rewritings of *Hamlet*.

Most of the plays cited in this essay are fairly recent, so it is worthwhile to follow subsequent rewritings, in order to establish whether deconstructive tendencies in adapting *Hamlet* persist in the twenty-first-century drama, and how they affect our understanding of Shakespeare's *oeuvre*. Moreover, since the theory of dewriting does not encompass all contemporary offshoots of this play, it will be valuable to distinguish alternative strategies of its dramatic appropriation. A further reflection on adaptations of *Hamlet* is essential, since to whatever "uses" we "return" it, this tragedy continues to shape our thinking about drama, history and culture.

NOTES

1. William Shakespeare, *Hamlet*, ed. Ann Thompson and Neil Taylor (London: Thomson Learning, 2006).
2. Ibid., 423.
3. Vincent Leitch quoted in Brian Vickers, *Appropriating Shakespeare: Contemporary Critical Quarrels* (New Haven and London: Yale University Press, 1993), 182.
4. James Calderwood, *To Be and Not to Be: Negation and Metadrama in Hamlet* (New York: Columbia University Press, 1983), XV.
5. Vickers, 180; Hugh Grady, *The Modernist Shakespeare: Critical Texts in a Material World* (Oxford: Clarendon Press 1991), 190.
6. John Drakakis, ed., *Alternative Shakespeares* (London and New York: Methuen, 1985); Patricia Parker and Geoffrey Hartmann, eds, *Shakespeare and the Question of Theory* (New York: Methuen, 1985); G. Douglas Atkins and David Moore Bergeron, eds, *Shakespeare and Deconstruction* (New York: Peter Lang, 1988).
7. Grady, 190.
8. Calderwood; David J. McDonald, "*Hamlet* and the Mimesis of Absence: A Post-Structuralist Analysis," *Educational Theatre Journal* 30, no. 1 (1978): 36–53; Annabel Patterson, "The Very Age and Body of the Time," in *Shakespeare and Deconstruction*, ed. G. Douglas Atkins and David M. Bergeron (New York: Peter Lang, 1991), 47–68.
9. John M. Kopper, "Troilus at Pluto's Gates: Subjectivity and the Duplicity of Discourse in Shakespeare's *Troilus and Cressida*," in Atkins and Bergeron, 149–71; William O. Scott, "Self-Difference in *Troilus and Cressida*," in Atkins and Bergeron, 129–48; Joseph Hillis Miller, "Ariachne's Broken Woof," *Georgia Review* 31, no. 1 (1977): 44–60.
10. Timothy Murray, "*Othello*, An Index and Obscure Prologue to the History of Foul Generic Thoughts," in Atkins and Bergeron, 213–43.
11. Howard Felperin, "The Dark Lady Identified or What Deconstruction Can Do for Shakespeare's *Sonnets*," in Atkins and Bergeron, 69–93; Ralph Flores, "Metatheater as Metaphorics: Playing Figures in Shakespeare's *Sonnets*," in Atkins and Bergeron, 95–127.
12. Peter Buse, "*Hamlet* Games—Stoppard with Lyotard," in Buse, *Drama + Theory: Critical Approaches to Modern British Drama* (Manchester: Manchester University Press, 2002), 50–68; Joanna Kokot, "'"All the world's a stage"'; Theatre-within-Theatre Convention in Tom Stoppard's *Rosencrantz and Guildenstern Are Dead*," in *Conventions and Texts*, ed. Andrzej Zgorzelski (Gdańsk: Uniwersytet Gdański, 2003), 113–39.
13. Francesco Fiorentino, "Heiner Müller e la *Hamletmaschine*," in *La Traduzione di Amleto nella cultura europea*, ed. Maria Del Sapio Gerbero (Venice: Marsilio, 2002), 77–107; Erika Fischer-Lichte, "Zwischen Differenz und Indifferenz. Funktionalisierung des Montage-Verfahrens bei Heiner Müller," in *Avantgarde und Postmoderne. Prozesse struktureller und funktioneller Veränderungen*, ed. Erika Fischer-Lichte and Klaus

Schwind (Tübingen: Stauffenburg, 1991), 231–45; Klaus Peter Steiger, *Moderne Shakespeare-Bearbeitungen. Ein Rezeptionstypus in der Gegenwartsliteratur* (Stuttgart, Berlin, Köln: Verlag W. Kohlhammer, 1990); Małgorzata Sugiera, *Wariacje szekspirowskie w powojennym dramacie europejskim* (Kraków: Universitas 1997); Steven Taubeneck, "Deconstructing the GDR: Heiner Mueller and Postmodern Cultural Politics," *Pacific Coast Philology* 26, no. 1/2 (1991),: 85–95; Arlene Akiko Teraoka, *The Silence of Entropy or Universal Discourse. The Postmodernist Poetics of Heiner Müller* (New York: Peter Lang Publishing, 1985).

14. Calderwood, 189.
15. Normand Berlin, "Death in *Rosencrantz and Guildenstern*: I," in *Critical Essays on Tom Stoppard*, ed. Anthony Jenkins (Boston: G. K. Hall & Co., 1990), 43.
16. Andy Lavender, *Hamlet in Pieces. Shakespeare Reworked by Peter Brook, Robert Lepage, Robert Wilson* (London: Nick Hern Books, 2001), 22.
17. Jan Kott, *Shakespeare our Contemporary*, trans. Bolesław Taborski (London: Routledge, 1994), 57.
18. T. S. Eliot, "Hamlet," in Eliot, *Selected Essays* (London: Faber and Faber, 1941), 145.
19. Gary Waller, "Decentering the Bard: The Dissemination of the Shakespearean Text," in Atkins and Bergeron, 32.
20. Richard Burt, ed. *Shakespeare After Mass Media* (New York: Palgrave, 2002), 13.
21. A. C. Bradley, *Shakespearean Tragedy* (New York: Fawcett Premier, 1986), 80–81.
22. Margareta de Grazia, *Hamlet without Hamlet* (Cambridge: Cambridge University Press, 1997), 1.
23. Jacques Derrida, *Of Grammatology*, trans. Gayatri Chakravorty Spivak (Baltimore: Johns Hopkins University Press, 1976), 158–63.
24. Michael Fischer, *Does Deconstruction Make Any Difference? Poststructuralism and the Defense of Poetry in Modern Criticism* (Bloomington: Indiana University Press, 1985), 33–4.
25. Christopher Norris, *Deconstruction. Theory and Practice* (London: Routledge, 2002), 32.
26. Derrida, *Of Grammatology*, 144–5.
27. Derrida, "Différance," in Derrida, *Margins of Philosophy*, trans. Alan Bass (Chicago: University of Chicago Press, 1982), 3.
28. Ibid., 6.
29. Derrida, *Of Grammatology*, 167.
30. Derrida, "Différance," 24.
31. Derrida, "Semiology and Grammatology: Interview with Julia Kristeva," in Derrida, *Positions*, trans. Alan Bass (Chicago: University of Chicago Press, 1981), 27.
32. G. Douglas Atkins, "Introduction," in Atkins and Bergeron, 14.
33. Grady, 209.
34. Heiner Müller, *Hamletmachine*, trans. Dennis Redmond, 2001 http://www.efn.org/~dredmond/Hamletmachine.PDF, 1, 5 (accessed 29 June 2010).
35. Derrida, *Of Grammatology*, 24.
36. Jonathan Kalb, *The Theatre of Heiner Müller* (Cambridge: Cambridge University Press, 1998), 109.
37. Linda Hutcheon, *A Poetics of Postmodernism. History, Theory, Fiction* (New York and London: Routledge, 1988), 124.

38. Sandra Clark, *Shakespeare Made Fit: Restoration Adaptations of Shakespeare* (London: J. M. Dent; Rutland, VT: Charles E. Tuttle, 1997).
39. Elinor Fuchs, *The Death of the Character: Perspectives on Theater after Modernism* (Bloomington and Indianapolis: Indiana University Press, 1996); Lavender, *Hamlet in Pieces*.
40. Hutcheon, *A Poetics of Postmodernism*; Patricia Waugh, *Metafiction: The Theory and Practice of Self-Conscious Fiction* (London and New York: Methuen, 1984) and *Practising Postmodernism, Reading Modernism* (London and New York: Edward Arnold, 1992); Brian McHale, *Postmodernist Fiction* (London and New York:Routledge, 1987).
41. Worthen provides an illuminating account of interrelationships between drama and theatre in the context of Shakespearean performance in *Shakespeare and the Authority of Performance* (Cambridge: Cambridge University Press, 1997) and *Drama: Between Poetry and Performance* (Oxford: Wiley-Blackwell, 2010).
42. Kott, 52.

11 Rethinking Shylock

Andrew Gurr

In the winter of 1596–97 Richard Burbage got into desperate financial trouble. It came from his father, who died in February 1597, bequeathing his first major source of income, the Theatre, to his elder son Cuthbert, and the new venue, the Blackfriars, to Richard. Both properties were costly gifts. The Theatre's lease was due to expire in April 1597, and its landlord, Giles Allen, had sworn that he would turn his property to better use than a playhouse. As Cuthbert reported of his half of the inheritance, the Theatre, in 1635, "The father of us ... built this house upon leased ground, by which meanes the Landlord & Hee had a great suite in law & by his death, the like troubles fell on us, his sonnes."[1] Richard suffered the like troubles to Cuthbert's conflict with Allen over the Theatre with his own inheritance, the Blackfriars, since his father in 1596 had borrowed nearly a thousand pounds to buy its freehold and build the playhouse, and in November had lost any means of repaying his creditors when the Privy Council banned performing there. That was when Shakespeare started writing his play about Shylock the moneylender.

Shylock is distinctive in the Shakespeare canon in quite a number of ways. In *Shakespeare and the Geography of Difference*, John Gillies points out how many times Shakespeare made use of exotic characters who are alien to the society of the plays they appear in.[2] All of them are at first tolerated, but later generate disaster. Such notable aliens as Tamora and Aaron, Othello, and Cleopatra can be allied with Shylock as figures whose acts prove to be what Gillies calls "innately transgressive." Shakespeare took a lot of trouble to identify Shylock as not just a resident of Venice but an alien there, one whose "tribe" made him the archetypal outsider, in Venice as much as in Belmont's Christian society. His alien role in *The Merchant of Venice* has attracted a massive cloud of commentary, and yet nothing has been said about the likelihood of his role being applied to the immediately dire and local circumstances of the Shakespeare company just when it was written.

Shylock as moneylender was a distinctly inconspicuous but far from insignificant link between the play's story and the players it was written for in the winter of 1596–97. There is ample evidence that this activity became a potent source of hostility for the performers of the play in its early showings on the Theatre's stage, and to its leading player in particular.[3] By the end of 1596, when the play was being written,[4] the company's financier, James Burbage, was in precisely the situation that Antonio finds himself in when he went to Shylock for his loan and then became bound to repay it without the means to do so. By February of the next year, after Burbage died and his younger son inherited the new playhouse, it was Richard who the hostile creditors besieged. Shylock has attracted an enormous amount of attention for his alien character. The highlighting of the non-Venetian with which Shakespeare so wonderfully camouflaged his villain has prevented us from seeing the immediate and entirely current London-based reason he had for incorporating such a potent story in the heart of a romantic comedy set in that remote and mythical great city and seaport, so unlike familiar London.

Close behind this feature of Shakespeare's play stands the Lord Chamberlain, Henry Carey. On 8 October 1594, as the new company's patron, he sent a strange letter to the Lord Mayor. Written when the first winter of the year that he set up the Shakespeare company was approaching, on the face of it his letter simply asked the Lord Mayor to let his new company perform through the coming season of cold weather at an indoor venue. Carey cited the old practices, asking:

> where my nowe companie of Players have byn accustomed for the better use of their qualities, & for the service of her Majestie if need soe require to plaie this winter time within the Citye at the Crosse kayes in Gracious street. These are to require & praye your Lordship the time beinge such as thankes be to god there is nowe no danger of the sicknes) to permit & suffer them soe to doe.

In an article I wrote some years ago about this letter,[5] I suggested that the Lord Mayor who came into office at the end of that month, Michaelmas 1594, Sir John Spencer, who was an alderman particularly hostile to playing, would have refused Carey's request. That refusal, I argued, was why early in 1596 Burbage bought a property in the "liberty" of the Blackfriars, and converted it into a new roofed playhouse. We know that Carey helped Burbage to acquire the Blackfriars property. He wrote about it to Sir George More, owner of part of the site that included a section Carey himself had once owned. On 9 February 1596, he wrote saying, knowingly, "you have all redie parted with part of your howse to somme that meanes to make a playe howse in yt." Such a comment implies Carey's approval of the project. His previous letter of 1594 to the Lord Mayor shows that he wanted to help his new company establish its playing venues, one for summer and one for winter. In view of the Mayor's rejection, James Burbage must have assumed that the Blackfriars, located in a precinct independent of his authority, would make an admirable replacement inside the city for the Cross Keys inn.

Carey's son, however, whose own dwelling-place was a set of chambers literally underneath the new playhouse, took a different view. He became the second signatory on the petition of the residents which that November asked the Privy Council to stop the project. The first was Lady Russell, sister-in-law to Lord Cecil who chaired the Council. These Blackfriars residents had plenty of clout, and the Council immediately approved what they asked for. Carey himself had died on 22 July of that year. Soon after his death Thomas Nashe reported that the company, "however in their old Lords tyme they thought there state setled, it is now so uncertayne they cannot build upon it."[6] All too soon that proved to be an appallingly appropriate pun.

Burbage bought the Upper Frater of the Blackfriars site on 4 February 1596 for £600, to which he added the cost of constructing a completely new playhouse inside it. The total price of his commitment to build the playhouse must have been well over £1,000, far more money than he could possibly have possessed within his personal resources. Of his debts entailed by the later Blackfriars, Cuthbert's 1635 declaration went on to say that "our father purchased it at extreame rates & made it into a play house with great charge & trouble." Such charge and trouble at "extreame rates" meant going to London's moneylenders, securing massive loans taken up at extortionate rates of interest. William Ingram has noted how the revised terms of the interest chargeable by moneylenders laid out in the Usury Act of 1571 helped to precipitate the flood of money that went into theatre-building from 1575 onwards.[7] Moneylending at high rates of interest was routine by the 1590s, and London's venture capitalists saw building playhouses as a thoroughly profitable activity. In November 1594, once the Privy Council's new regulations about playing meant that only suburban playhouses could be used for plays and the mayoralty ignored Carey's letter asking for the Cross Keys, two venture capitalists, Francis Langley and Oliver Woodliffe, neither of them previously involved with playing, each started building a playhouse in London's suburbs. On the south bank of the Thames Langley built the Swan, and in the east Woodliffe converted the Boar's Head in Stepney from an inn to a playhouse. Clearly they both expected to make good profits from their ventures. The recurrent phrase "take interest," used in *The Merchant*'s first exchange between Shylock and Antonio (1.3.43, 67, 68, 86), was applicable to their involvement in two ways.

Shakespeare started writing his play at the end of 1596, and the company first staged it early in 1597. That was precisely when James Burbage—and after he died in February his son Richard—would have come under direct attack from the loan sharks who had financed his new theatre. They of course found, once it was completely blocked from use, that they were equally blocked from taking any profit out of their investments. We can only imagine how much pressure these investors immediately applied to the old man to get their money back. Richard already knew such pressure at first hand. He is recorded back in 1591, in a lawsuit laid against him by the widow of Burbage's brother-in-law and financier John Brayne, which demanded payment of arrears on Brayne's loans to old Burbage. The testimony claimed that he defended his father's holdings against his creditors by wielding a fierce broomstick and twisting one complainant's nose in defence of his father's profits.

The events surrounding the Blackfriars crisis—from the residents' petition, sent to the Privy Council in November 1596, to the death of James Burbage in mid-February 1597—make the play's composition and first staging at such a time almost certain, and certainly apposite to its leading player's misfortunes. What is perhaps most intriguing is whether it was being prepared while James Burbage was still alive but coming near to his death, or whether Richard's subsequent inheritance prompted its composition. At either time, Portia's fortunate rescue of both Antonio and Bassanio was an act largely of wish-fulfillment, one that both the dying James and his younger son would have welcomed through that dire period.

The longer-term consequences of the Blackfriars disaster on the Burbages, with its largely fortuitous replication of Portia's rescue, should hardly surprise us. But its reality was distinctly less than an act of fortune, except in the most material sense. One substantial consequence of James's argosy-like and ineffective venture of 1596 revealed its impact on his sons two years later, at the end of 1598. As part of their hopeful because underfunded project to build a new playhouse for the company on Bankside out of the stolen remains of the old Theatre, Cuthbert and Richard needed a major injection of cash to help them redeploy the retrieved timbers to make the Globe. It must have been as a direct result of their father's unhappy experience over his loans for the Blackfriars that they turned for their funding not to London's loan sharks but to their fellow players. As company sharers, the interests of Heminges,

Shakespeare, Phillips, Pope, and Kempe were already sunk deep in its activities, so they were the best source of new cash free from loan-shark pressure to supply the funds for the new playhouse. All of them would profit equally from the company's collective success. *The Merchant of Venice* was still there in the company repertory as a reminder of the troubles James and Richard had suffered from London's moneylenders. Within less than a year the play was in print as a quarto. In February 1599 it must have been in clear and potent recall of the sunken Burbage argosy of two years before that Shakespeare and four other sharers signed up to each of them giving the Burbage sons £100 to build the company's new home. Such a request can hardly have startled them, since they had all been sharing in the performances of the play through most of the previous two years.

As sharers in the new building and in the company whose future they were gambling on, this act did not turn the players into moneylenders themselves. In any case, as company sharers they were clearly confident that they would soon get their money back. That, of course, they did, and more. The unique new deal that got the Globe built soon proved so successful, with a majority of the company sharers owning the playhouse they used, that when in 1608 Richard Burbage did finally retrieve his expensive inheritance, the Blackfriars, for the company's own use, he allocated its shares equally among the Globe's sharing housekeepers, mostly to the same owners. That sharing became the ultimate guarantee of the Shakespeare company's unique success as a commercial theatre enterprise. Other companies tried to imitate their financial structure, but rarely with any success.

Such a reading of the immediate background to the Shylock play raises many questions. Given the stressful conditions of moneylending in London, and the Burbages' experience of the perils that came from usurous borrowing, we have first to ask why Shakespeare should have taken such care to convert his model from a local London moneylender to someone as thoroughly exotic as the Jewish Shylock. The play is packed with information emphasizing the local colour of mythical Venice, the great Mediterranean trading and shipping centre that so easily outshone London with its Rialto and its synagogue. The wholly alien character of Shylock's culture, his ally Tubal, his daughter Jessica, his hatred of the Christian Antonio, his emphasis on having the prosperity of the heirs of Jacob, all his moneys and usances as Antonio describes them, make such elaborate colorification into a comprehensive disguise. It seems that Shakespeare would not do what Jonson might have opted to try, making his Shylock into a version of what many of London's citizenry such as Langley and Woodliffe were practising routinely at London's Rialto, the Royal Exchange.

We do, of course, know something about the Shakespeare family's own familiarity with usury. As Charles Edelman notes, both John Shakespeare and his eldest son were quite used to charging exorbitant rates of interest in Stratford when they lent their fellow-citizens money. We also know that one of Shakespeare's Stratford friends and business contacts was the venture capitalist John Combe. Shakespeare's own financial dealings were extensive, and even as early as 1596 we can assume he knew at first hand some of the processes of venture capitalism. It is a major pity that we lack much detailed information about his London contacts and possible dealings, so cannot know how familiar he was with some of the venture capitalists of that time. The few items of hard information we do have, such as the court order that William Wayte took out in 1596 to protect himself from Langley, Shakespeare, and two women, are tantalizing, but what it imports is quite obscure. Although the date of Wayte's order is intriguing, and seems significantly close in time to the Blackfriars affair, we have no idea why he should have named Shakespeare along with the loan shark Langley as the people against whom he took out his surety of the peace. We do know that Wayte's stepfather, William Gardiner, was a justice for the South Bank area including the Swan's Paris Garden, which was enough to make Leslie Hotson think Shakespeare made him the model for Justice Shallow in 1597. Few scholars now take that seriously, but the fact that Wayte took out his surety indicates that Shakespeare had got himself involved in a fracas in a part of the suburbs of London that three years later was to accept the Globe, but where he had no obvious interest in 1596.[8] Langley had recently completed the Swan and filled it with a new company of Pembroke's Men. Shakespeare seems to have been involved with a former company under the same patron around 1593, but we know no more than that. As with Hotson, this almost empty terrain is ripe for planting with wild conjecture.

If we refuse to speculate over why Shakespeare chose to set his play in Venice, the location for the old tale he was dramatizing, and not in London, we still have to face the perennial question of the story's more likely applications. Using a tale in which moneylending was only one relatively minor element in what was essentially a love-romance did offer the company a wish-fulfilling diversion from its current crisis. But even in such a routine view Shylock still stands out as an exceptional creation. At its crudest, we might fit melancholy Antonio to the dying James Burbage, father-figure to his son's Bassanio, while the outsider Shylock deliberately misrepresents the thwarted moneylenders now pestering old Burbage for repayment of their bonds. Such applications must have been in the author's mind, certainly in the minds of at least some of the players, and just conceivably in the minds of a few audience members familiar with the company's financial struggles at the end of 1596. The success of the residents' petition against the Blackfriars playhouse was a talking-point for many Londoners besides Thomas Nashe and his contacts.

Given Richard Burbage's close personal commitment to his father's financial troubles, the question which part he might have taken in the play, or been expected by the author to take in the first performances, is another intriguing question that, regretfully, can promote only speculative answers. Nothing survives to say who took which parts originally. Richard is usually assumed to have played Bassanio, the romantic hero. Who played the first Shylock we have no idea. Counting the number of lines spoken by the main characters, Tom King found that Shylock has 335 against Bassanio's 329 (Portia's is the largest part, with 557).[9] It is almost too easy a presumption that Richard would have taken Bassanio's role rather than playing Shylock. Playing Bassanio would have been a dangerous stimulus to make people apply the story to local circumstances. If the pressure from the debt collectors had any direct impact at the end of 1596, Richard might have played Antonio, who has only 188 lines but is generally thought to warrant the title role as Venice's merchant. On the other hand, Richard's opposite Edward Alleyn did play the bottle-nosed Barabbas in *The Jew of Malta* for the other duopoly company, and it is possible that Burbage might have found taking the part of Shylock in his own play an ironically apt inversion of his father's recent experiences. On this issue we are left with guesswork at best.

A possibly more rewarding question is what else in the theatrical culture of the time might signal the aftereffect of the players staging this radical parable about their collective experience as a shipwrecked company. Much has been made in the past of Marlowe's precedent for Shylock in *The Jew of Malta*'s Barabbas, and the public uproar in July 1594 over the trial and execution of the Portuguese Jewish doctor Ruy or Roderigo Lopez, which may have prompted the Admiral's Men to revive Marlowe's play. We can see Shakespeare openly diverging from Marlowe in his portrait of Shylock, and especially, despite the two similar balcony scenes with their caskets of gold and jewels, his use of Jessica as one of the sets of lovers in the finale, in contrast to Barabbas who poisons his own Abigail. For all its punishment of Shylock, Shakespeare's play was an overt comedy, not at all what T. S. Eliot called the "terrible farce" of Marlowe's ostensible tragedy.

One oblique hint survives to suggest an effect the portrayal of Shylock by the Chamberlain's might have had on the Admiral's company and its writers, and whether they showed any sign of knowing its immediate and local application to the Burbage troubles. This is linked to the choice of the

Venetian setting for Shylock, and more broadly with the distinctly gradual acceptance by both companies that London itself was a respectable setting for their comedies. Shakespeare's avoidance of the possibility of any direct application of Shylock to James Burbage's financial troubles is easily read as a tribute to his tact and general discretion over the popular but mostly crude business of making satirical applications. He may have been following company policy, which seems to have been discreet enough to avoid overt use of local conditions and settings except where it was unavoidable, as in the English history plays with their scenes at Court and in Eastcheap. That was not the common response, though. Early in 1598 Jonson did choose to locate *Every Man in his Humour*, written for the Chamberlain's, in a version of Italy's Florence, however obviously it was London-set, and which he changed openly to London in the 1616 Folio version. Some time before that the Chamberlain's Men had performed what was probably their first and almost only surviving play largely set in London, the tragedy *A Warning for Fair Women*, published in 1599. It had to use the London setting, since it dramatized a known murder story about Londoners, one previously told at length by Holinshed, like *Arden of Feversham*. As such, the company had no choice but to maintain the original London location, as did Arden with its town in Kent. Otherwise, both of the duopoly companies, at least before 1598, seem to have avoided setting any of their plays explicitly in London. The fact that Shakespeare wrote the Eastcheap scenes of the two Henry IV plays through 1596–97 at roughly the same time as he wrote *The Merchant*, and that subsequently he never set any comedy closer to London than Windsor, could be read in two ways—either as a show of his innate discretion, or as a more positive tactic of avoidance. That would mean he emphasized Shylock's alien status precisely in order to avert direct applicability to the Blackfriars catastrophe. The fact that no scholar has seen Shylock as a possible allusion to James Burbage's crisis at the end of 1596 might be seen as a tribute to such discretion.

The other dominant company of the time was less cautious. William Haughton was the first known writer who does seem to have openly used a London setting for a comedy, and he did so in a strikingly close rewrite of Shakespeare's play. He was an inventive playwright, starting the fashion for comedies in which the Devil visited London in 1600, a fashion imitated by several others, including Jonson with *The Devil is an Ass* in 1616. Late in 1597, not long after *Merchant*, Haughton wrote *Englishmen for my Money*, set explicitly and firmly in the city, and staged in February 1598. Full of overt references to the Exchange, Crotched Friars, Leadenhall, and other sites in the city of London, it borrows many features from *The Merchant*. Its central figure is a Portuguese financier Pisaro, an alien moneylender, rich from trading usurously in the city. The avaricious but ultimately defeated father of not one but three English daughters, he boasts in the play's opening speech that he owns thirty-two ships all coming successfully to London from Spain, and declares that he has become rich "by the sweet lovde trade of Usurie, / Letting for Interest, and on Morgages."[10] Though not specified as a Jew, on stage he wore the same bottle nose that Alleyn had worn when he played Barabbas in Marlowe's play and the usurer Leon in the parodic *Blind Beggar of Alexandria*.[11] Shylock-like, he tells the audience that three English lovers of his daughters

> Have pawnde to mee their Livings and their Lands:
> Each severall hoping, though their hopes are vaine,
> By mariage of my Daughters, to possesse
> Their Patrimonies and their Landes againe.
>
> (TLN 23–7)

That is the basis for Haughton's plot. Pisaro adds that they are deceiving themselves, and "though I guild my Temples with a smile, / It is but Judas-like, to worke their endes."

Haughton found Shylock's alien character a good starting-point for his own comedy, openly set in London. His play reflects his company's own *Jew of Malta* by making Pisaro a Portuguese as Lopez was, although Haughton seems to have avoided any extra anti-Semitism by making his appeal to his audiences entirely through exploitation of xenophobia. Besides Pisaro himself, outwitted by the three young English gentry who are his daughters' lovers, he made Pisaro's own favoured candidates for their hands three other foreign merchants, a Dutchman, an Italian, and a Frenchman. Like Pisaro himself, all three are fooled by the ingenuity of the three English lovers and the trio of daughters, who prefer their English suitors to the aliens. One of them charges Pisaro with precisely what the 1571 Usury Act forbade: "You take Tenn in the hundred more then Law," he says (TLN 1948). Later Pisaro himself admits "I take two and twenty in the hundred, / When the Law gives but ten" (TLN 2395–6). Such practices define him as the play's comic villain, much as was Shylock in contemporary views. Unlike Shylock, though, while also making him an alien Haughton openly located his work at London's Royal Exchange, and explicitly inflated Shylock's moneys and usances into Royal Exchange-based usury.

Haughton's plot develops the element represented in Merchant by the love between Shylock's Jessica and the Venetian Lorenzo. Like Jessica, Pisaro's daughters betray their father by marrying their English lovers. In the process they succeed in achieving what Pisaro announces in his first speech that he will prevent, returning to their husbands the wealth they had mortgaged to Pisaro before the play begins. At the end, a London citizen, Mr Moore, a pleader to Pisaro at the Exchange and witness to all the turmoil of the play's finale, tells him that fretting about his loss is pointless:

> These Gentlemen have with your Daughters helpe,
> Outstript you in your subtile enterprises:
> And therefore, seeing they are well descended,
> Turn hate to love, and let them have their Loves.
>
> (TLN 2668–71)

Pisaro accepts the inevitable, and all ends happily. Like *Merry Wives*, the core of the romantic plot has young gallants achieving financial gain by marrying the daughters of a rich citizen, a means of getting money that anticipated the practices in the boy company plays of the next decade, mostly staged, ironically for us and the Burbages, at the Blackfriars.

In its English setting Haughton's play, besides trebling the number of the alien's daughters, suffers none of the Shakespeare play's problems with Jessica's disloyalty to her father. Their own Englishness eliminates her sense of cultural distance. It is the four foreigners—Pisaro and the suitors with their comically poor command of English—who suffer as the play's fools. Xenophobia is a familiar knee-jerk reaction for most crowds, whether Elizabethan playgoers or the gatherings who bay at modern World Cup matches. Haughton's farcical treatment strips out the awkward corners from Shakespeare's play. The Admiral's play takes for granted the inherent xenophobia of Venetian attitudes to Shylock as something that could readily be exploited as a feature of contemporary London. Pisaro's pleasure in his gains from usury is only one part of what he loses at the conclusion. In his London setting Haughton found ample evidence for the hatred of such greed that his play expects his audiences to share and to boo at.

Haughton, perhaps knowingly, gives no direct sign of any possible application of Shakespeare's play to the Burbage crisis of 1596–97. He marks its differences quite clearly. Whereas at 1.3.27 Shylock rejects the idea of dining with Bassanio and having to "smell pork," Pisaro's guest, the Frenchman Delion, says he will relish eating Pisaro's beef and his bacon when he dines at his house (TLN 421). In one major scene characterizing Pisaro's business practices at the Exchange there is much talk of shipping being seized off Italy by Spanish galleys. Later in the same scene the Italian suitor asks Pisaro why he is so melancholy, and when he answers that it is because his ships are in peril replies that the galleys were set back by the wind, and Pisaro's ships are safe. His dealings with London citizens at the Exchange show him sharp and selfish with his money. The comic post who brings him information about his argosies arriving safely in Plymouth gets no payment for his good news. Haughton used the most notable elements in *The Merchant* while ignoring its most immediate local application. This avoidance might be seen as unhelpfully negative, but it fits the case quite as well as the idea that Shakespeare chose to set his play in Venice in order to avoid any charge of application to local people. If *Englishmen*'s author knew of the pressure that the Blackfriars catastrophe laid on the Burbages, he was evidently discreet enough to avoid any mention of it in his own play.

Some of Shakespeare's variations on the moneylending theme in *Merchant* need pursuing, if only to meet a few other likely targets for company hostility. Only forty lines into the play Antonio declares "my ventures are not in one bottom trusted." He has three argosies at sea, and he does not expect what Graziano in his blunt epistrophe twice calls the "strumpet wind" (2.6.17 and 20) to block their successful passage. James Burbage had two ventures, the Theatre as well as the Blackfriars, for his own argosies, leaving one of them to each of his sons. By April 1597 both of them were hopelessly lost. The sons' and their company's consequent financial troubles must have become known to many people besides Thomas Nashe. This calls to mind, however obliquely, the sharpness of Shylock's assurance to Antonio that he will "take no doit / Of usance for my monies" (1.3.133–4). Taking no interest other than the pound of flesh is one thing. When the playing company's whole concern was for a place they could use for playing, the Privy Council, which banned its use of the Blackfriars, might have taken no doit of interest from it but they certainly got the equivalent pound of flesh by killing the work of the most interested party. The players participating in *The Merchant* had no magical Portia to wave her legal or financial wand and rescue them from their troubles.

Portia's rescue of Antonio from the knife came from Shakespeare's source, as did the forfeit the Duke lays on Shylock. Antonio then asks that Shylock be required to convert himself into a Christian, and give all his remaining wealth to his daughter. This double punishment seems a curiously oblique way of punishing Shylock as a Jew for his use of usury. Only in this, perhaps, was Shakespeare emphasizing the English law that Haughton later chose to underline as Pisaro's chief fault. The fact that in Shakespeare's play it clears Shylock out of the way in Act 4, so that the lovers at Belmont, above all Lorenzo and his Jessica, are free to indulge themselves, in their lengthy self-indulgence released from all that Bassanio was fraught by in the earlier Acts, is part of the comforting process the final Act so thoroughly provides.

In a larger perspective, Antonio's insistence that Shylock convert himself into a Christian consorts well with Portia's rescue of Antonio and Bassanio from the hateful loan shark. If nothing else, it can be seen as a comfort Shakespeare gave his company, a trick of wish-fulfillment. It does not touch on one of the worst features of the current issue. When Nashe wrote his wry pun about the company not being able to build after Henry Carey's death it was the entire working group, the company, that he recorded as the victim, not James Burbage in person. Nashe must have known that Carey's son George, the company's new patron, did not share his father's position over supporting the idea of the Blackfriars playhouse. As second signatory of the hostile petition, George Carey was active, if not instrumental, in blocking the playhouse from use by what with his father's death had become his own company as its patron. He did, after all, live directly under the new playhouse. Haughton picked out Pisaro the usurous moneylender from *The Merchant* as his victim without making any acknowledgement, or possibly not realizing, that there was a further reason for the company playing at the Theatre to grieve over the loss of the Blackfriars besides the pressure from the moneylenders.

In an extreme view, Shylock might even be seen as not just a London loan shark but an even more oblique target, the company's new patron himself. Shylock was a substitute, a straw man that they could thwack with their double grievances. Beyond his identity as an alien, the man with the vengeful knife might have been imagined not just as a London loan shark but as their own new patron. Shakespeare himself did not view all the signatories of the petition with much personal animosity, since he maintained regular contact with another of them, his fellow-countryman Richard Field. He stayed in touch with him well enough to read copies of a number of Field's later publications, at least up to 1599, and lodged in Silver Street with a Huguenot family, the Mountjoys, who he must have met through Field's wife Jacqueline Vautrollier. But the company as a whole can hardly have ignored the heavy implication of George Carey's signature on the petition. He was not going to help them in the many ways that his father did.

Essentially all that the portrait of Shylock in Shakespeare's play offered the company, and especially Richard Burbage, was an outlet for their anger. Perhaps even more than the pressures applied by the sharks swimming round their leader, Shylock could have given them a self-comforting means of expressing on stage the grievance that they felt over George Carey's hostile action in November 1596. If the latent identity of Shylock as straw man can be applied to the London loan sharks, he might with equally good reason be applied to the company's new patron.

NOTES

1. Quoted from the "Sharers' Papers" in Andrew Gurr, *The Shakespeare Company, 1594–1642* (Cambridge: Cambridge University Press, 2004), 278.
2. John Gillies, *Shakespeare and the Geography of Difference* (Cambridge: Cambridge University Press, 1994), 99ff.
3. Studies such as John Gross, *Shylock: A Legend and Its Legacy* (New York: Simon and Schuster, 1992), and James Shapiro, *Shakespeare and the Jews* (New York: Columbia University Press, 1996), are brilliant at identifying the effects of the invention of Shylock, but ignore its immediate cause.
4. The date of *Merchant* is generally seen as determined chiefly by the reference in line 27 of the first scene to a ship that Salarino calls "my wealthy Andrew," a prize captured from the Spanish at Cadiz and brought to England in June 1596. Composition in late 1596 and staging in 1597 fits the time of the Blackfriars crisis perfectly. We might even use that dreadful fiasco as a determining factor for dating the play. The story from Ser Giovanni's *Il Pecorone* on which the whole play is based must have come into Shakespeare's mind as its apposite basis only after the petition went to the Privy Council in November 1596.
5. Andrew Gurr, "Henry Carey's Peculiar Letter," *Shakespeare Quarterly* 56 (2005) 51–75.
6. *Thomas Nashe, Works*, ed. R. B. McKerrow, revised edn (Oxford: Oxford University Press, 1958), vol. 5, 194. The addressee of Nashe's letter was most likely William Cotton, one of Carey's many servants.
7. William Ingram, "The Economics of Playing," in *A Companion to Shakespeare*, ed. David Scott Kastan (Oxford: Blackwell, 1999), 315–16. The law of 1571, which coincided with the completion of Gresham's Royal Exchange, redefined the terms for lending at interest, condemning usury but accepting interest charges so long as they ran at a level set by the state, initially 10 per cent; this led to a surge of money for new building becoming available from then on. The issue was essentially one of interpreting the Bible's injunction over usury. Thomas Wilson's *Discourse of Usury*, a dialogue published in 1572 but written before the revisions announced in the 1571 Act were passed, makes his Merchant declare as his last words: "It had been my part, having had such wealth, to have vysited the prisons, where men lie long for smal debt, and have beene oppressed wyth usurye to their utter undoing: to have ayded the pooore householders, the fatherlesse chyldren and the widowes. But hereafter I will vysite Christ more often in hys afflicted members, and lend freely by gods grace to suche and so many as I shalbe able and know to be honest, godly men, and relieve them chieflye, and make also restytucyon unto them whom I have most oppressed, and get my goods hereafter by lawfull means" (p. 380). (Wilson's *Discourse* was edited by R.

H. Tawney in 1925; his Introduction provides an extensive account of many aspects of moneylending at the time, in face of the much-exercised biblical declaration that usury is a damnable sin.) The law about chargeable interest was an ass that bore heavy burdens. Charles Edelman has sensible things to say about the Elizabethan definitions of usury, in "Which is the Jew that Shakespeare Knew? Shylock on the Elizabethan Stage," *Shakespeare Survey* 52 (1999), 103–4.

8. Hotson's theories about this are described with some vigour and a lot of conjecture in *Shakespeare Versus Shallow* (Boston: Little, Brown and Company, 1931), 9–83. See Park Honan, *Shakespeare. A Life* (Oxford: Oxford University Press, 1998) 260.
9. Tom King, *Casting Shakespeare's Plays. London Actors and Their Roles, 1590–1642* (Cambridge: Cambridge University Press, 1992), 184–5.
10. Quotations are taken from the Malone Society text of the 1616 edition of the play, entitled "ENGLISHMEN For my Money, OR, A pleasant Comedy, called, A Woman will have her Will." The MS edition was edited by W. W. Greg and published in 1912. This is TLN 19–20.
11. At TLN 1424 the English lover Harvey calls him "signor bottle-nose." By 1598 Alleyn himself had withdrawn from acting, but the player of Pisaro could still have worn his familiar fake nose. See Andrew Gurr, *Shakespeare's Opposites. The Admiral's Company 1594–1625*, Cambridge: Cambridge University Press, 2009, esp. 38, 232–3.

PART III

12 The Field in Review: New Biography Studies, Queer Turns in Theory, and Shakespearean Utility

Rebecca Chapman

Scholarship produced over the past two years in the international field of Shakespeare studies has focused heavily on Shakespeare's constitutive power. From the contested ways in which Shakespearean works entertain, educate, incite, and reflect various historical moments and cultural movements, to the degrees to which those works inflect the foundations upon which we make intellectual and affective sense of ourselves and our world, recent scholarship maintains that Shakespeare's utility matches his longevity. But how much is this utility worth? In the aftermath of harrowing natural disasters around the globe and economic crises that have hit our professions harder than many had imagined, liberal arts education has fallen under scrutiny. With increasing unemployment and decreasing endowments in mind, many have asked what claim the humanities have on dwindling resources.[1] The argument goes something like this: the humanities, by definition, encourages critical, analytical, and speculative thinking skills, by which one might explore what it means to be human, and all that that condition entails. Consequently, educators in the humanities tend to promote personal and civic growth as programmatic endpoints, rather than training students for particular vocations. In lean times, however, practicality and policy command more worth in cultural imaginaries than poetry and pontification. While no doubt many of us would challenge such an easy and unnecessarily Manichean distinction, the present situation poses a valuable opportunity—if not a mandate—in which we might examine what it is we think we are doing when we read and teach Shakespearean works. Recent scholarship in the field provides for us a wide variety of productive models.

It returns us to the time-held biographical tradition in Shakespeare studies, only this time, scholars are less concerned with answering the question of who Shakespeare was, seeking instead to uncover the ways in which our answers to this question reflect new cultural and technological developments and changing systems of value—questions, in other words, that feel particularly timely in the present moment. Performance and media studies continue to fascinate scholars and push archival boundaries. New work in these areas maintains that a nuanced understanding of such present-day *and* early modern English concepts as gender, sexuality, nation, race, and imperialism is needed to address the culturally sensitive issues raised in many Shakespearean works and adaptations. Emergent theoretical and philosophical approaches similarly question archival boundaries, and in the process foreground the educational, social, and political benefits of readdressing our professional activities. Metacriticism reigns, in other words. As we survey trends in the field, then, perhaps the best place to start is with the very signifier "Shakespeare," and our ever-continued desire to sketch its intractable ontological and epistemological contours.

The New Biography Studies

This desire operates as both theme and condition in James Shapiro's *Contested Will: Who Wrote Shakespeare?* The renewed interest in Shakespeare biography studies is as surprising as it is inevitable. That is, we have become so accustomed to the dull hum of the authorship controversy, we are often startled when it turns into an aggravated buzz, though it has shown itself able to do so every now and then. Many conditions can revitalize the genre: new author candidates, source evidence, recognized historical contexts, ways of imagining the role and life of the artist, approaches to autobiography. For Shapiro, those conditions include both change and constancy. Technological development as well as the unchecked insistence within the field on closeting the authorship question from "serious" academic work has created a socio-intellectual space in which those who would promote some of the likely candidates—Christopher Marlowe, the Earl of Oxford, Francis Bacon, for instance—can share their message. "Those who would deny Shakespeare's authorship, long excluded from publishing their work in academic journals or through university presses," he observes, "are now taking advantage of the level playing field provided by the Web, especially such widely consulted and democratic sites as Wikipedia" (8). Ignoring the question of authorship, in other words, has not made it disappear; if anything, curiosity about the real life and identity of the Bard has proliferated along with the number of websites, blogs, and podcasts produced on the topic. The recent political thriller *Anonymous* (2012), from director Roland Emmerich, whose credits include the apocalyptic *2012* (2009) and *Independence Day* (1996), supports Shapiro's claim that the controversy has gone mainstream—the film, for instance, advances Edward De Vere, Earl of Oxford as the true author. "The desire to feel the presence, experience a sense of intimacy with Shakespeare" (55), is not going away, nor are the serious questions of how and what we understand as literary genius and the relationship between art and life that attend it. On the contrary, Shapiro's historical examination of the doubters of Shakespeare, such as Helen Keller, Sigmund Freud, Henry James, and Mark Twain, demonstrates how our desire for epistemological certainty has led to the falsification of evidence and a vast web of conspiracy, since "[i]t was easier for critics who shared that desire to make stuff up rather than admit defeat" (55). His treatment of the topic is as generous as it is rigorous, and his is a book that will no doubt interest a wide range of readers.

Perhaps most fascinating, though, the two aims of Shapiro's book weave together a paradoxically performative point: while we may interrogate the desire to answer those unanswerable questions surrounding who Shakespeare was and whether he wrote the complete works, that desire is a compulsive one. Shapiro's first aim, he makes clear, is to provide insight into the debate and trace its history. "My interest," he writes, "is not in what people think—which has been stated again and again in unambiguous terms—so much as why they think it" (8), which concerns the constructions of concepts such as factuality and credibility. David Bevington's recent *Shakespeare and Biography* makes a similar move. It provides a history of biography, which intersects with rather than intervenes in the authorship debate. He surveys the primary and contradictory methodologies of archival and documentary research as well as the fictionalization and artistic license some biographers have taken, especially when confronting the question of whether or not Shakespeare was happy in his marriage. Along with these methods, Bevington explores the central topics of sex, politics, religion, Calvinism, and predestination that fascinate biographers most, and the danger of employing "the standards of twenty-first-century morality" to understand them, which "may well be at variance with those of the sixteenth and early seventeenth centuries" (14). No doubt, scholars concerned with constructions of cultural value in and surrounding Shakespearean works will find his second chapter useful, which outlines the eighteenth-century conventions by which Shakespeare biography took shape, with relatively little change today. In conclusion, however, Bevington breaks from his even-handed tone, and assures readers of his own take on the authorship question: "a counterargument can be offered to the Oxfordian position ... if one were to seek today for brilliant reporting of goings-on in 10 Downing Street or the White House or the Élysée Palace, would one choose to hear from some strategically placed cabinet member or from investigative reports like Woodward and Bernstein at the time of Washington Watergate?" (160). He suggests that as an outsider Shakespeare of Stratford "was in better position to see life steady and see it whole" (160) than aristocratic Oxford. Shapiro, too, makes a claim for the Stratfordian case, which he explains as the second aim of his book. He makes a strong case, and reintroduces fascinating but forgotten material like Richard Hunt's copy of William Camden's 1590 Latin edition of *Britannia,* which includes marginalia describing the author knows as Shakespeare as a famed actor. Performing the very practice he interrogates, Shapiro's intervention into the authorship debate raises the question of the stakes in the present moment of affirming that Shakespeare of Stratford did indeed author the plays attributed to his name. What precisely are we afraid of losing? Shapiro confesses in his final chapter, "What I find most disheartening about the claim that Shakespeare of Stratford lacked the life experience to have written the plays is that it diminishes the very thing that makes him so exceptional: his imagination" (277).

The anxiety over misrecognizing Shakespeare's singularity similarly motivates Stephen Greenblatt's newest narrative on the Bard's greatness, *Shakespeare's Freedom*, which maintains that Shakespeare linguistically, rhetorically, and stylistically pushed against the systems of absolutes that structured life in Renaissance England. He bases his argument regarding Shakespeare's personal genius on a series of well-grounded and astute close readings of those numerous moments in which Shakespearean characters negotiate the relationship between self-authorization and self-negation, individuation and prescription. For example, Cleopatra fears to see "Some squeaking Cleopatra boy [her] greatness / I'th' posture of a whore;"[2] King Richard II laments to his friends, "How can you say to me I am a king?;"[3] and Coriolanus insists that he will "but stand / As if a man were author of himself."[4] Greenblatt mines these complicated and rich moments, ultimately finding that "Shakespeare's great innovation is that the magic is, if anything, heightened when he turns, as he does again and again, to forms of beauty that violate the prevailing cultural norms" (41). Greenblatt organizes the book along the "four underlying concepts to which Shakespeare's imagination was drawn consistently and across the multiple genres in which he worked"

(4), which include beauty, hatred, authority, and autonomy. He examines the literary and dramatic codification of these tropes alongside their implications for Renaissance systems of aesthetics, and argues that Shakespeare worked with and against social imperatives, "at once embrac[ing] those norms and subvert[ing] them, finding an unexpected, paradoxical beauty in the smudges, marks, strains, scars, and wrinkles that had figured only as signs of ugliness and difference" (15). The radical sense of social questioning Greenblatt finds within Shakespearean characters suggests to him that "[i]n the sphere of his sovereign genius the authority of the playwright and poet seems absolutely free and unconstrained" (5). In fact, he notes, "The only power that does not seem limited in Shakespeare's work is the artist's own" (5).

The easy slide here from poet/playwright to character, however, warrants pause, not the least because it conflates speculative philosophy and textual analysis. Greenblatt's diction implies as much. For instance, he maintains as a central facet of his argument:

> if some form of subjection is the inescapable human condition, Shakespeare may nonetheless have thought that radical freedom was possible for a made object, that is, for a poem or a play. He may have thought too that such freedom was possible for the artist in the act of making those objects. (112)

Greenblatt surveys the obsessive degree to which Shakespearean works meditate on the power of art, and the ways in which artist figures grasped paradoxicality, only to privilege the act of art making as a space of freedom. As he recalls in Shakespeare's Sonnet 63, the speaker claims that the beauty of the young man "shall in these black lines be seen, / And they shall live, and in them still be green" (ll. 13–14). Yet, Greenblatt's diction is symptomatic of his larger point: Shakespeare "may have thought" about the radical freedom of artistry. Lapses into the subjunctive offer productive modes by which to interrogate cultural assumptions, to challenge perceived inevitabilities and historical or moral teleologies. In *Shakespeare's Freedom*, however, the "may have"s point to Greenblatt's desire to turn possibility into historical fact, or to at least pin it down long enough to sustain aesthetic analysis in the guise of biographical criticism. The argument on Shakespeare's will is a secondary one in this book, but it is also the one Greenblatt frames with the most gusto.

Both Shapiro's and Greenblatt's books are largely concerned with Shakespeare's imagination and autonomy, which would suggest that we ought to consider returning to what has perhaps become too rhetorical a question within our field: what is the trouble with intentionality as an analytical rubric?

And why do we seem driven to return to it as a means of approaching and understanding Shakespearean works, even if, as Shapiro maintains, we refuse to acknowledge it?

QUEER TURNS IN THEORY

The overwhelming number of emergent and reconsidered theoretical approaches to Shakespeare produced internationally not only suggest that the rumors of the death of theory are spurious ones, but also that we as a field have taken up the question of intentionality and complicated it with considerations of embodiment and social consequence. In the Introduction to her comprehensive and much-anticipated edited volume *Shakesqueer: A Queer Companion to the Complete Works of Shakespeare*, Madhavi Menon surveys the recurrent ways Shakespeare's plays and poetry raise questions of language, identity, and temporality, concepts that today's queer theory continues to work through. "The point of this volume," she explains, "is not to provide queer 'readings' of Shakespeare. It is, instead, to bring queerness into varied engagements with those texts without chronological or conceptual privilege" (25). Bringing together a variety of scholars—including Shakespeare and early modern scholars, to queer theorists, and scholar, who work between these fields—*Shakesqueer* appeals to a range of thinkers, and provides new, fresh ways of framing common cruxes in the plays many of us address in research and in the classroom: uncertainty as socially productive in *Comedy of Errors,* global culture as a form of open secrecy in *Othello,* legitimacy as social contract in *King John,* amnesia as amnesty in *The Tempest.* The volume also includes a bibliography for further reading, which will certainly provide students with a wealth of resources for their research papers. The volume offers essays on every piece attributed to the complete works; but it also includes essays on "nonexistent" plays such as *Cardenio* and *Love's Labour's Won.* Menon groups these under "lost plays," a category that demonstrates the playful, provocative, and rigorous ways in which this collection interrogates the notions of recognizability and identification, as themes we explore in the literature and theory we study and teach, as well as in the practical engagements in our day-to-day professional lives.

Central to the volume is a discussion on the contested use of the term "queer" in academic practices. Many have and continue to liken queer theory as a mode of inquiry with the Ides of March—a foreboding sign of impending doom. Others have been predicting for nearly two decades that it is a fad that will soon fade into our field's version of the embarrassing teenage hairstyle: it seemed like a good idea at the time, but we can't seem to remember why. Menon goes to great lengths to situate "queer" in her Introduction and for the larger volume. Because queer's efficacy lies, in part, in its transient quality, defining the term has presented notorious problems and incited disagreement among those who practice queer theory. While she leaves the term appropriately capacious, Menon summarizes:

> Queerness is bodily and that which challenges the limits of what we understand as the body. It expands its ambit to include discussions on the universe, animals, and rationality. While sexual desire sometimes lurks in the background or looms in the foreground, it is not always recognizable as desire. (7).

Understanding queer as often related to but not exclusively contingent upon sexuality, sexual orientation, or sexual desire, disjoins it from the synonymous relationship it has had with "homosexual." "Shakesqueer," or bringing together the signifiers "Shakespeare" and "queer," a willfully anachronistic term, then, "ruthlessly destroys the very idea of a singular identity—[Shakespeare's] and our own" (25). As Menon elaborates,

> Hitching queer theory to Shakespeare forces us to consider the posts we currently occupy: if ideas can be brought together over centuries, then what is the locus standi of the centuries themselves? What would we be if we had to dislocate who we are and what we do—if we had to, that is, queer ourselves? (3).

She answers this question in tones that inflect the concerns over the position of the humanities with which I began. "If Shakespeare were to be considered queer, that would change the ways in which we advertise our jobs, undertake our dissertations, theorize queerness, and carve out our identities" (3). If Shakespeare were to be considered queer, would the private, public, and social sectors understand Shakespeare studies in academia as worth more, able to have more of an effect outside the classroom, offer or students more purchasing power when they matriculate? Perhaps it is impossible to say, but it does raise questions as to the ways in which academic uses of "queer" diverge from those outside of academia, and whether those differences would change the scope of Menon's volume. Either way, I believe *Shakesqueer* will be indispensable over the next decade. It takes on the topic of bardolatry and the social in a refreshingly aggressive way and with a fabulous style. For instance, one of Menon's many colorful and cutting turns of phrase: "The conservative impulse to venerate Shakespeare stems from the same source as the desire to ignore his queerness. Both involve circumscribing him as untouchable: if we mount him, it can only be behind glass" (2).

Bruce Smith also wants to touch Shakespeare, and be queerly touched in return, like Menon, in ways that call attention to understandings of Shakespearean works that certain critical practices have foreclosed. He wonders, in *Phenomenal Shakespeare*, "What's so touching about Shakespeare?" (xvii): that is, he wishes to examine bardolatry as a bodily phenomenon. "In several senses," he explains, the book operates as a "manual for how to do historical phenomenology" (xvii), or a study of historical knowledge as produced through the phenomenon of our five senses and in the present moment. This approach to Shakespeare places emphasis on common experiences of receiving those works such as the creation and feeling of emotion, and the acts of reading, watching, and listening in the theater. Smith acknowledges up front:

> Inner gestures that inspire speech, the kinesthetic knowledge that comes with reading, and the pleasurable twinge of watching and hearing characters suffer on stage are difficult to talk about, not only because bodily sensations do not have a transparent relationship to language but because our keen awareness of cultural differences makes the project of talking about them look presumptuous if not impossible. (xvi)

Conceptualizing Shakespeare as an embodied practice could potentially destabilize Cartesian logic, while also paving the way for new approaches to reading Shakespeare that we have yet to imagine. "When you touch yourself, you trouble the usual distinction between subject (the toucher) and object (the touched)," Smith theorizes, and "[w]hat comes between the toucher and the touched remains a mystery to the rational mind—indeed, it defies the rational mind" (xviii). *Phenomenal Shakespeare* models an innovative way into Shakespeare, and its emphasis on affect and aesthetics, I suspect, will usher in a distinct new trend in the field.

Smith's organization is as clear as his writing. A Prologue briefly introduces the concept of historical phenomenology and explains how Smith will refer to "Shakespeare" through a series of acronyms—WSA (William Shakespeare as Author), THWS (The Historical William Shakespeare), CWWS (Collected Works of William Shakespeare), and WSCI (William Shakespeare as Cultural Icon). The first chapter supplies a survey and interrogation of the goals, assumptions, and working methods of historical phenomenology. Three subsequent chapters provide case studies from different facets of the Shakespearean corpus, focusing on Sonnet 29, *Venus and Adonis*, and *King*

Lear, respectively. For instance, Chapter Two, entitled "How Should One Read a Shakespeare Sonnet?," critiques the limitations of the two primary models of language: the linguistic turn of the 1960s and the influence of the concept of the *langue*, or the structures that make the marking of meaning possible. These models, he contends, foreclose an exploration of the affective connections and queer temporalities opened through the reading experience. Answering the question his title poses, Smith suggests that when we read a Shakespeare Sonnet, "[b]y assuming the subject position of 'one'" (81), we create intersubjective connections with the past and with Shakespeare.

Smith contributes an article to Lowell Gallagher and Shankar Raman's edited volume *Knowing Shakespeare: Senses, Embodiment, and Cognition*, which calls upon historical phenomenology to interrogate the ambivalent results of scholarly attempts to engage with the topic of the body in early modern culture. In their Introduction, Gallagher and Raman identify the primary problem:

> Taking into account gender, ethnicity, sexuality, and class rightfully acknowledges the need to differentiate among societal bodies. But such distinctions still rely on a body—*any* body—as the neutral and elemental unity of analysis, a post-Cartesian stance that privileges dualistic formulations opposing body to mind, soul, world, society, and so on. (3)

The eleven essays in the volume point toward the many ways in which Shakespearean works illuminate and trouble this distinction. Raman's "Hamlet in Motion" argues that the trope of sensory breakdown in *Hamlet* suggests early modern anxiety over the body as merely mechanical and motiveless. Allison Kay Deutermann's fascinating essay examines Samuel Pepys' account of attending his seventh performance of *The Tempest*, to demonstrate the degree to which "Pepys' audition is key to the production of his bodily hexis or disposition, a process through which he creates a coherent sense of himself as a social and embodied subject" (172). Diana E. Henderson examines how representations of the voice of "Shakespeare's Hero moves us to notice the unresolved problems of [*Much Ado about Nothing*], including fraternal murderousness and unabated male jealousy as well as the dilemmas of sense perception" (215). Each article explores to varying degrees problems we as a field have encountered in addressing material and immaterial bodies, with an ultimate suggestion that, "Only a final translation into the realms of the aesthetic can the avowedly conjectural, at the very edge of the known, can hope to communicate what eludes even the senses, however reconfigured" (29).

Smith's answer also takes us to aesthetics, while differentiating it from theory. This differentiation, however, is a tenuous one. As much as Smith's innovative approach will no doubt enrich theoretical engagement in the field, *Phenomenal Shakespeare* ostensibly positions literary theory along with theories of history as mutually "closed systems of thought" (186) that have detracted from our understanding of precisely why Shakespeare continues to resonate so strongly. We have moved from "the thesis of New Criticism [to] the antithesis of post-structuralism" (7), apparently, with little pause. New Historicism's insistence, too, on the "differentness of the early modern past" (23) has obscured the notion that the past and future are merely points on a continuum ever in flux. Menon calls this latter notion queer temporality, as does Carla Freccero's sharp article in *Shakesqueer,* entitled "Romeo and Juliet Love Death" (302–8). Again on the topic of temporality, Smith is careful to explain that his methodology "must inevitably be a *present* phenomenology, but not a *presentist* phenomenology if that means willfully turning one's back on the past" (36). The wide ranging articles in Evelyn Gajowski's recent edition, *Presentism, Gender, and Sexuality in Shakespeare*, go to great lengths to explore and begin to codify presentist approaches to Shakespeare, which, as Gajowski rightfully claims, have been under-theorized, if not un-theorized. The explanation she offers in her Introduction troubles the distinction Smith makes between present-inflected analysis and "Presentism":

> It is true to respond to a Shakespeare text is to enter into a dialogue with the past … Entering into such a conversation means entering into a dialogue not only with Shakespeare and his contemporaries, I would add, but also with the tradition of theatrical and critical responses to Shakespeare's texts that have accumulated over the past four centuries. And these themselves constitute not merely passive responses but also active constructions of meaning in their own right. (6)

According to Gajowski's collection, then, Presentism tempers analysis of the past with a concern over the multiplicity of archives and modes of knowledge circulating in the present moment. Smith's dismissal of Presentism, while seemingly making a presentist argument, demonstrates the ways in which *Phenomenal Shakespeare* makes sophisticated theoretical points while also questioning the use-value of such theoretical thought.

Stanley Stewart similarly theorizes the futility of theory in *Shakespeare and Philosophy*, which examines how philosophers from Richardson, Kant, Hume, Wittgenstein, Nietzsche, and Dewey have used Shakespeare as a subject of philosophy since the seventeenth century. Using Jean E. Howard's

2001 volume *Marxist Shakespeares* as an extended point of reference and example in his Introduction, Stewart warns, "[s]ometimes credulity takes the place of healthy skepticism" (26)—a dynamic he laments in the present state of the field. He observes that theorists who are "sometimes called 'social constructionists,' would raze to common ground any and all literary works that history's extraordinary praise has elevated above the status toward which…all works of art inevitably move, namely toward that of a lifeless document" (26). Again, we confront the problem of intentionality. Stewart concludes:

> Philosophy has gone a long way towards absorbing Shakespeare into philosophical discourse. As we have seen, thinkers like Bacon, Descartes, Hobbes, and Locke had different ends in view, and so the subject of 'Shakespeare' is as absent as the rhetorical tools one might use to address him and his works as a subject. (196)

Shakespeare's philosophical efficacy, then, empties out the signifier "Shakespeare" as a singular, stable subject of inquiry, but in a way that, apparently, keeps it hovering however slightly above that "common ground" upon which social constructionists would level it. No doubt, the contributors to *Marxist Shakespeares* would have plenty to say on the use of commonness and value in Stewart's thinking. More to the point, though, Stewart's informative and comprehensive account of Shakespeare in philosophy offers a fascinating take on the circulation and mutation of cultural capital conferred upon particular subjects, and the anxiety that the act of questioning the construction of value can bankrupt that value in the process.

After all, to disregard the use-value of literary theory in Shakespeare studies, including or excluding the theories of the social to which Stewart enigmatically refers, is, to a large degree, to disregard Shakespeare's works themselves; in *Shakespeare and Literary Theory*, Jonathan Gil Harris demonstrates the degree to which contemporary literary theory is Shakespearean in provenance. "[W]hen we contemplate Shakespeare's writing—whether by viewing the plays on the stage or by speculating about the texts on the page—we enter into theory," he maintains, "whether or not we know it" (5). Harris continually produces scholarship that is as interesting as it is sophisticated and challenging; this slim volume is no exception. He thematically organizes Shakespearean traces, some more indelible than others, in the formulation of theoretical movements from formalism and structuralism, to queer theory and actor-network theory—all of which combine in a surprising way under what we might call "Shakespearean theory." Twelve chapters constitute three parts, which are organized around the conceptual intersections that preoccupy Shakespearean works and theorists alike: language and structure, desire and identity, and culture and society. Taken together, the chapters call attention to the ways in which Shakespeare has provided symptomatic focus for literary theory, and "underscore how literary theory is less an external set of ideas imposed on Shakespeare's texts than a mode—or several modes—of critical reflection inspired by, and emerging from, his writing" (3). For instance, René Girard turns to *Troilus and Cressida* to articulate the dangers of mimetic desire; Jacques Derrida calls upon *Romeo and Juliet* to explore the consequences of countertime and the violence of naming; *Hamlet* becomes the reference against which Sigmund Freud and Jacques Lacan articulate their respective developmental models of the psyche, while it also provides Derrida with a model for what he calls hauntology, and Lee Edelman with a means of sketching out his highly influential theory of queer futurity; Elaine Showalter traces the literary and aesthetic history of Ophelia to question the possibility of a feminist ethics; and *The Tempest* and Aimé Césaire's appropriation *Une Tempête* acts as source material for Edward Said's understanding of orientalism in colonial enterprises. The causal relationships Harris draws across theories, histories, and texts are numerous. In this way, the book provides a productive resource for those who teach Shakespeare with or through theory, or vice versa. Establishing the symbiotic relationship between Shakespeare and theory, Harris explains, might allow us to "enter more self-consciously into theory when reading Shakespeare's plays and poems," (5) which, in turn, would demystify theory from an exotic critical practice to an already quotidian aspect of our professional lives.

POPULAR CULTURE

The topic of the "everyday" in our personal lives, however, has inspired slightly different though nonetheless dismissive critical ideologies as to what constitutes academic rigor and viable cultural artifacts. The proliferation of recent work on Shakespeare and popular culture both confronts this tendency and suggests its cessation. Owen Terris, Eve-Marie Oesterlen, and Luke McKernan's edited volume *Shakespeare on Film, Television and Radio: The Researcher's Guide* offers a first of its kind resource of "essays, archive documents, recommendation of notable productions and some essential reference tools to support the study of Shakespeare on film, television and radio" (viii), while paying particular attention to popular cultural artifacts, broadly defined. It is intended as a practical, hands-on tool for researchers, but also offers an introduction of the primary topics that have concerned studies of Shakespeare in popular media. It is divided into four parts: articles, documents, resources, and a reference guide. The first part offers original critical articles, though few, and its strength lies in its analysis of radio appropriations, a medium still underrepresented in Shakespeare media studies. In particular, Terris's "Shakespeare and British Television," examines "the changes in technology, cultural policies, politics and management" (20) that contributed to the significant decline of Shakespeare-based appropriations in the 1980s, while Oesterlen's article cites 1920s and 1930s British broadcasts to demonstrate how "Shakespeare played a crucial role in the development of radio drama's distinctive characteristics and opportunities, and how the new medium, in turn, helped to shape the contemporary reception of Shakespeare in performance" (51). The documents section includes original sources from the British entertainment industry such as Hitchcock's 1937 retort to critics who claimed Shakespeare films are either poor quality or that Shakespearean works simply could not translate well into film. The reference section will no doubt prove useful for students or scholars newly interested in media Shakespeare studies. It includes a comprehensive list of archives, guidance on their use, and advice on copyright and citation. Also valuable, the last section offers a comprehensive list of archives and libraries for researchers, as well as suggestions for further reading. Published through the British Universities Film and Video Council, the guide will appeal to those working with British popular culture in particular, and may have limited purchase for those working in other cultural registers or on global and international phenomenon.

Linking ideology to practice, Robert Shaughnessy, in his edited volume, *The Cambridge Companion to Shakespeare and Popular Culture*, identifies the multiple and often conflicting ways in which Shakespeare and popular culture have mutually shaped the perception of one another. In his Introduction, Shaughnessy observes that the study of popular culture has transformed from ephemeral and anecdotal to one of increasingly recognized significance. He attributes this shift, in part, to scholarly recognition of the valuable role that popular cultural appropriations play in helping us to address vexed questions of cultural ownership, aesthetic value, and social accesses, among other topics—questions, in other words, Shakespearean texts compulsively explore. Broadening the scope of "popular" beyond "contemporary," it explores "the factors that determine the definitions of and boundaries between the legitimate and illegitimate, the canonical and the authorized, and the subversive, the oppositional, the scandalous, and the inane" (5) to address how "Shakespeare has been consumed and reinvented, allowing for interface between cultural, literary, performance, and cinema studies" (2).

This volume reflects a simultaneously productive and problematically fractured image of Shakespeare. In addition to Shaughnessy's valuable Introduction, it offers twelve discrete articles that address unique case studies. Particularly astute, Emma Smith's article examines the historic precedent of shaping Shakespearean works to fit generic conventions in media other than theater. She focuses on the BBC's serial adaptation of the history cycles, *The Age of Kings* (1960), which melds historical epic with the conventions of soap opera. Smith's attention to generic specificity echoes Susan Greenhalgh's "Shakespeare Overheard: Performances, Adaptations, and Citations on Radio," which examines the simultaneous ubiquity and scholarly occlusion of broadcast transmissions of Shakespeare. Douglas Lanier's "Shakespeare™" spans genres in search of iconicity, Lanier arguing that:

> Like the Shakespearean trademark, fuller pop treatments of Shakespeare the man—in fictional biography, in children's literature, in genre fiction, period costumes, musicals, comic books, TV and film biographies—dwell in the long shadow of nineteenth-century conceptions of Shakespeare, in particular the outsize mythos surrounding Shakespearean authorship which had its roots in the cult of the Romantic genius. (100)

Both Shapiro's and Greenblatt's recent biographical scholarship supports Lanier's claim. Also noteworthy, W. B. Worthen identifies a paradox within digital culture. "[W]hile there's an abundance of Shakespearean imagery and textuality online, there's little Shakespeare performance there" (228), he notes. The Fall 2010 special issue of *Shakespeare Quarterly,* "Shakespeare and New Media" edited by Katherine Rowe, suggests the degree to which performances are indeed abundant online, and the issue "invite[s] us to look not only at familiar literary works but also at some familiar methodological assumptions with fresh eyes" (iii), which may help us to see performance where we least expect it. Shaughnessy's volume offers a new take on what happens when Shakespeare is popularized, and when the popular is Shakespeareanized. Articles in both sketch the remarkable variety of forms that Shakespeare and Shakespearean works take. As Kate Rumold argues in her article, "From 'Access' to 'Creativity': Shakespeare Institutions, New Media, and the Language of Cultural Value,"[5] institutions associated with Shakespeare such as the RSC and the Globe often co-opt the types of popular cultural Shakespeare-related artifacts that Shaughnessy's volume traces. Such institutions, Rumold writes, "present the remediation of their work by other, newer media forms as their own, deliberate appropriation of broadcast technology to extend the physical space of the stage—reclaiming value for the institution" (328).

Shaughnessy's volume is an important first step in disseminating critical work on pop culture Shakespeare, and has now opened the possibility of reading across and among the many registers in which we find Shakespeare. Parsing out discourses on genre, technological change, market, and cultural value in popular culture can make for illuminating case studies, but it threatens, as Rumold suggests, to suture over the process by which institutional imperatives can mask as subversive performances.

Emerging from the rubble of the 1980s hermetic subversion-containment debates, the conceptual power of subversion has returned, perhaps most conspicuously in recent scholarship on present-day, popular-culture live performances of Shakespeare. In part, this metaleptic shift stems from reconsiderations of how to reconceptualize performance and performativity, and Elizabeth Klett's *Cross-gender Shakespeare and English National Identity: Wearing the Codpiece* constructs a uniquely interdisciplinary case in point. She examines women's cross-gendered performances of Shakespeare on the English (primarily London) stage from 1995–2004, while noting its relationship to early modern English staging practices. At once theoretically, historically, theatrically, and politically grounded, she argues, "[t]he original purpose of the codpiece was to shield and emphasize male phallic power. By appropriating the appendage, either literally or figuratively, actresses can expose and dismantle the workings of masculinity, Shakespearean authority, and 'Englishness,' revealing how all three work to create cultural fictions of identity" (3). In the process, Klett prompts us to ask, how transformative is the performative? She works with Judith Butler's well-known understanding of "performativity" as the conditions that make ritualized and reiterable behavior, or "performance," possible. She intervenes, "[y]et defining performance as exclusively reiterable, as merely repeating familiar cultural norms, does not allow for the possibility of transformation of those norms … In this view, re-iteration is not a stale repetition of recognizable forms; instead, it allows for 'insubordination,' and for transformation through the act of re-production" (7). Klett suggests that, when we watch mimetic constructions of staged reality, we might also glimpse moments of misalignment.

Yet Klett interrogates binaristic logics that position the relationship between subversion and containment as oppositional. Perhaps the either/or framework gets in the way; perhaps it's both/and. For instance, she examines the controversial understandings of androgyny as "a transcendent union of opposites, or as a subversively embodied sexuality" (11). This controversy links contemporary women's cross-gendered performance with early modern Puritanical attacks levied against theatrical staging practices. Klett finds equally hostile reviews in both cases. "Androgyny" works as an analytical framework for cross-dressing theatrical performances, she explains, as long as we understand it as a complex, multiply textured practice. What is at stake for the public in both the present day and the early modern, she suggests, centers on the threat of gender disruption and its social consequences. Today, however, women's cross-dressing also poses a threat to Shakespeare iconicity, which she connects with the fact that "all-female productions at the Globe in 2003 and 2004 have seemingly marked an end, at least for now, of significant interest in women wearing the codpiece on the London stage" (168).

Klett's theoretical sophistication matches Steven Purcell's thoughtfully performative book *Popular Shakespeare: Simulation and Subversion on the Modern Stage*. No less theoretically rigorous, it questions how the multiple perspective at play in "popular theater might provide us with a destabilizing discourse, a means by which our habitually self-contained attitudes towards the texts might be disrupted" (24). Examining the theatrical device of disjunctive anachronism—or modes of theatricality which would call attention to discrepancies between past and present—so ubiquitous in contemporary, post-1990 British stagings of Shakespearean works, Purcell finds self-referentially political performances that bring to the forefront connections between theater and the social. Destabilizing boundaries—between theater and the social, past and present, Shakespeare and not Shakespeare—opens a conceptual space in which we spectators might question and address the myriad global inequalities that affect scholarly work, whether or not we directly address them. His chapter organization illustrates his point. Personal narratives alternate with formal and traditionally "academic" chapters. For instance, the book opens with a personal narrative Purcell entitles "Ambiguous Applause," which questions why he and his fellow audience members at a particular performance of *Titus Andronicus* applauded Aaron's final lines, "If one good deed in all my life I did / I do repent it from my very soul" (5.3.188–9). This personal narrative ushers in the first chapter, which examines the subtextual systems of power that construct the theatrical experience. The organizational structure of Purcell's book implicitly poses to the reader the question of precisely what counts as a body of serious, academic work, and why personal narrative so rarely finds its way explicitly into scholarship. In many ways, this book performs the historical phenomenology Smith promotes.

Purcell's examination of subject positions constitutes both the strength and slight limitation of this book. He offers this caveat early on: "This is ultimately a study of one observer's encounters with a set of cultural phenomena, and another writer in a different cultural context might experience the same subject very differently" (6). Such a statement calls important attention to the conventions by which spectatorship changes across cultures, nations, and demographics more generally. In this way, it provides a valuable lesson for those who engage in international Shakespeare studies on the importance of acknowledging difference. It also demonstrates the limitations of citing difference as an analytical rubric. The organizational structure of the book embraces the untidiness of discrete boundaries, shifting between the personal and the professional, the local and the global. Its analytical points do not. Framing analysis in terms of the singularity of a subject position can reduce sophisticated and experimental analysis to ineffectual navel-gazing, or alternately, as it threatens to do here, pull the political punch that Purcell swings at the notion of professional decorum and cultural transmission. The book ends with a reiteration of its politics of disturbance, though, and insists to its readers that, "where Shakespeare and popular culture appear most opposed, they might better expose one another: veneration might be undercut by irreverence, mythologising by parody, the impulse towards coherence through fracture" (221).

According to Melissa Croteau and Carolyn Jess-Cooke, a politics of disturbance unites intercultural Shakespeares through prolific visual citations of apocalypse. In their exciting edited volume *Apocalyptic Shakespeare: Essays on Visions of Chaos and Revelation in Recent Film Adaptations*, Croteau and Jess-Cooke call attention in their Introduction to the apocalyptic impulse that runs throughout history, from the eschatological doctrines of Zoroaster in Persia to the newest *Terminator* film. Our love of a well-told end-of-the-world story, however, takes a particularly political inflection when it comes to Shakespeare, in part because Shakespearean works and the discourse of British early modern theatricality link on- and off-stage performance with the threat of social dislocation. The volume delivers on its attempt to "provide a comprehensive examination of the ways in which recent Shakespeare films—in particular a body of predominantly late twentieth century and post-9/11 productions—register cultural concerns toward a global wasteland of literary nothingness, technological alienation, spiritual destruction, and the effects of globalization" (20). Articles sample films such as Baz Luhrmann's *William Shakespeare's Romeo + Juliet* (1996), Jean-Luc Godard's *King Lear* (1987), Michael Almereyda's *Hamlet* (2000), and Alex Cox's *Revengers Tragedy* (2002), all of which adopt spectacularly postmodern cinematic aesthetic. The essays provide us with a panoramic picture, revealing that these films dramatize the simultaneous threat of textual, relational, and material destruction along with the promise of Phoenician rebirth that attends apocalypse.

That Shakespeare occupies a paradoxically timely and timeless cultural position may confirm what many of us already sense when we teach Shakespeare. Students often have the comfortable and sometimes unchecked ability to understand Shakespeare as being able to weave life's secrets into the very words of his works, while also making the claim that his works are too old to be of use today. Recent studies in popular culture have begun to carefully trace these seemingly contradictory functions that Shakespeare plays today. More importantly, though, they illuminate the socio-political benefits and consequences of this paradox.

EMERGENT ARCHIVES

The inquisitive shift from what Shakespeare is to where we find him connects the analytical focus in popular cultural studies with the prolific and proliferating field of media Shakespeare studies; Judith Buchanan finds him in the extensive archive of silent film, and in the process challenges ontological relationship between Shakespeare and language. In *Shakespeare on Silent Film: An Excellent Dumb Discourse,* she explains, "a total of 250 and 300 films adapted from Shakespearean sources were made by the British, American, French, Italian, German, and Danish film industry" during the silent film era (1899–1927). Yet, not since Robert Hamilton Ball's pioneering 1968 work on silent Shakespeare film has a book-length project explored the genre. Buchanan continues Ball's work of sketching the contours of the archive. Beyond her goal "to bring into critical circulation some films not commercially available and so, as yet, scarcely known, if at all" (5), though, she demonstrates the capacity of wordless Shakespeare to defamiliarize central critical ideologies in Shakespeare studies more generally. The translation of Shakespeare's language into the visual semiotics of mise-en-scène and gesture, she argues, calls attention to "the aspiration of the theater and cinema as institutions, the tonal register of performance styles, the status of stars, the priorities of production companies and of national film industries, the history of Shakespeareana performance and even, at times, the nature of the plays themselves" (7). Buchanan organizes her chapters in broad chronological strokes to demonstrate how the industry reacted to its own economic, technological, and historical development. For instance, the historical focus in the first chapter pre-dates the invention of cinema, allowing Buchanan to confront the conventions by which Shakespeare became a suitable subject for cinema and for projection. Most fascinating, her second chapter calls upon Tom Gunning's concept of the "theater of attractions" to address the ways in which Shakespearean works, characters, and plots, were pictorialized rather than just narrated. "No longer could [cinematic Shakespeare] have functioned as an advertisement for the stage production, or even, more simply, as an 'actuality' celebration of the local" (69), she writes. "The film was thus marketed as being able to offer all that the stage production had done" (69), and thus we see how tensions between media competition and market demand have shaped that which we receive as "Shakespeare" in various cultural registers.

Whereas Buchanan explores the possibilities opened up with wordless Shakespeare, Kendra Preston Leonard capitalizes on sound—music in particular—as a sort of cultural metronome, with which to gage changing attitudes toward Shakespeare's works, the adaptations they inspire, and scholarly reaction to both. In *Shakespeare, Madness, and Music: Scoring Insanity in Cinematic Adaptations*, Leonard traces the condition of madness as a primary early modern trope for confronting anxieties over desire, prescription, politics, and aesthetics—topics we continue to explore. Across historical periods, too, music "was often used as a visible and audible symptom of a victim's disassociation from her—most cases of madness on the early modern stage involve women—surroundings and societal rules and her loss of self-control" (3). Leonard concentrates her analysis on *Hamlet*, *Macbeth*, and *King Lear* to trace a disruptive teleology. "As filmmakers have slowly departed from the aesthetic of the 'heritage' Shakespearean film as established by Olivier and the BBC's complete-works productions," she notes, "there has been a slow but undeniable dissolution of the traditional link between inappropriate performative behaviors, primarily singing, and madness" (127). While madness has constituted a general catch-all explanation in critical understandings of non-normative behaviors and representational strategies, Leonard makes a strong case that the musical language of some of the most well-distributed adaptations of *Hamlet*, *Macbeth*, and *King Lear* resists such reductive moves. Meanings we may stamp onto films, in other words, can fail to read the marginalized language of sound, which frequently presents counter-discourses to a film's visual language. Of course, first we must pay attention to music in Shakespeare screen adaptations. Leonard's study is the first of its kind and an important addition to the changing archives that comprise Shakespeare studies.

Alexander C. Y. Huang and Charles S. Ross's volume *Shakespeare in Hollywood, Asia, and Cyberspace* also expands archives in terms of genre as well as geography and technological medium. It brings unlikely discourses into conversation in an attempt to inspire critical reflection on the archives we work with. The articles collected here examine "a global array of interpretive strategies" (2), which illuminates the surprising ways in which these three traditions have developed in similar ways, or at the very least with similar concerns regarding spectatorship, translation, social effect, and reception. In many respects, this volume is redefining the field of Shakespeare in adaptation. In their Introduction, Huang and Ross note three distinct yet interrelated approaches to media Shakespeare that have developed since its increasing scholarly popularity in the 1990s. The first approach, which has been pioneered by "Michael Bristol, James Bulman, John Joughin, Barbara Hodgdon, Christy Desmet, and W. B. Worthen, among other key critics" (5), calls upon theoretical understandings to interrogate systems of representation adopted by appropriations. A second approach, which Buchanan and Leonard have adopted for their recent work, focuses on case studies to shift the critical attention to less familiar geographical, technological, or generic sites of appropriation. A third approach, they explain, "engages the histories and reception of Shakespeare's images, biographies, and reputation" (5), which Gary Taylor's *Reinventing Shakespeare* and Richard Burt's two-volume encyclopedia *Shakespeare and Shakespeare* both exemplify.[6] We might also consider recent biography studies as a hybrid mode of this last approach. Each approach offers a wealth of value, but the benefits of letting these modes collide and coalesce, Huang and Ross suggest, allows us to ask new questions. The volume shifts from an examination of what Shakespeare means in new contexts, or how these new contexts challenge perceptions of Shakespeare's works, to an interrogation of how "transnational Shakespeares animate and redirect the traffic between different geo-cultural or virtual realities" (1–2). The essays explore a range of case studies and responses, leaving the question productively open-ended.

Each section of the volume frames, as is tradition, the Shakespearean encounter as a mode of cultural translation, but also as one of redefinition. The collection is divided into four parts. The first, "Shakespeare in Hollywood," explores how Asian and Anglo-European modes of representation can and do influence one another, on and off screen, as comparative literature scholars, primarily from Japan and Taiwan, examine Hollywood productions. Mei Zhu finds that "the entire tradition of screwball comedy had its roots in Shakespearean comedies such as *Much Ado about Nothing*, *Love's Labour's Lost*, and *Comedy of Errors*" (24). Thus, treating contemporary films such as Kenneth Branagh's *Love's Labour's Lost* (2000) as a pop culture distortion or triviality minimizes cinematic tradition in an attempt to venerate the propriety of the Shakespearean corpus. Charles S. Ross examines the trope of the underwater woman in a cross-cultural context to identify Hollywood tendencies to display and condense onto the female body anxieties over social power. The second part, "Shakespeare in Asia," offers a geographical and historical survey of filmic traditions in Asia. Lei Jin identifies translational strategies by which "Kurosawa recreates that dramatic power of Shakespeare's *Macbeth* conveyed by dialogue" (88) rewritten in auditory conventions such as *noh* music. Also working with *Macbeth*, Huang argues that operatic *Macbeth*s "epitomize a paradigm shift from seeking authenticity to foregrounding artistic subjectivity in modes of cultural production that re-produce global texts" (104). Those interested in Asian Shakespeare will also find useful Huang's edited contribution to *Borrowers and Lenders* (4, no. 2, 2009), "Asian Shakespeares on Screen: Two Films in Perspective" and the open-access *Shakespeare Performance in Asia* (SPIA), a collection of videos of Asian Shakespeare performances. The third section, "Shakespeare in Cyberspace," confronts the effects of digital media on scholarly terminology and practice. Christy Desmet and Sujata Iyengar locate their co-edited print and online journal, *Borrowers and Lenders: A Journal of Shakespeare Adaptation* "between playground and Panopticon," (241), that is, "between new and emergent and old and institutionalized, and the desire for something creative but not creative enough" (241). These tensions suggest the benefits and difficulties of addressing the shifts and at times conflicts in how we as a field communicate with one another. Peter Holland closes the section by calling for a re-examination of our critical assumptions about community and performance, claiming that Shakespeare in cyberspace occupies a conceptual "space between the theater and the web in which new communities can be forged" (261). The final section provides a chronology and a bibliography—both of which would be valuable teaching guides for those of us who teach media Shakespeares. Taken together, the sections foreground the need to reconsider what we imagine as the conditions and consequences of the Shakespearean encounter.

While Huang and Ross illustrate the benefits of working with the tensions between local and global contextualizations, Greg Colón Semenza's volume *The English Renaissance in Popular Culture: An Age of All Time* rethinks Shakespearean universality by dislocating Shakespeare. He rightfully notes the Shakespeare-centric nature of scholarship on screen adaptations and translations, which is not to suggest scholars should exclude Shakespeare from critical examination. Rather, Semenza's collection brings together American and British scholars of Renaissance literature and popular culture to expand the conversation. He explains the scholarly stakes of the volume's intervention:

> Although English Renaissance literary scholars have written extensively on popular historical and political appropriations of Shakespeare—theorizing the cultural capital accrued through contact with the central canonical English author, such work has downplayed the fact that Shakespearean appropriations are merely part of a wider popular cultural interest and investment in the Renaissance as an imagined historical period. (10)

Widening the scope of analysis to music, sound, fairs, popular novels, the web, and media history, this volume concerns itself less with uncovering the past than it does with interrogating our uses of it in the present. In the process, the articles perform a productively complex historiography that illuminates the many ways in which we identify with and against the early modern period. As Semenza pithily remarks, "What happens in the Renaissance stays in the Renaissance. But what happens to the Renaissance in our own time gives the past new meaning," and paying close attention to this process promises to make one "more aware of the potential risks and rewards of doing so, and even experience the thrill and sense of renewal that comes with forgetting your past" (19).

The volume impressively grounds its theoretical developments with practical suggestions. In additional to the scholarly benefit, widening the scope of analysis from Shakespeare to the Renaissance can operate as a pedagogical tool. Examining cinematic artifacts such as *Elizabeth: The Golden Age* (2007) and *V for Vendetta* (2005), for instance, has the "value of making our students conscious of how adaptation operates" as a cultural process, which can likewise help "them to recognize their own historically contingent perspectives as readers of historical texts—and, consequently, of the contingent and contextual nature of historiography" (6). Each of its four sections—which focus on Renaissance icons, fantasies, sounds, and cinema—confront what I found to be a surprising and important binaristic divide. With a few exceptions, which are explored at length, "the sixteenth century, especially the later Elizabethan period, is represented as the English Golden Age, characterized by pageantry, intrigue, and a metaphorical and often literal colorfulness suggesting the vitality and infinite possibility of an England whose future greatness is already clear" (7). Conversely, the "seventeenth century—at least up through the Restoration—is usually depicted as a humorless and apocalyptic age, one clouded especially by the zeal and stereotyped asceticism of the godly" (8). This divide in representations of the Renaissance in popular culture, however implicit at times, structures the ways in which students received Renaissance texts. Understanding this dynamic offers educators a chance to readdress our own classroom practices accordingly.

Lisa Hopkins responds to a similar impetus to widen analytic scope, but in *Relocating Shakespeare and Austen on Screen* she does so by consolidating her examination to English iconography, placing cinematic adaptations of Shakespeare and Jane Austen side by side. She constructs a unique archive of popular cultural films, such as *William Shakespeare's Romeo + Juliet* (1996), *Clueless* (1995), *Hamlet* (2000), *Bridget Jones's Diary* (2001), *Shakespeare Wallah* (1965), *Bride and Prejudice* (2004), and *Becoming Jane* (2007). She finds that dislocating these iconographic figures from their traditional historical contexts allows for two primary benefits. First, paying close attention to media forms in which we receive English icons of the past can illuminate for us the larger systems of cultural value attributed to those icons. Second, and more central to Hopkins's theoretical goals of the book, the juxtaposition of Shakespeare and Austen, past and present, causes us to question "what 'Englishness' itself means, particularly in relation to two countries whose identities Britain helped to shape but which have now definitively broken away from it, the United States and India" (16). Both Shakespeare and Austen were writing at critical moments in colonial history, and each addresses issues of imperial enterprise in their writings. As theoretical circles within Shakespeare studies continue to explore the tensions between "post-colonial" and "transnational" as analytic terms, Hopkins demonstrates the benefits in allowing these tensions to remain in play. In this book, she treats timely and controversial topics of debate within the field in a delicate and sophisticated manner.

SHAKESPEAREAN UTILITY

To return to the question I posed at the outset of this review, what worth lies in humanities scholarship and education? Many of us, because of our educational background in the humanities, undoubtedly contest what precisely ideologically laden terms such as "humanities," "education," and "worth" mean in this context. Which is to say, many of us cut our critical thinking teeth in consuming Shakespearean works and their adaptations or the theoretical principles they helped to develop. Shakespeare holds a special place in most humanities programs, and crises may hit Shakespeare studies differently because of that. As scholarship over the past two years has explored, the intrinsic value associated with Shakespeare's works has provided momentum to sometimes troubling, sometimes subversive, and sometimes failed social and political movements. They do still, and each of these movements sends waves of disciplinary and epistemological change in approaches to Shakespeare and within the humanities more generally. We might look to Steven Mentz's new book *At the Bottom of Shakespeare's Ocean* as a case study. He develops a new "maritime humanities"—which is also referred to as "blue studies," "blue cultural humanities," and "the new thalassology"—which combines in scholarly and creative ways the discourses of post-colonialism, globalism, and environmentalism to explore the capacious, symbolic ways in which culture has come to understand the ocean. This exciting model of humanities examines the relationship between humans and the sea in a variety of contexts, including, but not limited to, literature, historical documents, and works of art. Paying close attention to the sea—one of the most "versatile symbols" (xiii)—can reveal how material reality circulates beyond its reach. On the topic of "our uncertain future," Mentz finds that "Shakespeare, sitting at the heart of English literature, has more to say ... than we might expect" (xiii). The wide range of readings and plays Mentz manages to fit into this slim volume is impressive. It also suggests that, for Mentz, the one inexhaustible resource indeed is language. "[I]t's through language and narrative that our culture has always grappled with living in an unstable" condition, he argues, "[w]e just don't often put them in the center where they belong" (98). The innovative methodologies and archives that have emerged in recent scholarship enforce the need to rethink our understandings of how what we do in our offices and classrooms translates beyond those spaces. In other words, it feels incredibly appropriate to question the use-value of humanities education. Shifting the terms of the question, however, seems equally important. How do we measure the social use-value of the humanities, and if resources were to be funneled in new directions, where would they go? Perhaps, like Shakespeare, the humanities have become fodder for our desire for apocalypse stories. The humanities are dead. Long live the humanities.

WORKS REVIEWED

Bevington, David. *Shakespeare and Biography.* Oxford and New York: Oxford University Press, 2010.
Buchanan, Judith. *Shakespeare on Silent Film: An Excellent Dumb Discourse.* Cambridge and New York: Cambridge University Press, 2009.

Croteau, Mellissa and Carolyn Jess-Cooke, eds. *Apocalyptic Shakespeare: Essays on Visions of Chaos and Revelation in Recent Film Adaptations.* Jefferson, NC: McFarland and Co., 2009.

Gajowski, Evelyn. *Presentism, Gender, and Sexuality in Shakespeare.* Basingstoke and New York: Palgrave, 2009.

Greenblatt, Stephen. *Shakespeare's Freedom.* Chicago: University of Chicago Press, 2010.

Harris, Jonathan Gil. *Shakespeare and Literary Theory.* Oxford: Oxford University Press, 2010.

Hopkins, Lisa. *Relocating Shakespeare and Austen on Screen.* Basingstoke and New York: Palgrave, 2009.

Huang, Alexander C. Y. and Charles S. Ross, eds. *Shakespeare in Hollywood, Asia, and Cyberspace.* West Lafayette, IN: Purdue University Press, 2009.

Klett, Elizabeth. *Cross-gender Shakespeare and English National Identity: Wearing the Codpiece.* New York: Palgrave, 2009.

Leonard, Kendra Preston. *Shakespeare, Madness, and Music: Scoring Insanity in Cinematic Adaptations.* Lanham, MD: Scarecrow Press, 2009.

Menon, Madhavi. *Shakesqueer: A Queer Companion to the Complete Works of Shakespeare.* Durham and London: Duke University Press, 2011.

Mentz, Steve. *At the Bottom of Shakespeare's Ocean.* London: Continuum, 2009.

Purcell, Stephen. *Popular Shakespeare: Simulation and Subversion on the Modern Stage.* Basingstoke and New York: Palgrave, 2009.

Raman, Shankar and Lowell Gallagher, eds. *Knowing Shakespeare: Senses, Embodiment and Cognition.* New York: Palgrave, 2010.

Rowe, Katherine, ed. *Shakespeare Quarterly* 61, no. 4 (2010): Special issue: "Shakespeare and New Media."

Semenza, Greg Colón, ed. *The English Renaissance in Popular Culture: An Age of All Time.* New York: Palgrave, 2010.

Shakespeare Performance in Asia. (2008): at http://web.mit.edu/shakespeare/asia/.

Shapiro, James. *Contested Will: Who Wrote Shakespeare?* New York: Simon & Schuster, 2010.

Shaughnessy, Robert, ed. *The Cambridge Companion to Shakespeare and Popular Culture.* Cambridge and New York: Cambridge University Press, 2007.

Smith, Bruce. *Phenomenal Shakespeare.* Chichester, UK and Malden, MA: Wiley-Blackwell, 2010.

Stewart, Stanley. *Shakespeare and Philosophy.* New York: Routledge, 2010.

Terris, Owen, Eve-Marie Oesterlen, and Luke McKernan, eds. *Shakespeare on Film, Television and Radio: The Researcher's Guide*. London: British Universities Film & Video Council, 2009.

NOTES

1. The *New York Times* ran a particularly salient article reporting the problematic position of the humanities and liberal arts education in our current climate; see Patricia Cohen, "In Tough Times, the Humanities Must Justify their Worth," *New York Times* C1, 25 February 2009, at http://www.nytimes.com/2009/02/25/books/25human.html.
2. *Antony and Cleopatra*, 5.2.216; all Shakespeare citations are taken from *The Norton Complete Shakespeare,* ed. Stephen Greenblatt, Walter Cohen, Jean E. Howard, and Katherine Maus, 2nd. ed. (New York: W. W. Norton, 2008).
3. *Richard II*, 3.2.173.
4. *Coriolanus*, 5.3.35–6.
5. Rumold's article appears in the special issue of *Shakespeare Quarterly,* "Shakespeare and New Media" (Fall 2010).
6. See Gary Taylor, *Reinventing Shakespeare: A Cultural History from the Restoration to the Present* (New York: Weidenfeld and Nicolson, 1989) and Richard Burt, *Shakespeares after Shakespeare: An Encyclopedia of the Bard in Mass Media and Popular Culture*, 2 vols (Westport, CT: Greenwood Press, 2007).

13 The Field in Review: Textual Studies, Performance Criticism, and Digital Humanities

Niamh J. O'Leary

Undertaking to discuss several of the scholarly monographs and edited collections published about Shakespeare in the last year has been a fascinating and inspiring experience. While this essay will focus on five specific subject areas, it is clear that scholarship is flourishing in many different directions and that a recounting like this can only reveal the tip of the iceberg, both in terms of any particular argument, and of the field as a whole. From Shakespeare's poetry, to his plays in performance and adaptation across the world, to textual history, to online databases, this essay will provide brief discussions of fourteen books and four digital archives.

As I state in the conclusion, having reviewed this body of work, it seems evident that the liveliest vein of scholarship in the last year is that which examines Shakespeare in a global context. Manfred Pfister and Juergen Gutsch's anthology presents translations of the Sonnets in seventy-three different languages. Three of the four digital archives represented below are devoted to examining Shakespeare's afterlives in non-European locations, among them Canada, China, and New Zealand. One whole section of this review essay focuses on monographs and edited collections published about Shakespeare around the globe, and particularly, Shakespeare in Asia. For the most part, scholarship in this area attends to performance traditions and adaptation, rather than, say, a particular Chinese tradition of Shakespeare scholarship. And yet, this criticism is by no means narrowly focused. Rather, it embraces a myriad of critical approaches, dealing with Shakespeare's poetry, questions of gender and politics, performance and pedagogy, textuality and transmission. As I will discuss below, this new and growing field both encompasses and expands known scholarly approaches, and throws open many new doors for Shakespearean scholarship. It demands interdisciplinarity and technological awareness, and it urges us to embrace less familiar narratives of Shakespearean tradition, becoming globally-aware scholars in a global profession.

SHAKESPEARE'S POETRY

Within the last year, two new volumes were released that focus on Shakespeare's poetry: a creative new anthology, and a companion. In *William Shakespeare's Sonnets for the First Time Globally Reprinted: A Quartercentenary Anthology*, editors Manfred Pfister and Juergen Gutsch, along with the aid of seventy-five contributors, present Shakespeare's Sonnets in seventy-three different languages, including Pennsylvania Dutch, Sign Language, Maori, and Klingon. The sheer immensity of the project is impressive. Each individual chapter includes a brief introductory essay discussing the history of Shakespeare's Sonnets, the sonnet form, and translation in each particular culture, while offering brief biographies of the translators and discussions of critical response to the translations. The introductions are followed by sample translations, and in many cases, multiple translations of the same sonnet. In addition to literal translations, the anthology contains "translations or transpositions into other genres of literature and other media" (12). These transpositions are available on the included DVD's "multimedial archive" (13).

The Sonnets, which were not internationally popular until the nineteenth century, are now translated all over the world, though in many international cultures, they were translated as much as a century after the plays (14). Some issues that come to the forefront in tracing translations of the Sonnets in different cultural contexts include the potentially subversive sexual aspect of the poetry; the question of whether or not "to render the Sonnets as closely as possible to their original aesthetic form"; whether or not to burden/enhance translations with extensive commentary and editorial apparatus; and the extent to which various translators "take liberties" with the Sonnets, rewriting them rather than translating them (16–19). Because translations were often "second hand"— that is, translated from French or German into Icelandic or Maori, rather than from English—the translated Sonnets are in a "double dialogue ... with both the original English text and with the extant target language translations past or present" (21). In addition, translations by poets engage in a third strand of dialogue—with that particular poet's own body of work (22). Pfister and Gutsch also note that these translations were frequently completed by men and women who were imprisoned or exiled. They tie this to the unique prevalence of Sonnet 66 in translations which, the editors argue, spoke particularly to "a continental Europe suffering under Nazism or Stalinism" because it focuses on "the political abuses of the times" (26).

The accompanying DVD provides a wealth of information. Here I have chosen to focus on two of its most useful applications. First, in terms of pedagogy, the many sound recordings of recitations of the Sonnets, both in English and by native speakers of every language represented in the anthology, provide a plethora of auditory experiences. There are also recordings of the Sonnets set to music in a variety of languages, films of the Sonnets being performed, and image files of book jackets advertising the Sonnets in different languages. Any of these materials could be used to provoke classroom discussion. Secondly, the DVD contains an extensive archive of images both of the Sonnets and of sonnet-related artwork. Pfister comments on the dearth of scholarship attending to the graphic afterlives of the Sonnets, and as scholarship increasingly becomes interested in the graphic afterlives of the plays, I imagine this collection will provide an excellent starting point for any who wish to engage the Sonnets in this way.

Michael Schoenfeldt's *The Cambridge Introduction to Shakespeare's Poetry* is a helpful companion text for Shakespeare's nondramatic poems. Schoenfeldt contends that, aside from the Sonnets, Shakespeare's poems "have been almost completely ignored outside the academy" (2). The introductory chapter situates the poems in relation to Shakespeare's dramatic oeuvre as well as the poetic traditions of early modern England. He aligns himself with Patrick Cheney's characterization of Shakespeare as poet-playwright and connects what Shakespeare does in his non-dramatic poetry to what he does in the plays. For example, he comments that Shakespeare "possesses a remarkable capacity to unfold and then overturn a position, either in the couplet or in the next poem," continuing to observe that "this ability to imagine various perspectives" may have contributed to his success as a playwright (7–8).

Schoenfeldt's enthusiastic admiration of the poems coupled with his rigorous close readings evokes an equal enthusiasm in his readers. Commenting on how much of Shakespeare's dramatic language has passed into common usage, Schoenfeldt suggests that "our comparative ignorance of the poems can be an asset, allowing us to hear them with fresh ears" (4). This is a good argument for beginning a Shakespeare course with the less-familiar poetry, helping our students to hear Shakespeare for the first time again, before turning to the well-trod ground of the plays. While devoting whole chapters each to *Venus and Adonis* and *The Rape of Lucrece*, and a single chapter to both *A Lover's Complaint* and "The Phoenix and the Turtle," Schoenfeldt addresses the Sonnets in three separate chapters, focusing respectively on the questions of textual mysteries, the thematic representations of time, and the thematic representations of desire. The textual mysteries chapter discusses in detail the publication history of the Sonnets, considering the dedication and the debate about the dedicatee, the debates surrounding the ordering of the Sonnets, and the mysteries surrounding the identity of the young man and the Dark Lady. Concluding his chapter on the Sonnets' interest in time, Schoenfeldt summarizes aptly "the poems propose the partial compensations of poetry, progeny, and memory against time's relentless and pervasive devastation" (87). He redirects our attention away from *who* Shakespeare was writing to and toward *what* he wrote about: that is, "the matrix of complex and conflicted emotions aroused by another person" (87). This leads into his chapter focusing on the Sonnets' interest in desire, a chapter that is, in part, an answer to the question, "why should we still read the poems?" Schoenfeldt comments both that "much of our current iconography and vocabulary of erotic experience derives from the love poetry that emerged in Shakespeare's lifetime" and that we are better equipped to read and appreciate the poems now because "the specific subjects of Shakespeare's poetry—ideas of race and color, the relation between same-sex and opposite-sex desire, connections between sex and death, the sexual power of women—have recently become intellectually and socially central to contemporary life in a way that they were not before" (18).

His closing chapter considers the question of why we are still so curious about who wrote Shakespeare. Schoenfeldt provides a two-page digestion and dismissal of authorship "conspiracy theories" that some may find useful in the classroom once the 2011 Roland Emmerich film *Anonymous* hits theaters. The rest of the chapter considers the early modern "fantasy of Shakespearean authorship"—a desire to locate new poems by Shakespeare—and the history of the textual scholarship required to recognize the illegitimacy of various such claims.

Schoenfeldt concludes that, even if Shakespeare's poems had been his only surviving works, he "would still be one of the greatest English writers, a poet who disturbed and advanced every genre he deployed, and who helped create the vocabulary and syntax with which we will still talk about love" (143)). The book works to prove this through making clear and interesting discussions of the poems available to a general audience, and ultimately, such a volume would be incredibly useful in the classroom.

TEXTUALITIES

In this broadly-defined subject area, two new books deal with more traditional questions of textual history, and one takes up related questions about the intersections of text and genre. I will discuss the latter first. Catherine M. S. Alexander's edited collection, *The Cambridge Companion to Shakespeare's Last Plays,* consists of two halves, the first of which focuses on how we have thus far conceived of Shakespeare's late plays and how we need to think of them differently, particularly focusing on historicizing them in the less-familiar Jacobean period. The second half of the collection features essays that look at the afterlives of these late plays.

I focus here on two excellent representative essays from the volume. First, in "What Is a 'Late' Play?," Gordon McMullan proposes two "thought-experiments" in order to rectify what he sees as an incomplete approach to the plays. The first is to consider Shakespeare's *last* plays, rather than his late plays. This category, according to McMullan, includes the ten plays written between 1607 and 1613, as dated by the Oxford Edition.[1] These plays share, if not "the traditional centrality of the *father/daughter* binary," then certainly a "gender-unspecific *parent/child*" concern (15–16). Secondly, they all hinge on "the issue of *return,*" in terms of the romance genre's interest in journey and reunion; in the plays' "rehearsing, reshaping and reinventing past concerns in new contexts"; and in the sense of revision, as evident in the revised *Lear* and the reworking of the Theseus tale from *A Midsummer Night's Dream* in *The Two Noble Kinsmen* (16–17). McMullan's second "thought-experiment" requires imagining the last plays in relation to other plays performed by the King's Men during the years 1607–13, and by competing companies, attending to "the place of the play in the commercial structures of the theatre" (21). This is an effort to decentralize the author, and a well-argued one. McMullan is convinced that "treating Shakespeare as the interpretive hub of the plays in question" is "to miss a certain amount (or even a great deal) of the point, to take a view which is at best partial" (24).

Another outstanding contribution to the volume is Russ McDonald's essay, "'You speak a language that I understand not': Listening to the Last Plays," in which he describes and analyzes the distinctive style of the last plays, a poetic style he calls "audacious, irregular, ostentatious, playful, and difficult" (91). He catalogues and provides examples of an impressive number of stylistic characteristics, glossing them with such clarity that this essay will be extremely useful in teaching the last plays. Turning to analysis, McDonald argues that Shakespeare's altered poetic style in the last plays is indicative of "imaginative recuperation of the female and a concentration on the redemptive associations of femininity" (104) He claims that Shakespeare's investment in increased ornamentation marks a return to an older style "left behind" by Jacobean playwrights and denigrated by anti-theatrical and anti-Catholic sentiment, which viewed the ornamentations of elaborate rhetoric as of a piece with cosmetics, idolatry, and other offensive worldly interests. According to McDonald, this stylistic renaissance is "consistent with [Shakespeare's] passage from tragedy to romance"—whereas excessive ornamentation and rhetorical fireworks often indicated subterfuge and danger in the tragedies, in the last plays, they provide "consolation and creativity" (105–6). However, he notes that the verbal flourishes could also be "a stylistic manifestation of the ambivalence Shakespeare encourages his audience to consider and to relish" (109).

Other excellent essays include Suzanne Gossett's exploration of co-authorship in *The Two Noble Kinsmen* and *Henry VIII*, and Virginia Mason Vaughan's discussion of the afterlife of *The Tempest* in various literary appropriations and adaptations. On the whole, the volume brings together an impressive set of critical approaches to these last plays.

In the preface to *Shakespeare's Errant Texts*, Lene B. Petersen sets out to answer the increasingly complex question, "how indeed do we define what constitutes a 'Shakespearean text'?" (xi). She sets up her book as a response to Laurie Maguire's *Shakespearean Suspect Texts* (1996) and Brian Vickers' *Shakespeare, Co-Author* (2002),[2] seeing her major contribution as an attention to "the many formal and stylistic synergies, interchanges and reciprocities between oral/memorial and authorial composition," focusing on "the site of interaction between actorly and authorial input" (xi). To accomplish this goal, Petersen brings in theories borrowed from folklore studies and devises a "series of stylo-statistical tests" that are designed to help elucidate authorship. Petersen sees herself following both theatre historians in her attentiveness to the practices of performance in Renaissance theatre, and scholars like Tiffany Stern and Simon Palfrey in their assertion that the playtexts we have today are a "composite product." Thus, she seeks to combine an understanding and study of Renaissance theatre practices with a more textually-driven study of "the playwright's stylistic imprint" (xvi).

Petersen's book begins with a history of the Elizabethan and Jacobean theatre, focusing in particular on what she identifies as its "oral-memorial dimensions," and combining this with methodologies derived from folklore study. She then applies this knowledge, along with formalist analysis and "computer-facilitated quantitative linguistics" to *Romeo and Juliet* and

Hamlet. She argues that "memorial retention in, and oral reproduction from, the minds of actors are significant factors in the morphology of the early modern playtext" (xvii). She insists that, when studying omissions in early modern playtexts, we must attend to "the idiosyncrasy of the matter omitted," stating that idiosyncratic, stylistic complexity could only be ensured through "repeat performance *and* print distribution over time," which she calls "tradition" (140). In addition, as "oral delivery and memorial retention operated as key formative factors in early modern play composition," Peterson feels we must bring together folklore studies of "the transmission of folktales and traditional ballads" with our study of the textual history of Shakespeare's plays (141).

In the second half of her book, Petersen turns to careful analysis of authorial style and linguistics, locating authorial fingerprint and tracing its disappearance over time as the text was revised through collaborative interference. She argues that it is not merely the author who contributed "stylistic components" to the plays, but rather, that the plays were affected by "oral contamination" among a host of other "extra-authorial influences" (237). Petersen introduces and demonstrates particular "stylo-statistical methods" of analysis which are helpful in "question[ing] certain *a priori* assumptions of textual categorization," such as the three categories of good quarto, bad quarto, and folio texts. In particular, Petersen applies these methods and metrics to demonstrate that *Romeo and Juliet* is not immediately separable into these three categories (237).

Clearly one of Peterson's main goals and greatest contributions is to introduce methodologies that will be useful in future studies of the "multi-text plays". Furthermore, Petersen's insistence on attending to oral/memorial traditions through lenses borrowed from folklore studies will certainly make an impression upon the field. It seems that the world of textual scholarship will soon have to answer to her call to action and "learn to map" tradition in order to understand its stylistic impact on developing play texts (241).

Gabriel Egan's *The Struggle for Shakespeare's Text: Twentieth-Century Editorial Theory and Practice* provides a history of the twentieth-century struggle to make sense of the many early editions of Shakespeare's works. Egan's history is not impartial; he argues "that authors are the most dominant agents in the constellation of forces (personal, cultural, political, and institutional) that come together in the publication of books" (3). Egan proposes to offer a different sort of history of editorial controversies by focusing on "how they seemed to the people who were making the arguments at the time" (9). He feels this kind of historically-located perspective, one that does not attempt "to discern [the theorists'] unconscious motives" will provide a clearer explanation of the controversy (10). Egan expresses frustration with scholarship that offers psychological interpretation of various editorial practices and promises that, while "a certain kind of historiography would read arguments about Shakespeare editions as symptomatic of other, wider conflicts ... this book pays its subjects the compliment of taking them at their word and it deals with their overt differences of opinion without trying to discern their unconscious motives" (9–10).

The body of the book consists of a chronological presentation of the rise of New Bibliography and the conflicts it encountered. Egan separates from this narrative a brief essay on "the rise and fall of the theory of memorial reconstruction," a theory that he argues "is not integral to the New Bibliography" (11). The book also contains three appendices. The first, "How early modern books were made: a brief guide" is exactly what it claims to be. The second provides a table of editions of Shakespeare prior to the 1623 First Folio, listing also who produced the editions and whether or not there were subsequent editions. The third, "Editorial principles of the major twentieth-century Shakespeare editions," lists "significant Shakespeare editions since 1899 with descriptions of their editorial approaches, cross-referenced to discussions of the editions or their ideas in the main body of [the] book" (240). Egan includes in this appendix only those editions that "stimulated debate about what editors should do or that helped establish Shakespeare's texts" (241–71).[3] Each edition is accompanied by an explanation of the editorial theory it deployed, and this contextual and comparative information is perhaps one of the book's most useful contributions as it provides a clear introduction to understanding how editorial theory has impacted our study of Shakespeare directly through the texts we choose to read and teach. Interestingly, Egan observes in this appendix "how seldom people at the heart of the [development of theory] were engaged" in the "practice" of editing Shakespeare's texts (240).

A brief conclusion examines the current state of editorial theory and practice, focusing on the influence of New Textualism, with its insistence that each edition "has its own integrity," and how editorial theory might respond to Lukas Erne's argument that Shakespeare was a professional writer, "concerned with his growing readership" as well as a man of the theatre (207–10). Egan's observations on editorial theory's need to respond to Erne are quite compelling and point the way for continuing advancements in editorial theory and practice. According to Egan, Erne's focus on Shakespeare as a man of the page provides a valuable corrective to the "stage-centered 'new' New Bibliography" (221). Egan also calls for editorial theory to turn more fully to the pressing concerns of co-authorship.

Shakespeare in Performance

Several books in the last year have turned to the well-trod and extremely rich area of performance studies. In *Shakespeare and the Problem of Adaptation*, Margaret Jane Kidnie argues "that a play, for all that it carries the rhetorical and ideological force of an enduring stability, is not an object at all, but rather a dynamic *process* that evolves over time in response to the needs and sensibilities of its users" (2). Kidnie asks what differentiates adaptation from production and is particularly interested in the way critics insist on being able to distinguish between what is and what is not Shakespearean adaptation. Kidnie's book "challenges sometimes unspoken assumptions that adaptation is synonymous with performance, or that performance is somehow more vulnerable than text to adaptive practices" (5-6). One of her chief contributions is the conception of "work as process," something which "continually takes shape as a *consequence* of production," and which Kidnie argues will make available "alternative critical practices" that consider the "politics of reception" (6–7).

In the first chapter, Kidnie expands on her definition of adaptation. Importantly, she recognizes that drama will always be a troubling genre because of the equal importance of text and performance. Like Petersen, she works to bring together histories of performance and text in order to understand the full richness of a work. She points to all the problems critics encounter when they operate under the assumption that there is a single correct "text" and offers the following important corrective: "textual production is subject to its own interventionist conventions" (23). So, the authenticity or legitimacy of a work is "continually produced among communities of users through assertion and dissension" (31). These "communities of users" are comprised of readers and spectators.

In the second chapter, she examines two Royal Shakespeare Company productions—the Warchus *Hamlet* (1997) and Doran *All's Well that Ends Well* (2003)—pointing out the "potentially temporary and limited currency" of any production that we call authentically Shakespearean today (9). The third chapter turns to the politics of Shakespearean adaptation, especially in terms of the "conception of the work" and the difficulties of sustaining a permeable category of "the work". Kidnie's third chapter, about "the politics of production," looks at "cases that openly declare an adaptive distance from Shakespeare's works," stating that they "disrupt Shakespearean production by making the works seem at once recognizable and strange" (65). Here, she focuses on Djanet Sears' *Harlem Duet* and Robert Lepage's *Elsinore*. She claims that, despite their outspoken claims of difference, these adaptations must and do "enter into a sustained interaction with the dominant theatrical-critical legacies of *Othello* and *Hamlet*" and that their "disruptive potential" arises from "the way they assert yet at the same time display as flexible and porous the boundaries separating a work from its adaptation" (70). In Chapter Four, Kidnie turns to Shakespeare on television, focusing on the BBC's *ShakespeareRe-Told* series (2005). This chapter looks at how new technologies can shape our ability to recognize Shakespeare's work. This seems a timely concern to pursue, as online Shakespeare archives such as those discussed below, continue to proliferate.

In the introduction to their collection of essays, *Shakespeare and Character: Theory, History, Performance, and Theatrical Persons*, editors Paul Yachnin and Jessica Slights argue "character has made a comeback," suggesting that for characters such as Desdemona, Hamlet, and Shylock, character-driven criticism is relevant, even essential (1). Yachnin and Slights claim that it is now time to return to this mode of scholarship because it is both "the organizing formal feature of Shakespeare's drama" and "the heart of audience engagement with his plays" (12). While this volume may at first seem misplaced among other scholarly contributions to the field of performance studies, Yachnin and Slights assert that "much greater attention needs to be paid to the contributions made by the theater and the performance environment as we attempt to re-articulate a notion of character in the twenty-first century" (3). Thus, the book deals at least in part with issues of performance.

Yachnin and Slights provide a history of character criticism. Interest in Shakespeare's characters migrated away from the concept that they "were best understood as mimetic representations of imagined persons," to the idea that we should "[explore] human nature through an analysis of Shakespearean character" (2). This approach reached its apex in A. C. Bradley's *Shakespearean Tragedy* (1904), which Yachnin and Slights call "the grand finale of nineteenth-century Shakespeare criticism" and "the definitive synthesis of this long tradition of celebrating Shakespeare's ability to portray psychological depth" (2). Character criticism was eclipsed by the critical movements of the twentieth century, including New Criticism, New Historicism, and Poststructuralism. But Yachnin and Slights feel that it is time to return to this mode of scholarship, based on their assertion "that character is the organizing principle of Shakespeare's plays ... [and] character is the principal bridge over which the emotional, cognitive, and political transactions of theater and literature pass between actors and playgoers or between written texts and readers" (7).

The essays in the book are divided into four separate sections. The first examines the basic questions of character criticism, and the second considers the Renaissance approach to Shakespeare's characters. The third looks at character in terms of performance, and the fourth examines specific characters from *Timon of Athens*, *King John*, and *King Lear*. The many essays provide a rich assortment of approaches to character criticism. Among the most intriguing are those by Michael Bristol, James Berg, and Leanore Lieblein.

Bristol's essay, "Confusing Shakespeare's Characters with Real People: Reflections on Reading in Four Questions," suggests that it is alright to think of Shakespeare's characters as real people. Considering Lear, Rosalind, and Viola, Bristol finds that Shakespeare's concept of human nature is one of "vulnerability to harm." He continues to argue that "authority" is more important to Shakespearean character than interiority, and "personhood" is comprised of "singularity and aloneness" in Shakespeare's plays (23–4, 29–30). He closes by reflecting on the fact that "character" as a verb means "to write," as well as to construe the contents of another's character, and that Shakespeare's characters spend a great deal of time attempting to understand one another, which is an essential aspect of human experience. In fact, as he points out, "[w]e learn about our own complex human nature by thinking about and coming to respect Shakespeare's characters" (38). In his chapter on "The Properties of Character in *King Lear*," James Berg takes a material history approach to Shakespeare's character, arguing that in *King Lear*, "all character *is* property, where property represents not just what persons seem to own, but the *things* that properly belong *with* them. And all property is character, symbolic *reading material*" (99). Berg states, "feebleness at the core of formidable persons is ... the play's central theme" (99), as all persons can be reduced to what they possess.

Leanore Lieblein's essay, "Embodied Intersubjectivity and the Creation of Early Modern Character," returns to the issue of performance, considering Shakespearean character as created out of an interaction between the actor's "own embodied subjectivity" and his experience of "the emotions and thoughts" of the "person personated" (127). Referencing Thomas Heywood's *Apology for Actors* (1612), Lieblein argues that "[r]hetorical theory of the early modern period suggests that the process of personation is understood as an intersubjective relationship between embodied subjects in what today are phenomenological terms" (127). Whether or not one agrees that character needs to "make a comeback," as Yachnin and Slights suggest, the essays in this volume provide many new and thought-provoking readings of Shakespeare's most-loved and most complex characters.

Like Lieblein, Erica Sheen looks to seventeenth-century rhetorical and theatrical theory. Sheen's *Shakespeare and the Institution of Theatre: The Best in this Kind* sets out to rectify what she sees as a critical failure to properly theorize the theatre as an institution and apply that theory to further readings of the plays. Sheen feels that the existing American theories of the institution of theater in the Renaissance are "[correlated with] the contemporary transition from Cold War to global market (and back again)" and that "the way this correlation is back-projected onto early modern and Shakespearean theatre ... might be doing both Shakespeare and contemporary Shakespeare studies a disservice" (11).[4] She turns instead to Anthony Giddens' "theory of structuration ... in an effort to review and renew the application of the concept of the institution to the study of Shakespearean theatre" (11). This theory emphasizes "agency rather than discourse," a mode that Sheen considers especially relevant to a study of Renaissance theatre, particularly because "it encourages us to recognize institutionalization as fundamentally a creative process" (12). Central to the book is what Sheen identifies as "the notion of a theatrical agency free from political accountability" (14).

Sheen applies her theory of the institution of theatre to readings of nine different plays, spanning from *The Taming of the Shrew* to *The Tempest*. She considers the transition in the 1590s away from theatrical dependence upon patronage to what she calls "financially induced autonomy," which can be read in the plays: "Shakespeare's plays in the 1590s chart the transformation of prestigious but unsupportive patronage into profitable popularity" (13–14). For example, Sheen compares the relative positions of the mechanicals in *A Midsummer Night's Dream* (1595–96), performing a specially prepared play expressly for a court occasion; and the players of *Hamlet* (1600), who belong to an autonomous group that arrives at the court by coincidence and remains "resolutely aloof" from the court politics that motivate Hamlet's request for their specific performance.

Sheen notes that, while Theseus's position as evaluator of the mechanicals' performative efforts may suggest that their success rests entirely on his patronage, the play undermines that notion. Not only does it offer clear statements of each player's individual motivation, but also, it contrasts Theseus's "obviously limited insight into the action" with Hippolyta's—who Sheen likens to the intelligent spectator, Elizabeth (99). Turning to *Hamlet*, Sheen argues that the leading player's speech in 2.2 demonstrates "that Shakespeare saw literary readership as a structural element ... of theatre at its best" (105). Sheen notes Hamlet's excellent memory of the speech, despite having never seen the play performed: "In strong contrast to Theseus, the skills he brings to the selection of this speech for performance, particularly in his emphasis on style, are those of a reader, not a prince or courtier" (105). She also points out the "chain of spectatorships" in this scene: Hecuba looking at Priam, the Player "looking" at them and narrating the scene, Hamlet watching the player, and us watching Hamlet. These layers only further enrich a much more complex narrative of "the exchange that takes place between the disparate positions of interest mapped out by this collective public gaze" (107). Moving then to a sharp reading of Elizabeth I's 1601 claim "I am Richard II. Know ye not that?", Sheen suggests that the queen "articulates the iterative nature of a habit of spectatorship now naturalized as a general form of social competence" and that "by 1601, [Shakespearean theatre] was above political accountability" (109).

As she explores various plays, Sheen considers the playhouse as property and the changing needs and demands of the theatrical traditions, spanning from the early 1590s when Shakespeare operated quasi-independently in the London theatre scene; to the mid-1590s, when the Chamberlain's Men had residence at the Theatre; to the late 1590s, as they moved to the Globe and began to anticipate Elizabeth's death; to the early 1600s, as Shakespeare responded to the altered expectations of a new monarch and the potential for change that the Blackfriars offered.

John Astington's *Actors and Acting in Shakespeare's Time: The Art of Stage Playing,* provides a very helpful and insightful history of the profession of actors and the habits of acting during the Renaissance. He identifies "the lack [of acting schools] in England before the later seventeenth century" and "the player's role as an instructor" as two of his major concentrations (1). He begins with the assertion that the theatre was a rapidly growing and changing profession in Renaissance England. Astington estimates there were 150–200 actors in London in the early seventeenth century. In addition to these professional actors, he also mentions "a vigorous amateur theatre" both in schools and universities and among communities as varied as "apprentices, sailors, lawyers, and aristocratic families" (8–9).

Astington's first chapter, about the vocabulary of the theatre in Renaissance England, is perhaps the most immediately compelling. First, he examines the "dismissive" language used by some of Shakespeare's characters to describe acting, such as "counterfeit," "in jest," and "shadows." He looks in particular at Theseus in *A Midsummer Night's Dream* and Hamlet speaking to the players. Using this evidence to contrive a historical vocabulary of acting, Astington argues that early modern performance focused on "action" and "accent" as the "central terms in whatever we might tentatively call a theory of acting in the

Shakespearean period" (20). These terms, Astington claims, are a Renaissance revision of Quintilian's and Cicero's emphasis on voice, facial expression, and animation (or *vox*, *vultus*, and *vita*) (23). He also considers the Renaissance emphasis on the term "presentation" rather than "representation" to refer to stage performances, commenting that it both evokes a sense of "the current living moment," and contrasts the artifice and "rigidity" that Shakespeare mocks in the mechanicals' presentation of Wall and Moon (30).

In later chapters, Astington addresses the relationship between theatre and education and the professional lives of actors. The third chapter provides a fascinating history of how professional actors made use of the traditions of apprenticeship: actors like John Hemminges would be registered apprentices and eventually practitioners in "legitimate" trades, such as grocery. These actors would use the apprenticeship to become official "citizens of London [and] freemen of London companies" (77–8). They would go on to take on apprentices of their own, nominally as apprentice grocers, but would actually train the boys in the ways of the theatre.

At the end of the book, Astington provides an amazing appendix. Totaling 36 pages, this lists principal actors known to have performed in 1558–1660 and includes a brief paragraph biography of each. On the whole, Astington's book provides a helpful history and would be a good intro text to assign chapters from for classes on early modern drama.

Lina Perkins Wilder's *Shakespeare's Memory Theatre: Recollection, Properties, and Character* traces the way that "the materials of theatre are, for Shakespeare, the materials of memory" (1). Wilder argues that props, the physical space of the theatre, and the actors "become the materials for a mnemonic dramaturgy that shapes language, character, and plot" (1–2). Props and actors appeared in multiple productions, and thus the memory of other performances and other stages that existed outside the experience of a single performance was important—a memory the viewer brought to each play he witnessed, and one frequently invoked by the actors and characters onstage. Wilder claims that "a means of staging something like subjectivity begins to develop in the disjunction between the audience's recollection of the fictional and theatrical 'past' surrounding the play and the character's" (12). In addition, Wilder theorizes the power of "absent objects" to evoke memories, such as Lady Macbeth's child and Prospero's books. Ultimately, she argues, "Shakespeare's memory theatre consists of props that are not there …, contained physical spaces located elsewhere than on the stage …, and props whose physical presence evokes physical absence" (2).[5]

Wilder considers the gendered aspects of memory, pointing out the distinction between the rhetorical understanding of recollection and memory. The former was characterized as "wandering" and thus, feminine, and must be "controlled through skills gendered male" (4). She sees these competing notions of male-gendered, orderly memory or recounting, and female-gendered, disorderly recollection, reflected in Shakespeare's plays: "As male bodily discipline breaks down in Shakespeare's memory theatre, accurate and orderly reporting of offstage events gives way to the rhetorical circulation of *dilatio*. The result is that in Shakespeare's plays women teach educated men how to think" (8).[6]

The first chapter provides a history of the memory arts and their intersection and conflict with theatrical memory practices in early modern England, looking in particular at embodied memory and uses of the body and physical space in creating and maintaining memory. Wilder then turns to readings of seven plays chosen because each "evokes a past vexed by war, by vendetta, or by usurpation, a past which makes socially stabilizing memory difficult to maintain" (19). The chapters include readings of Romeo's remembrance of the Apothecary's shop and the Nurse's remembrance of weaning Juliet; Falstaff as a memory figure in the *Henry IV* plays and *Henry V*; Desdemona and Lady Macbeth as figures of false or fractured memory; and the "absent mnemonics made present" in *The Tempest*'s daughters and wives and Prospero's cell and books. Altogether, these readings:

> [explore] a tragic mode informed by history and particularly by the role of women and other outsiders from history. ... Constructing a past from theatrical materials, such figures align themselves with the social and professional world of the theatre as much as, if not more than, with the fictional world of the plays in which they take shape. (19)

Perhaps the book's most promising chapter, Wilder's treatment of the *Henry IV* plays and *Henry V* identifies both Falstaff and the Hostess as figures of memory. In particular, the audience is challenged by Falstaff's conspicuous absence to attempt an impossible act of forgetting; one of many that the three plays demand. Wilder argues that the audience must "put aside" many "inconvenient memor[ies]" of Richard II's death and Henry IV's path to the throne and, most importantly for this argument, Falstaff himself, "with whom the future Henry V engages in conflict over the contents of the audience's memories" (39).

In her conclusion, Wilder notes, "staged remembering makes social business even of the supposed interior of the mind" (204). On the whole,

Wilder's book is wildly provocative and rigorously documented. Dealing in particular with rhetorical treatises and an intimate understanding of stagecraft and the materials of theatre, she offers many suggestive new readings of the plays, shedding new light on such old issues as Lady Macbeth's absent children and Prospero's books. Thickly written and densely theoretical, it can be a tough, but certainly rewarding, read.

GLOBAL SHAKESPEARES

It is only in recent years that American scholars have begun to pursue questions of Global Shakespeares, both in terms of how Shakespeare and his contemporaries conceived of the globe, and of how the globe has conceived of Shakespeare over the last four hundred years. Taking up the former vein of inquiry, Carole Levin and John Watkins undertake one of Hercules' endeavors in *Shakespeare's Foreign Worlds*: to undo the disciplinary boundaries that have kept historians and literary scholars from fully acknowledging their similarities. They begin by asking, "what would happen if we threw out the pretension of disciplinary divergence altogether and began to question the Elizabethan past, not as professors of literature and history but simply as early modernists?" (3). They lament that, while conferences and co-edited volumes propose to bring together historians and literary scholars, there is still a great deal of "institutional pretense" about the separation between the two approaches, and one sign of that is the lack of co-authored monographs. This book is their response.

While the question of disciplinary boundaries is interesting, Levin and Watkins' greatest accomplishment is their choice to apply this endeavor to an examination of Elizabethan nationhood. Combining Levin's interest in "Shakespeare's responses to marginalized sectors of English society" with Watkins's interest in "the context of broadly European historical movements," the volume argues that "the emergence of the 'foreign' as a portable category that might be applied both to 'strangers' from other countries and to native-born English men and women, such as religious dissidents, who resisted conformity to an increasingly narrow sense of English identity" is "an ideological development fundamental to the conception of English nationhood" (8). Focusing on the 1590s—prior to major colonial expansion and yet concurrent with great population growth and internal, European migration—the authors argue, "Shakespeare's England comes about by reducing an almost infinite number of groups and individuals to the general category of the foreign" (14).

According to Watkins and Levin, Englishness was defined by "coherence" within England, and "distinctiveness" from other European cultures. Each of these descriptors is, of course, problematic, and it is in these contradictions and problems that Shakespeare creates his richest drama. The authors chose to write about *1 Henry VI*, *The Merchant of Venice*, and *The Taming of the Shrew*, claiming that "Shakespeare's evocation of foreign and domestic settings ... creates the sense of an English identity continually threatened by a nebulous foreignness" (14). The book is structured in three sets of paired chapters, each set addressing one of the three plays. Each set of chapters is preceded by a brief introduction, and each set includes one chapter by Levin and one by Watkins. They collectively see *1 Henry VI* as Shakespeare's "earliest and most complex response to the Reformation's impact on English constructions of the foreign" (23). They both take up Joan of Arc in the play, locating gender "as a particularly charged site in the emergence of the foreign as a category of opprobrium defining the English nation" (23). Turning to *The Merchant of Venice*, Levin examines Jessica's conversion in the context of similar historical conversions, arguing that it "expose[s] the persistence of a fundamental Jewishness that could never fully assimilate to English society" (83). Watkins reads the play's fixation on the deteriorating economic state of Venice as reflective of English anxiety about similar economic collapse. And in the last paired chapter set, the authors consider *The Taming of the Shrew*, looking at how "new ways of thinking ... might be domesticated as fundamentally English, repudiated as alien and subversive, or occupy a controversial position somewhere in between" (141). Considering the effects of Reformation theology and Italian humanism, each author argues that the play raises interesting questions about these schools of thought through Katherine: "Shakespeare seems to have been less interested in theological and philosophical differences than in the effect that humanist and Protestant pedagogical traditions might have on the place of women within the home and, by implication, on English society at large" (142).

Levin and Watkins are right to remind us that "relatively few of Shakespeare's characters are English" (8). Their choice to focus on Shakespeare, "a notoriously unreliable historian," pays off well (6). Their readings of Shakespeare's foreign characters inject new life into the discourse of nationhood in scholarship, and their concerted effort to enter this discourse in a cross-disciplinary way is particularly refreshing.

While Levin and Watkins' text takes up Global Shakespeare on Shakespeare's own terms, Alexander Huang, Dennis Kennedy and Yong Li Lan, and Poonam Trivedi and Minami Ryuta pursue Global Shakespeare on the globe's terms. Alexander Huang's *Chinese Shakespeares: Two Centuries of Cultural Exchange* hinges on plurals. It is about Chinese Shakespeare*s*, and not Shakespeare in China; performance idiom*s*, rather than a single tradition; and localit*ies*, rather than a single site or cultural identity. The critical history offered in this book is incredibly rich. Huang begins by drawing a compelling connection between the narratives of Shakespeare's supremacy and those about "China's rise in global stature," pointing out that "few are aware that for almost two centuries, East Asian writers, film-makers, and theater directors have also engaged Shakespeare in their works in a wide range of contexts" (2). Huang argues that, in our cultural moment, we *ought* to be learning more about China, in all contexts (25). The book includes a select chronology, a ten-page timeline that runs from 1596 to 2008 and lists events in three parallel columns: historical events, worldwide Shakespeares, and Chinese Shakespeares (listing significant performances and publications). This chronology is helpful for those who know less about China and its history, for putting the material of the book in the context of more familiar Shakespeare chronologies, and for demonstrating the growth over time of Chinese interaction with Shakespeare's canon.

Huang makes a clear distinction between Shakespeare in China and Chinese Shakespeares. The former "obscures the dialectics of exchange between different cultures and implies the imposition of one culture upon the other, investing certain texts with a transhistorical status," whereas the latter suggests that "encounters of Shakespeare and China [are] a transformative process" in which both Shakespeare and China are effected (39). He identifies "three coexisting modes to engage ideas of China and Shakespeare." The first is "a trend to universalize rather than localize Shakespeare" by performing classically Anglo versions of the plays; the second "localize(s) the plot, setting, and meanings of a play"; and the third "has prompted artists to truncate and rewrite Shakespeare's plays so as to relate them to images of China" (16–17).

In order to analyze these traditions, Huang argues that we need an "in-depth critical history" of the local performances, and that is precisely what his book provides. He acknowledges the difficulty of "the ephemeral nature of live theater" and seeks to rectify this problem by offering thorough recounting specific performances (35). Structured as a series of case studies, the book first provides necessary history and theory background, spanning a period from 1839 until the present day, and then moves chronologically through various stages of Chinese engagement with Shakespeare, in each instance focusing on a handful of significant performances and films. Huang points out that, while Shakespeare was seen as a symbol of the West, and thus "both reviled and admired," Chinese approaches to Shakespeare are not burdened with the same post-colonial concerns as those of other nations. In this respect, his engagement with these performances is rich and varied, rather than focused on issues of colonial identity (26–7). The book endeavors to provide the critical engagement with these productions that has been lacking from prior discussion, which tends toward the descriptive, rather than analytical. This "overflow of 'reports' without theoretical reflection," Huang argues, is symptomatic of a failure to note the significance of performance and adaptation as critical engagements with a text (36). Overall, the book asks and seeks to answer the following questions: "what does 'Shakespeare' *do* in Chinese literary and performance culture?" and "how do imaginations about China function in Shakespearean performances, and what ideological work do they undertake?" (3). Of his book, Huang promises that "Much of this work will undermine the fantasies of cultural exclusivity of both 'Shakespeare' and 'China,' attending to the fact that even though every reading is a rewriting, more rewritings of a canonical text do not always translate into more radical rethinking of normative assumptions" (5).

In one chapter, Huang takes on silent film and early theater and examines how Shakespeare was adapted and reinvented during the 1930s and '40s through performances that emphasized "cosmopolitanism" and "the new woman." He discusses a silent-film version of *The Merchant of Venice* entitled *The Woman Lawyer* (1927), which highlighted "female agency throughout the story" (114–15). In the epilogue, he takes up two recent Chinese Shakespeares—the film adaptation of *Hamlet* directed by Feng Xiaogang, *The Banquet* (2006), and a stage production of *Richard III* (2001). In his analysis of the former, Huang points out the ways in which reception fixated largely on debating whether the film was Shakespeare or Chinese cinema, demonstrating at the close of the study what he stated at the start: that we must rethink our approaches to understanding and analyzing cross-cultural adaptations, and that we indeed need a capacious theory of intercultural engagement. Huang's extensive accounts and critiques of significant productions should provide ample basis for such a theory's development. Clearly, this has been recognized by the academy at large, as *Chinese Shakespeares* won the 2010 Aldo and Jeanne Scaglione Prize for Comparative Literary Studies.

Dennis Kennedy and Yong Li Lan's *Shakespeare in Asia* takes on a much broader geographical area than Huang's exploration of specifically Chinese Shakespeares. As an edited volume rather than a monograph, it also has less coherence, though this is not necessarily a weakness of the collection. Like Huang, Kennedy and Yong cite Patrice Pavis's 1991 claim that "it was too early to expect a formulated theory of intercultural performance." They respond that:

> the real difficulty in theorizing interculturalism lies in trying to identify what happens to spectators ... [as] inherent in the intercultural engagement of Shakespeare is the divergence of perspectives, defined by the position of the spectator within a community whose boundaries are redrawn and renegotiated as part of the heuristic of the performance ... Yet discursive terms that make productive use of a culturally relative position, or of the plurality and variability of reception, remain largely underdeveloped, in comparison to the settled critical idiom of objectivity which tends to totalize a single cultural standpoint. (12)

This issue grows more complex when Kennedy and Yong insist that "Asian intercultural performance has developed self-reflexive and self-conscious modes of treating its Asian-ness and its plurality of performance cultures, and demands a corresponding level of self-reflexivity from any spectator" (14).

In their volume, editors Kennedy and Yong look at "contemporary Shakespeare performance in Asia from theoretical and historical perspectives" in the last two decades, acknowledging that there is no "unified approach to Shakespeare" in Asia, nor does Asia "comprise a single market of competing regions" (1, 6). They note the expansion in Asian Shakespeare production and, resisting an Anglo-centric approach to the Shakespearean text, they argue, "whatever the linguistic losses that accompany translation, for theatre and film there have been significant gains" (6).

They define three ways in which Asian cultures came into contact with Shakespeare: "nationalist appropriation, colonial instigation, and intercultural revision" (7). Using Japan as an example of nationalist appropriation, Kennedy and Yong comment that Shakespeare's "introduction was part of the reform movement, allied with industry and open markets as an exemplary 'contemporary' writer, driven by the national project of modernization" (8). As an example of colonial instigation, they turn to India, where Shakespeare was "part of a general project of edification" and stood to symbolize "a conduit of the stability of the conqueror's mental landscape" (9). Intercultural revision, they claim, is "the most innovative type of contemporary Asian Shakespeare" and it "attempts to move away from political applications into more self-consciously aesthetic realms." This process of interaction leads to the creation of "a new text" (10). Kennedy and Yong comment that, as Asian performance styles privilege the visual and embodied performance over the verbal text, "Asian Shakespeare performances are collectively distinguished from Shakespeare produced in other areas of the world by the force of their visual, aural, and corporeal strategies for adapting the play, a shift of emphasis that gives Shakespeare an unfamiliar, powerful, but problematic, sensory force" (17).

The volume is divided into four parts. The first, called "Voice and Body," contains three chapters that engage with "the radical shift in meaning and effect that is brought by the self-conscious application of alien methods to Shakespeare or, ..., the application of alien Shakespeare to indigenous methods" (26). One of the strengths of the volume is that it includes several essays by people closely associated with or involved in performance, such as Fei Chunfang and Sun Huizhu, whose essay deals with adapting *Othello* into Beijing Opera. The second part of the volume, "Shakespeare in Asian Popular Cultures," looks at popular modes of performance and contemporary Asian audiences, examining their "significance ... within the arc of development of their particular social changes and performance movements" (71–2). The third section, "Transacting Cultures," proves how rich the field of Shakespeare in Asia/Asian Shakespeares is for criticism. Focusing on the suggestion that "the use of Shakespeare in Asian performance is founded on the desire to renegotiate the notion of cultural identity," the four essays in this section constitute two pairs of essays on the same production (153). The first two look at Wu Hsing-Kuo's *King Lear* and the second two at Ong Keng Sen's *Desdemona*. In each case, the two essays approach the production from different critical angles and come to very different conclusions. Clearly, there is much to mine here. The fourth and final section of essays, "Intercultural politics," takes up "the terms on which Shakespeare and Asian performance are brought together in contemporary productions." The essays ask how Shakespeare and Asian theatre "are mutually useful to each other," examining the "ideological, theoretical, and political implications" of combining the two traditions (217).

Poonam Trivedi and Minami Ryuta's edited collection, *Re-Playing Shakespeare in Asia*, is the most expansive of the three engagements with Asian Shakespeare(s). Trivedi and Ryuta state that the volume's sixteen essays discuss "over forty productions of thirteen plays in eight Asian countries" (3). Like Kennedy and Yong, they make no claim to universal understanding, but rather to unveiling the tip of the iceberg. Like Huang and Kennedy and Yong, they note that our present time is an era of what they call "Asian resurgence," and thus it is imperative that we direct our scholarly attention eastward, claiming "the recognition, circulation, and approbation of Asian versions of Shakespeare in the last few decades mark a shift in intellectual property relations" (2).

Also like Huang and Kennedy and Yong, they cite Patrice Pavis's call for a theory of intercultural performance, and seek to explain the reasons why we need one and why we don't yet have one:

> discussion of intercultural Shakespeare remains caught in a cleft stick of authenticity versus difference, of the universal versus the hybrid, and of the global versus the local, resulting in an unresolved tension between these polarities … Fully intercultural, that is, non-European, Shakespeare is routinely put down as impenetrably different and foreign and is thus rejected as "inauthentic" by the metropolis. … The purpose of this book is precisely to expose and revoke this persisting "orientalism" and to show the multiple ways in which Shakespeare "fits" in Asia, and how versions of Asian Shakespeare "make fit" beyond the confines of Asia. (5–6)

Trivedi and Ryuta agree with Kennedy and Yong about the richness translation can impart to a text: "foreign Shakespeare is certainly not a Shakespeare emptied of words. On the contrary, it is one with added languages and additional resonances, both linguistic and performative … Translation, which is linguistic, performative, and cultural, instead expands, not narrows, the range of reference for Shakespeare" (15). And this stand can be likened to Huang's claim that Shakespeare is changed by Chinese interaction with it.

The book is divided into four sections, dealing with intercultural, textual, post-colonial, and gender/genre issues. The first section takes on "larger issues of intercultural Shakespeare and its development in Asia" (6). These four essays provide a very good opening to the collection, beginning with James Brandon's broad introduction to Shakespeare in Asia. The other three essays consider Ariane Mnouchkine's early 1980s series of Asian-inflected Western stagings of plays, Indian Shakespeare, and Japanese theatre. The second set of essays considers the "place of the text in performed Shakespeares, the ways his words are to be conjoined to and embodied with 'other' theatrical languages, and the nature and extent of the malleability of texts required" (8). The most intriguing in this section is Li Ruru's essay on "Six People in Search of 'To be or not to be …'." Li examines six Chinese productions of *Hamlet* for how the famous soliloquy is translated. Her analysis is motivated by the fact that there is no direct Chinese translation for "to be," and thus, "all the Chinese translations have to make it more concrete and definite, and consequently limit the imagination or connection that readers or audiences might have when they read/listen to the original English" (119). Some sample translations include "to live, or not to live" and "existence, or destruction." Other essays in this section of the book look at Japanese pop Shakespeare and Bengali Shakespeare. The group of essays focusing on post-colonial questions offers a much-needed re-evaluation of knee-jerk understandings of post-colonial Asia. Trivedi and Ryuta state a desire to focus on "the place of smaller imperialisms and occupations in Asia." Thus, Part III examines how Shakespeare "was twinned with imperial authority either in an assertion or in a resistance to it" in the Philippines, Malaysia, Korea, Taiwan, and localized Chinese productions (in an essay by Alexander Huang) (10). The final section of the book looks at how intercultural performances effect genre and gender transformations, examining traditions of dance in particular.

While Trivedi and Ryuta express distress that "critical discourse does not seem to have the space for the new ways of seeing, hearing, and knowing that Asian Shakespeares have come to demand," the publication evidence seems to oppose this (15). With two edited collections and a monograph all centered on Asian Shakespeares just out in the last year, we may safely say that critical discourse is turning its eye and its mind Eastward.

DIGITAL RESOURCES

As scholarly interest in global Shakespeare expands, online digital archives are becoming increasingly useful and important. Considering this, I will review four major websites—archives and research tools that are pedagogically useful and ever-expanding. While the websites discussed below are not necessarily new in the last year, because their content is consistently growing and changing, they remain fairly current.

The *Internet Shakespeare Editions Incorporated* is a non-profit organization affiliated with the University of Victoria. The website contains three major categories of content: online editions of Shakespeare's works and contemporary or source texts; relevant historical materials in a section called "Shakespeare's Life and Times," and a "Theater" section that includes reviews and records of hundreds of performances and films. In the website's "Annex" section, one can find many online editions of Shakespeare's plays and poetry, as well as plays attributed to Shakespeare in the Third Folio, and other related works, such as Lyly's *Euphues* and Lodge's *Rosalind*. The texts are very useful, but most have not yet been peer-reviewed or annotated. Of the Shakespeare texts, only the Sonnets have online annotations. Once the annotations are available for all the plays, the site will become a good supplement or alternative to traditional classroom texts. Perhaps its greatest utility is its presentation of so much related source material. In addition, many plays are accompanied by helpful introductory essays. Again, once this is uniform throughout the site's holdings, it will be an incredibly rich resource.

In the "Shakespeare's Life and Times" section of the website, there is a wealth of informative pages covering Shakespeare's biography; early modern society; the history of England (with specific pages on Henry VIII, Elizabeth I, and James I); various ideas about education, gender, and family; a brief history of drama and a discussion of other early modern literature; a whole book on the stage; and a helpful reference section with a chronology.[7] The site claims to have "over 1,000 pages" in this section of its content. There are even embedded audio files of songs from some of the plays.

In the "Performance" section of the site, there is a single video file of King John's death scene from an 1899 performance starring Herbert Beerbohm Tree as King John. There are almost seventy audio clips of various scenes and speeches and songs, twelve interviews with directors and actors, over 2,500 production stills, almost 500 reviews, and much more. All of these are searchable by play. The performance section also links to *The ISE Performance Chronicle*, a journal "devoted to reviews of contemporary Shakespeare theater."[8]

There is a wealth of information here, and quite a lot of time could be spent digging around in it. The historical background materials available in the "Life and Times" segment could make useful supplementary reading in an undergraduate survey course, while the online source texts could be most helpful in graduate seminars or independent research. Once the plays themselves are fully annotated, this site will surely rise to greater prominence in the classroom.

The Canadian Adaptations of Shakespeare Project (CASP) boasts a more finessed and more immediately intuitive and useable website. The CASP is housed out of the University of Guelph's School of English and Theatre Studies and in 2004, director Daniel Fischlin launched the website. In 2007, Version 2 was released. On the website's homepage, the project claims to be "the first research project of its kind devoted to the systematic exploration and documentation of the ways in which Shakespeare has been adapted into a national, multicultural theatrical practice." The Version 2 release "more than double[d] the content."[9] The Home page features tabs for Canadiana, Shakespeare, and Canadian Theatre. There are also links to the various content areas of the site, including Shakespeare News, which includes an RSS feed, convenient for those who wish to subscribe to news releases from the CASP.

The Online Anthology features "over fifty playscripts with associated multimedia, research hyperlinks, original introductions, database information"

TEXTUAL STUDIES, PERFORMANCE, AND DIGITAL HUMANITIES   219

and more.[10] These entries span from the nineteenth century to today. One of the strengths of the site is the way that the information in one division—such as the anthology—links immediately and easily to related resources in another—such as multimedia. It is perhaps best to explain the site's holdings by pursuing a single source through its many content areas. For example, if one were to click on the Anthology entry for Allison McWood's 2006 play, *It was Kit: The TRUE Story of Christopher Marlowe*, one would find a general introduction to McWood's three stage adaptations and links to the PDF playtext, the original cast, an image gallery, and to the anthology entries for McWood's two other plays. The database link leads to the database entry for this adaptation. In that entry, a considerable amount of information is presented in extremely well-organized visual chart, including the performance history, a brief biography of the author, the original cast and production staff, the date and location of the first production, and links to reviews of the performance. (The Database content area holds this sort of information for "over 530 plays [CASP has] identified as Canadian Adaptations of Shakespeare."[11]) If one were to follow the link to the image gallery, one would find images associated with all of McWood's adaptations, including production stills, publicity photos, and posters.

The "Spotlight" content area features three themed content groups—Canadian Aboriginal Adaptations of Shakespeare; a spotlight on *Slings & Arrows*, the Canadian television show about a Shakespeare theatre troupe; and a spotlight in development about Shakespeare and French Canadian Theatre. Particularly intriguing is the motivating question "Pourquoi pas Molière?"[12] A quick glance at the spotlight on Aboriginal Adaptations of Shakespeare shows that this feature provides a brief introduction to the larger topic and then aggregates information throughout the archives related to Aboriginal productions.

The Multimedia section has three parts: image gallery, streaming audio, and streaming video. The video section contains all sorts of goodies, including a *South Park* episode in which the characters travel to see a Canadian Shakespeare Festival; Canadian comedy troupes' send-ups of various plays; excerpts from Paul Almond's noteworthy 1961 *Macbeth*, which starred Sean Connery; and selections from the 1983 Rick Moranis film *Strange Brew*. The audio section has musical performances as well as interviews and audio from productions.

The Learning Commons contains helpful pedagogical materials. The first section, designed for secondary school teachers, features five "courses," complete with teachers' guides, student instructions, worksheets, and other materials. These range from trivia, to history, to production design, to performance. The second section, designed for post-secondary school, contains sample syllabi from McGill University and The University of Guelph. The interactive folio and study guide is a flash-animated tool that claims to be "quite simply the most interactive and sophisticated version of *Romeo and Juliet* ever created."[13] As you click on the text, highlighted passages can reveal images, gloss, video, or audio. It is also fully navigable via act, scene, and page.

The site also includes a comprehensive bibliography of all the references in the archive, as well as a general reference bibliography, and a spotlight bibliography (relevant to the current "Spotlight" feature). The Essays section features many essays about Shakespeare theatre in Canada. There are also two youth games: 'Speare and Chronos. And there is a "virtual exhibit" based on "the *Shakespeare—Made in Canada* exhibition hosted by the Macdonald Stewart Art Centre from January to June 2007."[14]

Global Shakespeares is an open-access digital video archive that features content from productions around the world. Co-founded and co-edited by Peter Donaldson and Alexander Huang, the project features an impressive international list of scholarly contributors and an elegant design. A "collaborative project providing online access to performances of Shakespeare from many parts of the world as well as essays and metadata provided by scholars and educators," the archive (at the time of writing) contained "more than 296 productions, 75 video clips, and online videos of over 30 full productions."[15] It is a truly amazing resource for educators and scholars.

The content is allotted into five separate geographic areas: East and Southeast Asia, India, Brazil, the Arab World, and the United Kingdom and America. A click on one of these geographic titles summons an introductory essay and a set of video clips relevant to that particular region. The "All Productions" page contains an excellent searchable archive, organized according to Shakespeare play, and listing the title, director, year, company, language, and country of each production. Clicking on any title will bring you to a new page that provides any video material for that production, as well as links to interviews, performance reviews, scholarship, and "behind-the-scenes" information. You can limit the archive to only those with video available, which may be helpful for classroom use. For those with video, the embedded video streams easily. One can watch clips of "Sonho de uma noite de Verão," a Portuguese children's theatre *Midsummer Night's Dream*, and compare it with an animated Czech film based on the same play, *Sen noci svatojánské*, available in its entirety.

The resources page links to lists of production scripts, essays and interviews, theater companies, a relevant bibliography, and suggested external links. There is an option to follow an RSS Feed of website updates and project news, as well. This site is more streamlined and focused—in the sense that it is geared entirely toward providing videos of productions—than the CASP. As scholarship seeks to answer the call for further theorization of intercultural performance, as evidenced in Huang's book and Kennedy and Yong's and Trivedi and Ryuta's collections, certainly archives like this will be infinitely valuable. They will also give us the ability to more immediately implement these ideas in our classrooms, where students can be invited to look at how five different regions of the world reinvent Shakespeare.

The first phase of the *Global Shakespeares* project, *Shakespeare Performance in Asia* (SPIA) is another open-access digital archive of performances. Another project of Alexander Huang and Peter Donaldson, the site features 25 full videos, 22 clips, and an archive of 248 titles, and promises to "launch an innovative workspace with a suite of advanced research tools that allow users to make virtual clips of performances for replay within the system, to tag videos, to make and store annotations to visual and textual materials, and to compose multimedia essays."[16] Like Global Shakespeares, SPIA is directed and edited by Peter Donaldson and Alexander Huang and housed out of MIT. It is linked with a larger effort, the Asian Shakespeare Intercultural Archive (ASIA). This additional research archive makes available even more digital records of productions.

SPIA's easily searchable database of video records includes a helpful "search by play" menu, with director, genre, city, and country filters. The very high-quality videos play in Quicktime and range in production date from 1994 to 2007. The much larger catalogue of productions, "includes films, stage productions, TV series, and cartoons produced on the Indian Subcontinent, in South Asia, Southeast Asia, East Asia, Pacific Islands, New Zealand (in Maori), Europe, and in the US." The catalogue lists productions with "distinctive Shakespearean and Asian elements or references regardless of geo-cultural origins of the performances."[17] In the commentary section of the website, three essays address issues of Asian Shakespeare, and there are excerpts of interviews with directors, brief biographies of ten major artists and seven theatre companies, a helpful glossary of important terms relating to Asian performances, and a broad bibliography of fifty print sources.

The contents of this particular database provide a preview of what we can expect as the Global Shakespeares project expands. The availability of digital video archives will enhance our ability to research Shakespeare's contemporary presence around the world. These archives will also enable us to share, teach, and cite these productions in a way we never could before, and in a way similar to how we share, teach, and cite text resources. This is one of the main motivations behind the creation of these archives, according to Huang: to simultaneously expand awareness of Global Shakespeare and to provide a way for us to implement that awareness pedagogically and critically.[18]

CONCLUSION

The books coming out from major academic presses around the world in the last few years indicate that Global Shakesepeares is the fastest-growing vein of Shakespeare scholarship, and for good reason. The work done by Alexander Huang, Dennis Kennedy, Poonam Trivedi, and others, proves that not only can we no longer ignore the rich traditions of Shakespearean performance and scholarship arising from other parts of the world, but also that we have much to learn and many new avenues to explore. It seems to me that Global Shakespeares is the most important new vogue in Shakespeare scholarship, and a welcome one: one that allows us to dissolve disciplinary boundaries in the way that Carole Levin and John Watkins challenge us to. Global Shakespeares invites us, not merely to bridge the separations between habits of literary scholarship and historians, but also comparative literature departments, modern language departments, political science departments, and more. This new vein of scholarship is the melting pot in which so many individual interests—poetry, textual history, Shakespeare in performance, digital archives—suddenly grow richer and expand into new territories. Surely the handful of books reviewed here are only the tip of the iceberg, and what is to follow will include rich textual histories of international Shakespeares, advanced performance theories, a new disciplinary interest in Shakespearean poetry in other languages, and a sincere investment in how to expand accessibility to these international, cross-cultural concerns via digital archives.

As Bollywood knocks on the doors of major American cinemas, and as YouTube and other websites traffic international film with increasing speed, it will soon become irresponsible not to teach and study Shakespeare in an international, performative, adaptive context.

Notes

1. These plays are *All's Well That Ends Well*, *Pericles*, *Coriolanus*, *The Winter's Tale*, *The Tragedy of King Lear*, *Cymbeline*, *The Tempest*, *Cardenio*, *Henry VIII*, and *The Two Noble Kinsmen*.
2. Laurie Maguire, *Shakespearean Suspect Texts: The "Bad" Quartos and Their Contexts* (New York: Cambridge University Press, 1996); Brian Vickers, *Shakespeare, Co-Author* (Oxford: Oxford University Press, 2002).
3. This list includes each of the three Arden Shakespeare series, Peter Alexander's *Complete Works* (1951), Fredson Bowers' *Dramatic Works in the Beaumont and Fletcher Canon* (1966–96), G. Blakemore Evans' *Riverside Shakespeare* (1974), Stanley Wells' *Oxford Shakespeare Works* (1982–), and Gary Taylor and John Lavagnino's *Thomas Middleton: The Collected Works* (2007), among others.
4. The existing theories Sheen critiques include those offered by Greenblatt, Agnew, Bruster, Barroll, and Yachin and Dawson.
5. An example of this last category would be Yorick's skull.
6. Wilder follows this claim with a brilliant reading of *Richard III* 4.4, in which first Margaret teaches Elizabeth and the Duchess of York the best way to remember and mourn their losses, and then Elizabeth finds herself in the position of educating Richard about memory, under the guise of teaching him how to woo her daughter.
7. This section of the website was written by Michael Best and last updated in November 2010. Michael Best, "Shakespeare's Life and Times," *Internet Shakespeare Editions*, 25 May 2011, at http://internetshakespeare.uvic.ca/Library/SLT/index.html.
8. *ISE Performance Chronicle*, 25 May 2011, at http://isechronicle.uvic.ca/.
9. Daniel Fischlin, *Canadian Adaptations of Shakespeare Project*, 2 June 2011, at http://www.uoguelph.ca/shakespeare/.
10. Fischlin, "Online Anthology," *CASP*, 2 June 2011, at http://www.canadianshakespeares.ca/anthology.cfm.
11. Fischlin, "Database," CASP, 2 June 2011, at http://www.canadianshakespeares.ca/Production_Shakespeare/SearchPublic.cfm.
12. Fischlin, "CASP Spotlights," *CASP*, 2 June 2011, at http://www.canadianshakespeares.ca/spotlight_main.cfm.
13. Fischlin, "Interactive Folio and Study Guide: Romeo and Juliet," CASP, 2 June 2011, at http://www.canadianshakespeares.ca/rjfolio.cfm.
14. Fischlin, "Shakespeare Made in Canada," *CASP*, 2 June 2011, http://vsmic.canadianshakespeares.ca/.
15. Peter Donaldson and Alexander Huang, "About," *Global Shakespeares*, 2 June 2011, at http://globalshakespeares.org/about.
16. Alexander Huang, "About Shakespeare Performance in Asia," *Shakespeare Performance in Asia*, 2 June 2011, at http://web.mit.edu/shakespeare/asia/about/.
17. Huang, "Catalogue of Productions," *Shakespeare Performance in Asia*, 2 June 2011, at http://web.mit.edu/shakespeare/asia/collections/catalogue.html.
18. Alexander Huang, "Global Shakespeare 2.0 and the Task of the Performance Archive," *Shakespeare Survey* 64 (2011): 38–51.

WORKS REVIEWED

Alexander, Catherine M. S., ed. *The Cambridge Companion to Shakespeare's Last Plays*. Cambridge: Cambridge University Press, 2009.

Astington, John. *Actors and Acting in Shakespeare's Time: The Art of Stage Playing*. Cambridge: Cambridge University Press, 2010.

Donaldson, Peter, and Alexander Huang, eds. *Global Shakespeares*. 2 June 2011. http://globalshakespeares.org/.

Egan, Gabriel. *The Struggle for Shakespeare's Text: Twentieth-Century Editorial Theory and Practice*. Cambridge: Cambridge University Press, 2010.

Fischlin, Daniel, ed. *Canadian Adaptations of Shakespeare Project*. 2 June 2011. http://www.uoguelph.ca/shakespeare/.

Huang, Alexander C. Y. *Chinese Shakespeares: Two Centuries of Cultural Exchange*. New York: Columbia University Press, 2009.

———. "Global Shakespeare 2.0 and the Task of the Performance Archive." *Shakespeare Survey* 64 (2011), 38–51.

———, ed. *Shakespeare Performance in Asia*. 2 June 2011. http://web.mit.edu/shakespeare/asia/about/.

Internet Shakespeare Editions Incorporated. 25 May 2011. http://internetshakespeare.uvic.ca/.

Kennedy, Dennis and Yong Li Lan, eds. *Shakespeare in Asia*. Cambridge: Cambridge University Press, 2010.

Kidnie, Margaret Jane. *Shakespeare and the Problem of Adaptation*. New York: Routledge, 2009.

Levin, Carole and John Watkins. *Shakespeare's Foreign Worlds*. Ithaca, NY: Cornell University Press, 2009.

Petersen, Lene B. *Shakespeare's Errant Texts: Textual Form and Linguistic Style in Shakespearean "Bad" Quartos and Co-Authored Plays*. Cambridge: Cambridge University Press, July 2010.

Pfister, Manfred and Juergen Gutsch, eds. *William Shakespeare's Sonnets for the First Time Globally Reprinted: A Quartercentenary Anthology*. Dozwil, Switzerland: Edition SIGNAThUR, 2009.

Schoenfeldt, Michael. *The Cambridge Introduction to Shakespeare's Poetry*. Cambridge: Cambridge University Press, 2010.

Sheen, Erica. *Shakespeare and the Institution of Theatre: The Best in this Kind*. New York: Palgrave, 2009.

Trivedi, Poonam and Minami Ryuta, eds. *Re-Playing Shakespeare in Asia*. New York: Routledge, 2010.

Wilder, Lena Perkins. *Shakespeare's Memory Theatre: Recollection, Properties, and Character.* Cambridge: Cambridge University Press, 2010.
Yachnin, Paul and Jessica Slights, eds. *Shakespeare and Character: Theory, History, Performance and Theatrical Persons*. New York: Palgrave, 2009.

Bibliography

Editions of Shakespeare are not listed in this bibliography but can be found in notes to individual essays.

Agamben, Giorgio. *State of Exception*. Translated by Kevin Attell. Stanford: Stanford University Press, 2005.
Angoor, VCD, directed by Gulzar. 1981; Mumbai: Video Palace, 2011.
Arora, Keval. "Dabbling in Babble," http://www.stagebuzz.info/PAGES/Columnists/Keval%20Dabbling%20in%20Babble.htm.
Aristotle. *Poetics*. Translated by Ingram Bywater. Oxford: Clarendon Press, 1920.
Astington, John. *Actors and Acting in Shakespeare's Time: The Art of Stage Playing*. Cambridge: Cambridge University Press, 2010.
Atkins, G. Douglas. "Introduction." In *Shakespeare and Deconstruction*, edited by G. Douglas Atkins and David M. Bergeron. 1–17. New York: P. Lang, 1988.
Atkins, G. Douglas and David Moore Bergeron, eds. *Shakespeare and Deconstruction*. New York: Peter Lang, 1988.
Bagchi, Jashodhara. "Shakespeare in Loin Cloths: English Literature and the early Nationalist Consciousness in Bengal." In *Rethinking English; Essays in Literature, Language, History*, edited by Svati Joshi. 146–59. New Delhi: Trianka, 1991.
Bandyopadhyay, Akshay Kumar. *Hamlet*. Cuttack: Cuttack Trading Company, 1934.
Bandyopadhyay, Brajendranath. *Bangiya Natyashalar Itihasa 1795–1876*. Kolkata: Bangiya-Sahitya-Parishat, 1933.
Bapat, Gopal Vaman, *Natak Vishayak Vyapak Vichar*. Pune: Shankar Bapuji Mujumdar for *Rangabhumi*, 1910.
Barr, Pat and Ray Desmond. *Simla: A Hill Station in British India*. Delhi: B. R. Publishing Corporation, and London: The Scolar Press, 1978.
Bazin, Andre. *What is Cinema?* vol. 1, Berkeley: University of California Press, 1967.

Benjamin, Walter. "Critique of Violence." In *Reflections*, edited by Peter Demetz. 277–300. New York: Schocken Books, 1986.

Benjamin, Walter. *The Origin of German Tragic Drama*. Translated by John Osborne. London: Verso, 1998.

Bennett, Susan. *Performing Nostalgia: Shifting Shakespeare and the Contemporary Past*. Routledge; London, 1996.

Berg, James. "The Properties of Character in *King Lear*." In *Shakespeare and Character: Theory, History, Performance and Theatrical Persons*, edited by Paul Yachnin and Jessica Slights. 98–116. New York: Palgrave, 2009.

Berlin, Normand. "Death in *Rosencrantz and Guildenstern*: I." In *Critical Essays on Tom Stoppard*, edited by Anthony Jenkins. 43–50. Boston: G. K. Hall & Co., 1990.

Best, Michael. "Shakespeare's Life and Times," *Internet Shakespeare Editions*, 25 May 2011, http://internetshakespeare.uvic.ca/Library/SLT/index.html.

Bevington, David. *Shakespeare and Biography*. Oxford and New York: Oxford University Press, 2010.

Bharati, Ashvin. 1287 (August–September 1880). Reprinted in *Rabindra Rachanabali*, vol. 30, Kolkata, Visva-Bharati, 1998.

Bhole, Keshavrao. *Antara*. Mumbai: Mauj Prakashan Griha, 1996.

Billington, Michael. "Indian Summer," *The Guardian*, 31 May 2006. http://www.guardian.co.uk/stage/2006/may/31/theatre.india.

Billington, Michael. "A Midsummer Night's Dream," *The Guardian*, 9 June 2006. http://www.guardian.co.uk/stage/2006/jun/09/theatre.rsc.

Biswas, Moinak. "Mourning and Blood-ties: Macbeth in Mumbai." *Journal of the Moving Image*, 5 (December 2006), http://www.jmionline.org/jmi5_4.htm on 18 June 2011.

Bose, Rajnarain. *Atma-charit*. Kolkata: Kuntaline Press, 1909.

Bradley, A. C. *Shakespearean Tragedy*. New York: Fawcett Premier, 1986.

Bristol, Michael. "Confusing Shakespeare's Characters with Real People: Reflections on Reading in Four Questions." In *Shakespeare and Character: Theory, History, Performance and Theatrical Persons*, edited by Paul Yachnin and Jessica Slights. 21–40. New York: Palgrave, 2009).

Brougham, John, *Much Ado about a Merchant of Venice*. New York: Samuel French, n.d. Reprinted in vol. 5 of *Nineteenth Century Shakespeare Burlesques*, edited by Stanley Wells, 5 vols. London: Diploma Press Ltd, 1978.

Buchanan, Judith. *Shakespeare on Silent Film: An Excellent Dumb Discourse*. Cambridge and New York: Cambridge University Press, 2009.

Burnett, Mark Thornton. *Filming Shakespeare in the Global Marketplace.* New York: Palgrave Macmillan, 2007.

Buck, Edward J. *Simla Past and Present.* Calcutta: Thacker, Spink and Co, 1904.

Bulman, James. *The Merchant of Venice: Shakespeare in Performance.* Manchester: Manchester University Press, 1991.

Burt, Richard. "All that remains of Shakespeare in Indian film." In *Shakespeare in Asia*, edited by Dennis Kennedy and Yong Li Lan. 50–68. Cambridge: Cambridge University Press, 2010.

Burt, Richard. *Shakespeare After Mass Media.* New York: Palgrave, 2002.

Burt, Richard. *Shakespeares After Shakespeare: An Encyclopedia of the Bard in Mass Media and Popular Culture*, 2 vols. Westport, CT: Greenwood Press, 2007.

Buse, Peter. "*Hamlet* Games—Stoppard with Lyotard." In *Drama + Theory: Critical Approaches to Modern British Drama.* 50–68. Manchester: Manchester University Press, 2002.

The Calcutta University Calendar 1858–59. Kolkata: Bishop's College Press, 1858.

The Calcutta University Calendar 1860–61. Kolkata: Baptist Mission Press, 1860.

The Calcutta University Calendar 1862–63. Kolkata: Thacker, Spink & Co., 1862.

The Calcutta University Calendar 1863–64. Kolkata: Thacker, Spink & Co., 1863.

Calderwood, James. *To Be and Not to Be: Negation and Metadrama in Hamlet.* New York: Columbia University Press, 1983.

Campbell, Oscar James, ed. *The Reader's Encyclopedia of Shakespeare.* New York: Thomas Y. Crowell Company, 1966,

Carlyle, Thomas. *On Heroes, Hero-Worship and the Heroic in History* (1841). Oxford: Oxford University Press, 1963.

Chakravarti, Paromita. "Modernity, Postcoloniality and Othello: the case of *Saptapadi.*" In *Remaking Shakespeare: Performance across Media, Genres and Cultures*, edited by Pascale Aebischer, Edward J. Esche and Nigel Wheale. 39–55. New York: Palgrave Macmillan, 2003.

Chatterjee, Partha. "Whose Imagined Community?" In *Empire & Nation: Essential Writings 1985–2005.* Ranikhet: Permanent Black, 2010.

Chattopadhyay, Bankimchandra. "Shakuntala, Miranda ebang Desdemona." In *Bankimchandra's Bangadarshan: Selected Essays in Translation*, edited by Tapati Gupta. 220–32. Kolkata: Das Gupta & Co. Pvt. Ltd, 2007.

Chaudhuri, Sukanta. "Shakespeare in India." In *Internet* Shakespeare *Editions*, http://internetshakespeare.uvic.ca/Library/Criticism/shakespearein/india4.html.

Chiplunkar, Vishnushastri. "Bhashantar" [Translation]. In *Nibandhamaletil Vangmay Vishayak Nivadak Nibandha* [Selected Essays from the Journal *Nibandhamala*]. Pune: Chitrashal Prakashan, n.d.

Chiplunkar, Vishnushastri. "Tara Natak." *Nibandhamala*, 22 (1879).

Clark, Sandra. *Shakespeare Made Fit: Restoration Adaptations of Shakespeare*. London: J. M. Dent; Rutland, VT: Charles E. Tuttle, 1997.

Coleridge, Samuel Taylor. *Coleridge's Poetry and* Prose. Edited by Nicholas Halmi, Paul Magnuson, and Raimonda Modiano. New York: W. W. Norton & Company, 2004.

Conway, Christopher. "Tim Supple's A Midsummer Night's Dream at the Roundhouse Theatre, London," 22 March 2007. http://drconway.wordpress.com/2007/03/22/tim-supples-a-midsummer-nights-dream-at-the-roundhouse-theatre-london/

Croteau, Mellissa and Carolyn Jess-Cooke, eds. *Apocalyptic Shakespeare: Essays on Visions of Chaos and Revelation in Recent Film Adaptations*. Jefferson, NC: McFarland and Co., 2009.

Das, Nilakantha. "Fakir Mohan O Odia Shaitya" [Fakir Mohan and Oriya Literature]. In *Odia Bhasha O Shaitya* [Oriya Language and Literature]. Berhampur: New Student's Store, 1958.

Das, Sisir Kumar. "Shakespeare in Indian Languages." *Jadavpur Journal of Comparative Literature* 36 (1998–99): 111–36.

Dasgupta, Susmita. *Amitabh: The Making of a Superstar*. Delhi: Penguin Books, 2007.

De Grazia, Margareta. *Hamlet without Hamlet*. Cambridge: Cambridge University Press, 1997.

Denyer, P. H. *The Centenarian, Being a Summary of the History of Simla Amateur Theatricals during the Past 100 Years*. Simla: Liddells, 1937.

Derrida, Jacques. "Différance." In Derrida, *Margins of Philosophy*. Translated by Alan Bass. 1–27. Chicago: University of Chicago Press, 1982.

Derrida, Jacques. *Of Grammatology*. Translated by Gayatri Chakravorty Spivak. Baltimore: Johns Hopkins University Press, 1976.

Derrida, Jacques. "Semiology and Grammatology: Interview with Julia Kristeva." In Derrida, *Positions*. Translated by Alan Bass. 15–36. Chicago: University of Chicago Press, 1981.

Dey, Lalbehari. *Recollections of* Alexander *Duff*. London: T. Nelson & Sons, 1879.

Dobson, Michael. "Shakespeare Performances in England, 2006: 15 June 2006." *Shakespeare Survey* 60 (2007): 300–302.
Donaldson, Peter. "Disseminating Shakespeare: Paternity and Text in Jean-Luc Godard's King Lear." In *Shakespearean Films, Shakespearean Directors*. 189–225. Unwin Hyman: Boston, 1990.
Donaldson, Peter and Alexander Huang. "About," *Global Shakespeares*, 2 June 2011. http://globalshakespeares.org/about.
Drakakis, John, ed. *Alternative Shakespeares*, London and New York: Methuen, 1985.
Duff, James Grant. *History of the Mahrattas*, 3 vols. London: Longmans, Rees, Orme, Brown, and Green, 1826.
Dutt, Utpal. *Aajker Shahjahan*. In *Natak Samagra* [Collected Plays], vol. 7. Edited by Sova Sen, Bishnupriya Dutt and Souvik Raychaudhuri. Kolkata: Mitra and Ghosh Publishers, 1999.
Dutt, Utpal. *Shakespeare o Brecht* (1988). In *Gadya Sangraha* [Collected Prose], vol. 1, *Natya Chinta* [Thoughts on Theatre]. Edited by Samik Bandyopadhyay. 319–75. Kolkata: Dey's Publishing, 2004.
Dutt, Utpal. *Girish Chandra Ghosh*. New Delhi: Sahitya Akademi, 1992.
Dutt, Utpal. *Shakespeare-er Samaj Chinta*. Kolkata: M. C. Sarkar and Sons, 1999.
Dwyer, Rachel. "Amitabh Bachchan; The Angry Young Man." British Academy of Film and Television Arts, November 16, 2007.
Echeruo, Michael J. C. "Tanistry, the 'Due of Birth', and Macbeth's Sin." *Shakespeare Quarterly* 23, no. 4 (1972): 444–50.
Edelman, Charles. "Which is the Jew that Shakespeare Knew? Shylock on the Elizabethan Stage." *Shakespeare Survey* 52 (1999): 99–106.
Eden, Emily. *Letters From India*. London: Richard Bentley, 1872.
Eliot, T. S. "Hamlet." In *Selected Essays*. 141–6. London: Faber and Faber, 1941.
Egan, Gabriel. *The Struggle for Shakespeare's Text: Twentieth-Century Editorial Theory and Practice*. Cambridge: Cambridge University Press, 2010.
Felperin, Howard. "The Dark Lady Identified or What Deconstruction Can Do For Shakespeare's *Sonnets*." In *Shakespeare and Deconstruction*, edited by G. Douglas Atkins and David M. Bergeron. 69–93. New York: P. Lang, 1988.
Fiorentino, Francesco. "Heiner Müller e la *Hamletmaschine*." In *La Traduzione di Amleto nella cultura europea*, edited by Maria Del Sapio Gerbero. 77–107. Venice: Marsilio, 2002.

"FIR registered in journalist JD's murder case." *The Telegraph*, Kolkata, June 27, 2011. http://www.telegraphindia.com/1110627/jsp/frontpage/story_141646690.jsp

Fischer, Michael. *Does Deconstruction Make Any Difference? Poststructuralism and the Defense of Poetry in Modern Criticism*. Bloomington: Indiana University Press, 1985.

Fischer-Lichte, Erika. "Zwischen Differenz und Indifferenz. Funktionalisierung des Montage-Verfahrens bei Heiner Müller." In *Avantgarde und Postmoderne. Prozesse struktureller und funktioneller Veränderungen*, edited by Erika Fischer-Lichte and Klaus Schwind. 231–45. Tübingen: Stauffenburg, 1991.

Fischlin, Daniel. *Canadian Adaptations of Shakespeare Project*, 2 June 2011. http://www.uoguelph.ca/shakespeare/.

Fischlin, Daniel. "CASP Spotlights," *CASP*, 2 June 2011. http://www.canadianshakespeares.ca/spotlight_main.cfm

Fischlin, Daniel. "Database," *CASP*, 2 June 2011. http://www.canadianshakespeares.ca/Production_Shakespeare/SearchPublic.cfm.

Fischlin, Daniel. "Interactive Folio and Study Guide: *Romeo and Juliet*," *CASP*, 2 June 2011. http://www.canadianshakespeares.ca/rjfolio.cfm.

Fischlin, Daniel. "Online Anthology," *CASP*, 2 June 2011. http://www.canadianshakespeares.ca/anthology.cfm.

Fischlin, Daniel. "Shakespeare Made in Canada," *CASP*, 2 June 2011. http://vsmic.canadianshakespeares.ca/.

Flores, Ralph. "Metatheater as Metaphorics: Playing Figures in Shakespeare's Sonnets." In *Shakespeare and Deconstruction*, edited by G. Douglas Atkins and David M. Bergeron. 95–127. New York: P. Lang, 1988.

Foucault, Michel. "What is an Author?" In *Textual Strategies: Perspectives in Post-Structuralist Criticism*, edited by Josue V. Harari. 141–60. Ithaca: Cornell University Press, 1979.

Fraser, F. J. *The Merry Merchant of Venice: A Peep at Shakespeare Through the Venetians*. Allahabad: The Pioneer Press, 1895.

Freud, Sigmund. "The Uncanny." (1919). In *The Penguin Freud Library*, vol. 14: *Art and Literature*, edited by Albert Dickson, translated by James Strachey. 335–76. London: Penguin, 1990.

Fuchs, Elinor. *The Death of the Character: Perspectives on Theater after Modernism*. Bloomington and Indianapolis: Indiana University Press, 1996.

Gajowski, Evelyn. *Presentism, Gender, and Sexuality in Shakespeare*. Basingstoke and New York: Palgrave, 2009.

Ghose, Jagannath Ballabh. *Premika-Premika* [translation of *Romeo and Juliet*]. Cuttack: The Union Printing Works, 1908.

Gillies, John. *Shakespeare and the Geography of Difference.* Cambridge: Cambridge University Press, 1994.

Grady, Hugh. *The Modernist Shakespeare: Critical Texts in a Material World.* Oxford: Clarendon Press, 1991.

Green, David. "The Role of the Third Space in Inter-cultural Dialogue." Paper delivered at a conference on "Multilingualism and Intercultural Dialogue in Globalisation," University of Delhi, 11–12 December 2008.

Greenblatt, Stephen. *Shakespeare's Freedom.* Chicago: University of Chicago Press, 2010.

Greenhalgh, Susanne. "Theatre Reviews: A Midsummer Night's Dream," *Shakespeare Bulletin* 24 (Winter 2006): 65–9.

Gross, John. *Shylock: A Legend and Its Legacy.* New York: Simon and Schuster, 1992.

Gupta, Bipinbehari. *Puratan Prasanga.* Kolkata: Pustak Biponi, 1989.

Gurr, Andrew. "Henry Carey's Peculiar Letter," *Shakespeare Quarterly* 56 (2005): 51–75.

Gurr, Andrew. *Shakespeare's Opposites. The Admiral's Company 1594–1625.* Cambridge: Cambridge University Press, 2009.

Gurr, Andrew. *The Shakespeare Company, 1594–1642.* Cambridge: Cambridge University Press, 2004.

Guruji, Krishnaji Abaji, "Natakachi Sthityantate" [Transitions in Theatre], *Rangabhumi,* 1911 (in several instalments).

Harishchandra, Bharatendu. *Bharatendu Granthavali*, vol. 1. Edited by Shivprasad Mishra. Varanasi: Nagari Pracharini Sabha, 1970. (in Hindi)

Harris, Jonathan Gil. *Shakespeare and Literary Theory.* Oxford: Oxford University Press, 2010.

Hart, Christopher. "Oh, what a night." *The Sunday Times*, 18 March 2007.

Heraclitus. *The Complete Fragments: Translation and Commentary and the Greek Text*, translated and edited by William J. Harris, http://community.middlebury.edu/~harris/Philosophy/heraclitus.pdf).

Holinshed, Raphael. *The History of Scotland.* vol. 2, *The Chronicles of England, Scotland and Ireland.* London: John Hunne, 1577.

Honan, Park. *Shakespeare. A Life.* Oxford: Oxford University Press, 1998.

Hopkins, Lisa. *Relocating Shakespeare and Austen on Screen.* Basingstoke and New York: Palgrave, 2009.

Hotson, Leslie. *Shakespeare Versus Shallow.* Boston: Little, Brown and Company, 1931.

Huang, Alexander C. Y. "About Shakespeare Performance in Asia," *Shakespeare Performance in Asia*, 2 June 2011, http://web.mit.edu/shakespeare/asia/about/.

Huang, Alexander C. Y. "Catalogue of Productions," *Shakespeare Performance in Asia*, 2 June 2011, http://web.mit.edu/shakespeare/asia/collections/catalogue.html.

Huang, Alexander C. Y. *Chinese Shakespeares: Two Centuries of Cultural Exchange*. New York: Columbia University Press, 2009.

Huang, Alexander C. Y. "Global Shakespeare 2.0 and the Task of the Performance Archive," *Shakespeare Survey* 64 (2011): 38–51.

Huang, Alexander C. Y. and Charles S. Ross, eds. *Shakespeare in Hollywood, Asia, and Cyberspace*. West Lafayette, IN: Purdue University Press, 2009.

Hutcheon, Linda. *A Poetics of Postmodernism. History, Theory, Fiction*. New York and London: Routledge, 1988.

Hutcheon, Linda. *A Theory of Adaptation*. New York: Routledge, 2006.

Hutcheon, Linda. *Theory of Parody: The Teaching of Twentieth Century Forms*. New York: Methuen, 1985.

Huysen, Andreas. *Twilight Memories: Marking Time in a Culture of Amnesia*. New York and London: Routledge, 1995.

Ingram, William. "The Economics of Playing." In *A Companion to Shakespeare*, edited by David Scott Kastan. 313–27. Oxford: Blackwell, 1999.

ISE Performance Chronicle, 25 May 2011, http://isechronicle.uvic.ca/.

Jameson, Frederic. *PostModernism or, The Cultural Logic of Late Capitalism*. Verso: London, 1991.

Joshi, Namrata. "Krzysztof … In Meerut," *Outlook India Magazine*, 31 August 2009, http://www.outlookindia.com/article.aspx?261415 on 18 June 2011.

Joshi, Sumant. *Naman Natawara: Arthat Kahi Divangat Natyasevakanche Parichay*. Mumbai: Sahitya Sahakar Sangha Prakashan, 1971.

Kalb, Jonathan. *The Theatre of Heiner Müller*. Cambridge: Cambridge University Press, 1998.

Kanwar, Pamela. *Imperial Simla: The Political Culture of the Raj*. Delhi: Oxford University Press, 1990.

Kapadia, Parmita. "Shakespeare Transposed; The British Stage on the Postcolonial Screen." In *Almost Shakespeare: Reinventing His Works for Cinema and Television*, edited by James R. Keller and Leslie Stratyner. 42–56. Jefferson, NC: McFarland & Co., 2004.

Kashmiri, Agha Hashra [Hashr]. *Havas ka Putla [Said-e-Havas]*. Edited by Krishnadev Jhari. New Delhi: Sharada Prakashan, 1984 (in Hindi).

Kashmiri, Agha Hashra [Hashr]. *Khvabe Hasti [Khwab-e-Hasti]*. Edited by Krishnadev Jhari. New Delhi: Sharada Prakashan, 1986. (in Hindi)

Kellaway, Kate. "Indian summer of heat and lust," *The Observer*, 18 March 2007.

Kendal, Geoffrey. *The Shakespeare Wallah: The Autobiography of Geoffrey Kendal*. London: Sidgwick and Jackson, 1986.

Kennedy, Dennis and Yong Li Lan, eds. *Shakespeare in Asia*. Cambridge: Cambridge University Press, 2010.

Kesavan, Mukul, "Urdu, Awadh and the Tawaif: The Islamicate Roots of the Hindi Cinema." In *Forging Identities: Gender, Communities and the State*, edited by Zoya Hasan. 244–57. New Delhi: Kali for Women, 1994.

Kidnie, Margaret Jane. *Shakespeare and the Problem of Adaptation*. New York: Routledge, 2009.

King, Tom. *Casting Shakespeare's Plays. London Actors and Their Roles, 1590–1642*. Cambridge: Cambridge University Press, 1992.

Klett, Elizabeth. *Cross-gender Shakespeare and English National Identity: Wearing the Codpiece*. New York: Palgrave, 2009.

Kokot, Joanna, "'All the world's a stage'; Theatre-within-Theatre Convention in Tom Stoppard's *Rosencrantz and Guildenstern Are Dead*." In *Conventions and Texts*, edited by Andrzej Zgorzelski. 113–39. Gdańsk: Uniwersytet Gdański, 2003.

Kopper, John M. "Troilus at Pluto's Gates: Subjectivity and the Duplicity of Discourse in Shakespeare's *Troilus and Cressida*." In *Shakespeare and Deconstruction*, edited by G. Douglas Atkins and David M. Bergeron. 149–71. New York: P. Lang, 1988.

Kott, Jan. *Shakespeare our Contemporary*. Translated by Bolesław Taborski. London: Routledge, 1994.

Lal, Ananda. "The Dream—A journey through time." British Council playbill for *A Midsummer Night's Dream* (April 2006), unpaginated.

Lal, Ananda. "Edge of creativity." *The Telegraph*. Kolkata: 30 April 2006.

Lal, Ananda. "Language and the Dream." Royal Shakespeare Company playbill for *A Midsummer Night's Dream* (June 2006), unpaginated.

Lal, Ananda. "Post-script to a Dream." *Connecting*. New Delhi: May 2006, 9–11.

Lal, Ananda and Sukanta Chaudhuri, eds. *Shakespeare on the Calcutta Stage: A Checklist*. Kolkata: Papyrus, 2001.

Lavender, Andy. *Hamlet in Pieces. Shakespeare Reworked by Peter Brook, Robert Lepage, Robert Wilson*. London: Nick Hern Books, 2001.

Lawrence, Amy. "Daddy Dearest: Patriarchy and the Artist Prospero's Books." In *The Films of Peter Greenaway*. 140–64. Cambridge: Cambridge University Press, 1997.

Leiblein, Leanore. "Embodied Intersubjectivity and the Creation of Early Modern Character," In *Shakespeare and Character: Theory, History, Performance and Theatrical Persons,* edited by Paul Yachnin and Jessica Slights. 117–36. New York: Palgrave, 2009.

Lelyveld, Toby. *Shylock on the Stage*. Cleveland, OH: The Press of Western Reserve University, 1960.

Leonard, Kendra Preston. *Shakespeare, Madness, and Music: Scoring Insanity in Cinematic Adaptations*. Lanham, MD: Scarecrow Press, 2009.

Levin, Carole and John Watkins. *Shakespeare's Foreign Worlds*. Ithaca, NY: Cornell University Press, 2009.

Lewis, Wyndham. *The Lion and the Fox: the Role of the Hero in the Plays of Shakespeare*. London: Grant Richards, 1927.

Li, Ruru. "Six People in Search of 'To be or not to be …': Hamlet's Soliloquy in Six Chinese Productions and the Metamorphosis of Shakespeare Performance on the Chinese Stage." In *Re-Playing Shakespeare in Asia*, edited by Poonam Trivedi and Minami Ryuta. 119–40. New York: Routledge, 2010.

Long, Robert Emmet. *The Films of Merchant-Ivory*. New York: Harry N. Abrams, 1991.

Loomba, Ania. *Gender, Race, Renaissance Drama*. Manchester: Manchester University Press, 1989.

Loomba, Ania and Martin Orkin, eds. *Post-Colonial Shakespeares*. London: Routledge, 1998.

MacCabe, Colin. "A Post-national European Cinema: A Consideration of Derek Jarman's *The Tempest* and *Edward II*." In *Dissolving Views: Key Writings on British Cinema*, edited by Andrew Higson. 191–201. London: Cassell, 1996.

Machiavelli, Niccolò. *The Prince and the Discourses*. New York: Random House, 1950.

Maguire, Laurie. *Shakespearean Suspect Texts: The "Bad" Quartos and Their Contexts*. New York: Cambridge University Press, 1996.

Mahajani, Vishnu Moreshwar. *Tara Natak: Mahakavi Shakespearekrut Cymbeline Yachyavar Adharit*. Pune: Marathi Granthottejak Mandali, 1879.

Majumdar, Sarottama. "That Sublime Old Gentleman." In *India's Shakespeare: Translation, Interpretation, and Performance*, edited by Poonam Trivedi and Dennis Bartholomeusz. 232–9. Delhi: Pearson Education, 2006.

Mansinha, Mayadhar (transl.). *Othello*. Cuttack: Das Brothers, under the aegis of Sahitya Akademi, Delhi, 1959.

Maqbool. DVD, directed by Vishal Bhardwaj, 2003; New Delhi: Eagle Home Entertainment Pvt. Ltd, 2007.

Marathe, K. B. *Naval va Natak Hyanvishayi Nibandha*. Pune: Modern Prakashan, 1962.

Marlowe, Sam. "A Midsummer Night's Dream." *The Times*, 10 June 2006.

Mason, David. "Dharma and Violence in Mumbai." In *Asian Shakespeares on Screen: Two Films in Perspective*. Special issue of *Borrowers and Lenders: The Journal of Shakespeare and Appropriation* 4, no. 2 (Spring/Summer 2009), http://www.borrowers.uga.edu

Mazumdar, Ranjini. *Bombay Cinema: An Archive of a City*. Minneapolis: University of Minnesota, 2007.

McDonald, David J. "*Hamlet* and the Mimesis of Absence: A Post-Structuralist Analysis." *Educational Theatre Journal* 30, no. 1 (1978): 36–53.

McDonald, Russ. "'You speak a language that I understand not': Listening to the Last Plays." In *The Cambridge Companion to Shakespeare's Last Plays*, edited by Catherine M. S. Alexander. 91–112. Cambridge: Cambridge University Press, 2009.

McHale, Brian. *Postmodernist Fiction*, London and New York: Routledge, 1987.

McMullan, Gordon. "What is a 'late' play?" In *The Cambridge Companion to Shakespeare's Last Plays*, edited by Catherine M. S. Alexander. 5–28. Cambridge: Cambridge University Press, 2009.

Menon, Madhavi. *Shakesqueer: A Queer Companion to the Complete Works of Shakespeare*. Durham and London: Duke University Press, 2011.

Mentz, Steve. *At the Bottom of Shakespeare's Ocean*. London: Continuum, 2009.

Miller, Joseph Hillis. "Ariachne's Broken Woof." *Georgia Review* 31, no. 1 (1977): 44–60.

Miller, William. *Shakespeare's King Lear and Indian Politics*. Madras: G. A. Natesan, 1900.

Mishra, Narendra Nath. *Adhunika Odia Kavyadhara: Adiyuga* [The Development of Modern Oriya Poetry: The Early Phase]. Santiniketan: Visva-Bharati Gabeshana Prakashan Samiti, 1964.

Mohanty, Sachidanada. "Shakespeare in Orissa: Culture, Ideology and Translation Practice." In *Gender and Cultural Identity in Colonial Orissa*. 158–64. Hyderabad: Orient Longman, 2008.

Mondal, Monidipa. "Creating a Dream: An Interview with Tim Supple." 1 February 2008, http://exnihilomagazine.wordpress.com/2008/02/01/creating-a-dream-an-interview-with-tim-supple/

Mujumdar, Shankar Bapuji. *Jagaprasiddha nat Garrick Yache Charita*. Pune: Vijay, 1930.

Mukherjee, Meenakshi, "The Beginnings of the English Novel." In *An Illustrated History of Indian Literature in English*, edited by Arvind Krishna Mehrotra. 92–102. Delhi: Permanent Black, 2003.

Muñoz Valdivieso, Sofía. "'Mine ear is much enamour'd of thy note': Shakespeare's Intercultural Dream in the Indian Subcontinent." *SEDERI* 19 (2009): 99–119.

Murray, Timothy. "*Othello*, An Index and Obscure Prologue to the History of Foul Generic Thoughts." In *Shakespeare and Deconstruction*, edited by G. Douglas Atkins and David M. Bergeron. 213–43. New York: P. Lang, 1988.

Müller, Heiner. *Hamletmachine*. Translated by Dennis Redmond, 2001 http://www.efn.org/~dredmond/Hamletmachine.PDF, accessed 29 June 2010, 1–9.

Nashe, Thomas. *Thomas Nashe, Works*. Edited by R. B. McKerrow; revised edn. Oxford: Oxford University Press, 1958.

Nayak, Jatindra K. "Sacred Time Secular Space: The Printed Oriya Almanac." In *Science, Literature and Aesthetics*, edited by Amiya Dev. 781–9. New Delhi: Centre for Studies in Civilisations, 2009.

Newnham-Davis, Lt Col. "Amateurs in Foreign Parts." In *Amateur Clubs and Actors*, edited by W. G. Elliot. 221–46. London: Edward Arnold, 1898.

Niyogi De, Esha. "Modern Shakespeares in Popular Bombay Cinema: Translation, Subjectivity and Community." *Screen* 43, no. 1 (Spring 2002): 19–40.

Norris, Christopher. *Deconstruction. Theory and Practice*. London: Routledge, 2002.

Oak, Govind Ramachandra. "*Sawai Madhavrao Peshave Yancha Mrutyu*: Pustakpariksha" (book review), *Vividhadnyanavistar* 37 (1906): 464–72.

Omkara. VCD, directed by Vishal Bhardwaj, 2006; Mumbai: Shemaroo Entertainment Pvt. Ltd, 2009.

Parker, Patricia and Geoffrey Hartmann, eds, *Shakespeare and the Question of Theory*. New York: Methuen, 1985.

Pattanaik, D. P. "Introduction." In *Kabilipi* [Letters of Poets]. Kolkata: Visva-Bharati, 1957.
Patterson, Annabel. "The Very Age and Body of the Time." In *Shakespeare and Deconstruction*, edited by G. Douglas Atkins and David M. Bergeron. 47–68. New York: Peter Lang, 1991.
Petersen, Lene B. *Shakespeare's Errant Texts: Textual Form and Linguistic Style in Shakespearean "Bad" Quartos and Co-Authored Plays*. Cambridge: Cambridge University Press, July 2010.
Phadke, Narayan Seetaram. "Gadakaryanche Durjan." *Ratnakar*, June (1927): 435–43.
Pfister, Manfred and Juergen Gutsch. *William Shakespeare's Sonnets for the First Time Globally Reprinted: A Quartercentenary Anthology*. Dozwil, Switzerland: Edition SIGNAThUR, 2009.
Plato. *Republic*: *The Dialogues of Plato*. Translated by B. Jowett. New York: Random House, 1937.
Powell, Lucy. "In his wildest dream," *The Sunday Times* (London), 4 March 2007.
Prasad, Maheshchandra. *Daah ka Phal*. Arrah: the author, 1939. (in Hindi)
Prasad, Raekha. "All the world's on stage," *The Times* (London), 15 April 2006.
Purcell, Stephen. *Popular Shakespeare: Simulation and Subversion on the Modern Stage*. Basingstoke and New York: Palgrave, 2009.
Raman, Shankar and Lowell Gallagher, eds. *Knowing Shakespeare: Senses, Embodiment and Cognition*. New York: Palgrave, 2010.
Richardson, D. L. *Literary Leaves or Prose and Verse*. Kolkata: Samuel Smith and Co., 1836.
Richardson, D. L. *Selections from the British Poets: From the Time of Chaucer to the Present Day*. Calcutta: Baptist Mission Press, 1840.
Rothwell, Kenneth S. *A History of Shakespeare on Screen: A Century of Film and Television*. Cambridge: Cambridge University Press, 1999.
Rust, Jennifer R. and Julia Reinhardt Lupton. "Introduction: Schmitt and Shakespeare." In *Carl Schmitt's Hamlet and Hecuba*, translated by David Pan and Jennifer R. Rust. New York: Telos Press Publishing, 2009.
"Sangit Sharada Natak: Pustakpariksha" (book review). *Vividhdnyanvistar* 9 (1899): 279.
Sankaranarayanan, Vasanthi. "A Midsummer Night's Dream," 28 April 2006, http://www.narthaki.com/info/reviews/rev344.html.
Schoch, Richard W. *Not Shakespeare: Bardolatry and Burlesque in the Nineteenth Century*. Cambridge: Cambridge University Press, 2002.

Schoenfeldt, Michael. *The Cambridge Introduction to Shakespeare's Poetry.* Cambridge: Cambridge University Press, 2010.

Scott, William O. "Self-Difference in *Troilus and Cressida.*" In *Shakespeare and Deconstruction*, edited by G. Douglas Atkins and David M. Bergeron. 129–48. New York: Peter Lang, 1991.

Semenza, Greg Colón, ed. *The English Renaissance in Popular Culture: An Age of All Time.* New York: Palgrave, 2010.

Sen, Amrita. "*Maqbool* and Bollywood Conventions," in *Asian Shakespeares on Screen: Two Films in Perspective.* Special issue of *Borrowers and Lenders: The Journal of Shakespeare and Appropriation* 4, no. 2 (Spring/Summer 2009). http://www.borrowers.uga.edu/

Sen, Suddhaseel. "Indigenizing Macbeth: Vishal Bhardwaj's Maqbool," in *Asian Shakespeares on Screen: Two Films in Perspective.* Special issue of *Borrowers and Lenders: The Journal of Shakespeare and Appropriation* 4, no. 2 (Spring/Summer 2009). http://www.borrowers.uga.edu/

Shakespeare Performance in Asia. http://web.mit.edu/shakespeare/asia/

Shapiro, James. *Contested Will: Who Wrote Shakespeare?* New York: Simon & Schuster, 2010.

Shapiro, James. *Shakespeare and the Jews.* New York: Columbia University Press, 1996.

Shapiro, Michael. "Shylock the Old Clothes Man: Victorian Burlesques of *The Merchant of Venice.*" In *Shakespeare's World / World Shakespeares*, edited by Richard Fotheringham, Christa Jansohn, and R. S. White. 119–29. Newark: University of Delaware Press, 2008.

Sheen, Erica. *Shakespeare and the Institution of Theatre: The Best in This Kind.* New York: Palgrave, 2009.

Singh, Brahmanand. "Interview with Vishal Bhardwaj." In *Cinema in India.* Mumbai: National Film Development Corporation, 2003.

Singh, Jyotsna G. "Shakespeare and the Civilising Mission." In *Colonial Narratives/Cultural Dialogues: "Discoveries" of India in the Language of Colonialism.* 101–28. London: Routledge, 1996.

Smith, Bruce. *Phenomenal Shakespeare.* Chichester, UK and Malden, MA: Wiley-Blackwell, 2010.

Somaaya, Bhawana. *Amitabh Bachchan: The Legend.* Delhi: Macmillan, 1999.

Spencer, Charles. "A delirious Dream of India," *The Daily Telegraph*, 15 March 2007.

Spencer, Charles. "A fantastical, unforgettable Dream," *The Daily Telegraph*, 12 June 2006.

Steiger, Klaus Peter. *Moderne Shakespeare-Bearbeitungen. Ein Rezeptionstypus in der Gegenwartsliteratur*. Stuttgart, Berlin, Köln: Verlag W. Kohlhammer, 1990.

Stewart, Stanley. *Shakespeare and Philosophy*. New York: Routledge, 2010.

Sugiera, Małgorzata. *Wariacje szekspirowskie w powojennym dramacie europejskim*. Kraków: Universitas 1997.

Supple, Tim. "Making The Dream—a director's story," British Council playbill for *A Midsummer Night's Dream* [April 2006], unpaginated

Tagore, Rabindranath. *Jibansmriti [My Reminiscences]* in vol. 17 of *Rabindra Rachanabali* [Rabindranath Tagore, Complete Works]. Kolkata: Visva-Bharati, 1954.

Tagore, Rabindranath. *Jogajog* (Kolkata: Visva-Bharati, 1929); transl into English as *Jogajog/Relationships* by Supriya Chaudhuri. Delhi: Oxford University Press, 2005.

Talfourd, Francis, *Shylock, or the Merchant of Venice Preserved*. London: Thomas Hailes Lacy, 1860. Reprinted in vol. 3 of *Nineteenth Century Shakespeare Burlesques*, edited by Stanley Wells, 5 vols. London: Diploma Press Ltd, 1978.

Taubeneck, Steven. "Deconstructing the GDR: Heiner Mueller and Postmodern Cultural Politics." *Pacific Coast Philology* 26, no. 1/2 (1991): 85–95.

Taylor, Gary. *Reinventing Shakespeare: A Cultural History from the Restoration to the Present*. New York: Weidenfeld and Nicolson, 1989.

Taylor, Paul. "A Midsummer Night's Dream," *The Independent*, 12 June 2006.

Teraoka, Arlene Akiko. *The Silence of Entropy or Universal Discourse. The Postmodernist Poetics of Heiner Müller*. New York: Peter Lang, 1985.

Terris, Owen, Eve-Marie Oesterlen, and Luke McKernan, eds. *Shakespeare on Film, Television and Radio: The Researcher's Guide*. London: British Universities Film and Video Council, 2009.

The (Old Clothes) Merchant of Venice or The Young Judge and Old Jewry, A Burlesque Sketch For the Drawing Room. New York: De Witt's Acting Plays, no. 331, n.d.

Trivedi, Harish. *Colonial Transactions: English Literature and India*. Kolkata: Papyrus, 1993; Manchester: Manchester University Press, 1995.

Trivedi, Poonam. "Introduction," In *India's Shakespeare: Translation, Interpretation, and Performance*, edited by Poonam Trivedi and Dennis Bartholomeusz. 13–46. Newark: University of Delaware Press, 2005.

Trivedi, Poonam "'It is the bloody business which informs thus …': Local Politics and Performative Praxis, *Macbeth* in India." In *World-wide*

Shakespeares: Local Appropriations in Film and Performance, edited by Sonia Massai. 47–54. Abingdon: Routledge, 2005.

Trivedi, Poonam, "'Mak[ing] ... Strange / Even to the disposition that I owe: Vishal Bharadwaj's *Maqbool*." In *Asian Shakespeares on Screen: Two Films in Perspective*. Special issue of *Borrowers and Lenders: The Journal of Shakespeare and Appropriation* 4, no. 2 (Spring/Summer 2009), http://www.borrowers.uga.edu

Trivedi, Poonam and Minami Ryuta. *Re-Playing Shakespeare in Asia*. New York: Routledge, 2010.

Tweedie, James. "Caliban's Books: The Hybrid Text in Peter Greenaway's *Prospero's Books*," *Cinema Journal* 40, no. 1 (Fall 2000): 104–26.

Verma, Rajiva. "Shakespeare in Hindi Cinema." In *India's Shakespeare: Translation, Interpretation, and Performance*, ed. Poonam Trivedi and Dennis Bartholomeusz. 269–90. Newark: University of Delaware Press, 2005. Reprinted with revisions in *Shakespeare: The Indian Icon*, edited by Vikram Chopra. 742–58. New Delhi: The Reader's Paradise, 2011.

Verma, Rajiva. "*Hamlet* on the Hindi Screen," *Hamlet Studies* 24 (2002): 81–93.

Verma, Rajiva. "*Macbeth* in India, with Special Reference to Some Versions in Hindi," *Shakespeare Worldwide* (Tokyo) 14/15 (1995): 28–41.

Vickers, Brian. *Appropriating Shakespeare: Contemporary Critical Quarrels*. New Haven and London: Yale University Press, 1993.

Vickers, Brian. *Shakespeare, Co-Author*. Oxford: Oxford University Press, 2002.

Viswanathan, Gauri. *Masks of Conquest: Literary Study and British Rule in India*. New York: Columbia University Press, 1989.

Walimbe, R. S. *Marathi Natyasamiksha: 1860–1935 [Marathi Theatre Criticism: 1860–1935]*. Pune: Pune Vidyapeeth Prakashan, 1966.

Waller, Gary. "Decentering the Bard: The Dissemination of the Shakespearean Text." In *Shakespeare and Deconstruction*, edited by G. Douglas Atkins and David M. Bergeron. 21–45. New York: Peter Lang, 1991.

Waugh, Patricia. *Metafiction: The Theory and Practice of Self-Conscious Fiction*. London and New York: Methuen, 1984.

Waugh, Patricia. *Practising Postmodernism, Reading Modernism*. London and New York: Edward Arnold, 1992.

Wells, Stanley. ed. *Nineteenth Century Shakespeare Burlesques*. 5 vols. London: Diploma Press Ltd, 1978.

Wilder, Lena Perkins. *Shakespeare's Memory Theatre: Recollection, Properties, and Character*. Cambridge: Cambridge University Press, 2010.

Wilson, Thomas. *A Discourse upon Usury* (1572). Edited with a historical introduction by R. H. Tawney. London: Bell, 1925.
Worthen, William B. *Shakespeare and the Authority of Performance*. Cambridge: Cambridge University Press, 1997.
Worthen, William B. *Drama: Between Poetry and Performance*. Oxford: Wiley-Blackwell, 2010.
Yachnin, Paul and Jessica Slights, eds. *Shakespeare and Character: Theory, History, Performance and Theatrical Persons*. New York: Palgrave, 2009.

Notes on Contributors

Rangana Banerji is Assistant Professor in English at Muralidhar Girls' College, Kolkata, India. She is the author of *The Mahabharata Monologues* (Pages & Chapters, 2011) and she assisted as a researcher for *Shakespeare on the Calcutta Stage: A Checklist*, edited by Ananda Lal and Sukanta Chaudhuri (Papyrus, 2001). Her research interests include the institutionalization of English studies in Bengal and studies of the Mahabharata.

Urmila Bhirdikar teaches in the School of Language, Literature and Culture Studies at the Central University of Gujarat, Gandhinagar, India. Her research and publications are in the fields of translation, theatre and music, and gender and sexuality in the Maharashtra.

Tom Bishop is Professor of English at the University of Auckland, New Zealand. He is the author of *Shakespeare and the Theatre of Wonder* (Cambridge University Press, 1996), the translator of Ovid's *Amores* (Carcanet, 2003), and a General Editor of *The Shakespearean International Yearbook*. He has published articles on Elizabethan music, Shakespeare, Jonson, Australian literature, and other topics, and is currently working on Shakespeare's Theatre Games.

Graham Bradshaw, General Editor emeritus of the *Shakespearean International Yearbook*, is retired as Professor of English at Chuo University in Tokyo. He is Honorary Professor of English and Fine Arts at the University of Queensland. His publications include *Shakespeare's Skepticism* (St Martin's Press, 1987), *Misrepresentations: Shakespeare and the Materialists* (Cornell, 1993) and numerous essays. He is co-author, with Tetsuo Kishi, of *Shakespeare in Japan* (Continuum, 2005) and co-editor, with Michael Neill, of *J. M. Coetzee's Austerities* (Ashgate, 2010).

Paromita Chakravarti is Associate Professor in the Department of English and Joint Director, School of Women's Studies at Jadavpur University, Kolkata, India. She works on the history and gendering of madness, queer and sexuality studies, Shakespearean adaptations, film studies, women's writing, and education.

Rebecca Chapman is Assistant Professor of English and Director of the Writing Studio at Holy Names University, Oakland, California. Her primary research interests include gender and sexuality in early modern England, queer theory, and the intersections between Shakespeare and systems of cultural value. Currently she is completing a book project entitled *Rehabilitating Shakespeare: Cultural Appropriation, Queer Subjectivity,* which discusses the emerging use of Shakespeare in rehabilitation programmes worldwide.

Sukanta Chaudhuri is Professor Emeritus at Jadavpur University, Kolkata, India. His publications include *Infirm Glory: Shakespeare and the Renaissance Image of Man* (Clarendon Press, 1981), *Renaissance Pastoral and Its English Developments* (Clarendon Press, 1989), *Shakespeare on the Calcutta Stage* (co-edited with Ananda Lal, Papyrus, 2001), and *The Metaphysics of Text* (Cambridge University Press, 2010). He is currently editing an anthology of Renaissance pastoral poetry for Manchester University Press. He has authored the entry on 'Shakespeare in India' for *Shakespeare Internet Editions*, and is on the Executive Committee of the International Shakespeare Association.

Supriya Chaudhuri is Professor and Co-ordinator, Centre for Advanced Study, Department of English, Jadavpur University, Kolkata, India. She works on Shakespeare and the Renaissance, critical theory, cultural history, cinema and translation. Among her recent publications are *Conversations with Jacqueline Rose* (co-authored, Seagull/Chicago University Press, 2010) and articles on Spenser, Shakespeare, and modernism in India.

Andrew Gurr is Professor Emeritus at the University of Reading, and former Director of Research at the Shakespeare Globe Centre, London. While at the Globe he spent twenty years chairing the committee that fixed the Globe's shape and structure. His academic books include *The Shakespearean Stage 1574–1642*, now in its fourth edition (Cambridge University Press, 2009), *Playgoing in Shakespeare's London*, now in its third (Cambridge University Press, 2004), *The Shakespearian Playing Companies* (Clarendon Press, 1996), *The Shakespeare Company, 1594–1642* (Cambridge University Press, 2004), and *Shakespeare's Opposites: The Admiral's Company, 1594–1625* (Cambridge University Press, 2009).

Alexander C. Y. Huang, a General Editor of *The Shakespearean International Yearbook*, is director of the Dean's Scholars in Shakespeare Program and Associate Professor of English at George Washington University in Washington, D.C., research affiliate in literature at MIT, performance editor of *Internet Shakespeare Editions* (http://internetshakespeare.uvic.ca/), and the co-founder and co-editor of *Global Shakespeares* (http://globalshakespeares.org/). He received the MLA's Aldo and Jeanne Scaglione Prize and an honorable mention of NYU's Joe A. Callaway Prize for the Best Book on Drama or Theatre for *Chinese Shakespeares: Two Centuries of Cultural Exchange* (Columbia University Press, 2009), and has published widely on Shakespeare, performance, digital humanities, and globalization in English, German, and Chinese. His book *Weltliteratur und Welttheater: Interkulturelle Perspektiven des Humanismus* is forthcoming. He currently serves as the chair of MLA Committee on the *New Variorum Edition of Shakespeare*.

Aniket Jaaware teaches English at the University of Pune, India. His research interests and publications are in the areas of literary theory, translation studies, and science fiction.

Ananda Lal is Professor of English at Jadavpur University, Kolkata, India. His major books are *The Oxford Companion to Indian Theatre* (Oxford University Press, 2004) and *Rabindranath Tagore: Three Plays* (MP Birla Foundation, 1987). His work on Shakespeare includes *Shakespeare on the Calcutta Stage* (co-edited with Sukanta Chaudhuri: Papyrus, 2001), the dramaturgy for Tim Supple's *A Midsummer-Night's Dream*, and direction of theatre productions of *The Merchant of Venice* and *Measure for Measure*.

Aneta Mancewicz is Marie Curie Research Fellow at Central School of Speech and Drama, University of London, UK and Assistant Professor of English Literature at Kazimierz Wielki University, Bydgoszcz, Poland. She has also been Visiting Scholar at City University of New York, Graduate Center. Her book *Biedny Hamlet* (Poor Hamlet; Księgarnia Akademicka Press, 2010) examines deconstruction of *Hamlet* and Hamlet in contemporary European drama. She is currently preparing a book about intermediality in performances of Shakespeare in Europe.

Jatindra K. Nayak is Professor of English at Utkal University, Orissa, India. His research interests include translation and comparative literature. He has co-translated into English, with Paul St-Pierre, the classic Oriya novel *Chha*

Mana Atha Guntha (Six Acres and a Third; University of California Press, 2005). He was winner of the Hutch-Crossword Indian Fiction Translation Award, 2004.

Niamh J. O'Leary is an Assistant Professor of English at Xavier University in Cincinnati, Ohio. Her current research addresses questions of female community in the Renaissance—how it was formed, what it could accomplish, and how it was represented in English Renaissance literature. She is also interested in performance criticism, Shakespeare in popular culture, and Shakespeare on film. Her article on Feng Xiaogang's *The Banquet*, a Chinese adaptation of *Hamlet*, is forthcoming in *Upstart Crow*.

Poonam Trivedi is Associate Professor in English at Indraprastha College, University of Delhi, India. Her publications include *Re-playing Shakespeare in Asia* (co-edited with Ryuta Minami: Routledge, 2010), *India's Shakespeare: Translation, Interpretation and Performance* (co- edited with Dennis Bartholomeusz: Longman, 2005), a CD-ROM 'King Lear *in India*' (2006), and articles on Indian the atre, performance and film versions of Shakespeare in India, and on women in Shakespeare.

Rajiva Verma is the author of *Myth, Ritual and Shakespeare* (Spantech, 1990), and "Winners and Losers: A Study of *Macbeth* and *Antony and Cleopatra*" (*Modern Language Review*, 1986). His recent publications include essays on *Coriolanus* and *Hamlet*. A founding member and a former president of the Shakespeare Society of India and a former head of the Department of English at the University of Delhi, India, he is currently Advisor in the Institute of Lifelong Learning at the University.

Index

Editions of Shakespeare, authors of included essays, and references in footnotes and bibliography are not indexed.

Agamben, Giorgio 103
Alexander, Catherine M. S. 199
Allen, Giles 153
Alleyn, Edward 159, 161
Almereyda, Michael 185
Antoon, A. J. 65
Arambam, Lokendra 101
Aristotle 97
Arora, Keval 73, 75, 78
Astington, John 207–8
Atkins, G. Douglas 134, 138

Bandyopadhyay, Tarashankar 122
Bauersima, Igor 143–5, 147–8
Bazin, André 121
Beier, Karin 66
Benjamin, Walter 102–6
Berg, James 205
Berlin, Normand 135
Betts, Jean 139, 147–8
Bevington, David 171–2
Bhardwaj, Vishal 91, 92, 95, 101–3, 105, 107, 108, 110, 116, 117
Big Brother (TV show) 143
Billington, Michael 75, 76
Bose, Rajnarain 35, 36
Bradley, A. C. 135–7, 204
Brayne, John 156
Bristol, Michael 205
Brook, Peter 65, 66, 69, 70, 76, 95
Brougham, John 10, 15
Buchanan, Judith 186–8
Burbage family 153–60, 162–4
Burt, Richard 119, 188
Butler, Judith 183

Calderwood, James 134, 135
Canadian Adaptations of Shakespeare Project 218–19
Cardenio 174
Carey, George 155, 164–5
Carey, Henry 154–5, 164–5
Carlyle, Thomas ix, 3
Chandra, Vikram 109
Chatterjee, Satishchandra 65
Chattopadhyay, (Chatterjee), Bankimchandra (Bankim) 29, 30, 40
Chattopadhyay, Partha 30
Chiplunkar, Vishnushastri 43, 44
Clark, Sandra 146
Clarke, Margaret 139, 147
Coppola, Francis Ford 106
Cox, Alex 185
Croteau, Melissa 185

De Grazia, Margreta 136–7
De Vere, Edward *see* Oxford, Earl of
Derrida, Jacques 134, 137–8, 180
Desai, Anita 108
Desmet, Christy 188, 189
Deval, G. B. 46
Dobson, Michael 70, 72, 75, 76
Donaldson, Peter 115, 220, 221
dreamthinkspeak (theatre company) 148
Dryden, John 31, 38
Dutt, Utpal 65, 99, 100, 116–24, 126

Edelman, Charles 158
Eden, Emily 8, 11,
Egan, Gabriel 201–2
Eliot, T. S. 141, 159
Emmerich, Roland 171, 198

Field, Richard 164
Foucault, Michel 98
Fraser, F. J. 10, 16, 17
Freud, Sigmund 66, 93, 101, 136, 171, 180
Fuchs, Elinor 146

Gadkari, Ram Ganesh 49, 50
Gaiety Theatre, The (Simla) 9, 11–14, 16, 19, 21, 22–5
Gajowski, Evelyn 178
Gallagher, Lowell 177
Garrick, David 8, 45
Ghose, Jagannath Ballav 55, 61
Ghosh, Harachandra 98, 99
Ghosh, Rituporno 91, 115–19, 121–7
Gillies, John 153
Global Shakespeares 220–22
Głowacki, Janusz 139, 140–41, 147
Godard, Jean-Luc 115, 127, 185
Gowda, Srikanthesh 65
Greenaway, Peter 115, 127
Greenblatt, Stephen 172–3, 182
Greenhalgh, Susanne 74, 77
Gross, John 10, 24
Gutsch, Juergen 195–7

Hardinge, Lord 8
Harishchandra, Bharatendu 88
Harris, Jonathan Gil 179–80
Hashr, Agha 25, 84, 85, 100
Haughton, William 160–64
Henderson, Diana E. 177
Herzog, Werner 66
Holland, Peter 189
Hopkins, Lisa 191
Hotson, Leslie 158
Howard, Jean E. 178–9
Huang, Alexander C. Y. 187–9, 212–13, 215–17, 220, 222
Hussain, Akhtar 86
Hutcheon, Linda 22, 98, 145, 146

Internet Shakespeare Editions 217–18
Irving, Henry 8, 13, 20, 45
Iyengar, Sujata 189

Jameson, Frederic 124
Jarman, Derek 115, 127

Jess-Cooke, Carolyn 185
Jonson, Ben 157, 160

Kalb, Jonathan 142
Karanth, H. V. 100
Kashmiri, Agha Hashr 84, 85, 100
Kendal, Geoffrey 8, 119,
Kennedy, Dennis 213–16, 221, 222
Khadilkar, Krishnaji Prabhakar 45, 46–8, 50
Kidnie, Margaret Jane 203–4
Kieślowski, Krzysztof 102
Kipling, Rudyard 13, 14
Klett, Elizabeth 183–4
Kolhatkar, Mahadevshastri 43, 44
Kott, Jan 66, 146
Kurosawa, Akira 101–103, 189

La Ruina, Saverio 139, 142–3, 147
Langley, Francis 155, 157–8
Lanier, Douglas 182
Lavender, Andy 135, 146
Lei Jin 189
Lelyveld, Toby 10, 24
Leonard, Kendra Preston 187–8
Lepage, Robert 66, 203
Levin, Carole 210–11, 222
Lieblein, Leanore 205–6
Lodge, Thomas 217
Lopez, Roderigo 159, 161
Love's Labour's Won 174
Luhrmann, Baz 185
Lyly, John 217

Mansinha, Mayadhar 60–62
Marlowe, Christopher 159, 161, 170, 219
McDonald, Russ 199–200
McKernan, Luke 180
McMullan, Gordon 199
Mehta, Suketu 109
Menon, Madhavi 174–6, 178
Mentz, Stephen 192
Merry Merchant of Venice, The 8–10, 14–25
Miller, William ix, 7, 25
Modi, Sohrab 83, 84, 86–90
Mujumdar, Shankararao 45
Müller, Heiner 135, 141–2, 147

INDEX

Nashe, Thomas 155, 159, 163–4
Neill, Michael ix
Ninagawa, Yukio 66

Oesterlen, Eve-Marie 180–81
Omkara 91–5, 108, 116–17
Oxford, Earl of 170–72

Pavis, Patrice 213, 216
Petersen, Lene B. 200–201, 203
Pfister, Manfred 195–7
Poole, John 9
Purcell, Stephen 184–5

Quiles, Eduardo 139, 147

Rakshit, Haranchandra 55
Raman, Shankar 177
Ray, Radhanath 54, 57, 62
Ray, Satyajit 101, 125, 126
Richardson, D. L. 30–39
Ross, Charles S. 187–9
Rosset, Caca 66
Rowe, Katherine 182
Rowe, Nicholas 37
Rumold, Kate 182–3
Rushdie, Salman 66, 109,
Ryuta, Minami 211, 215–17, 221

Sahu, Kishore 86, 89–90
Samuel Taylor Coleridge 32, 33, 136
Sanzio, Socìetas Raffaello 148
Schmitt, Carl 103
Schoch, Richard W. 9
Schoenfeldt, Michael 197–8
Semenza, Greg Colón 189–90
Shakespeare, William
    A Lover's Complaint 198
    A Midsummer Night's Dream ix, 3–4, 14, 43, 65–79, 199, 206, 207, 220
    All's Well that Ends Well 203, 223
    Antony and Cleopatra 51, 128, 153, 172
    As You Like It 25, 63, 205
    Coriolanus 31, 32, 172, 223
    Cymbeline 24, 25, 36, 44,
    Hamlet 10, 31–33, 35–6, 40, 43, 45, 47–50, 51, 52, 56–60, 76, 83, 86–91, 98, 103, 123, 133–49, 177, 180, 185, 187, 191, 201, 203–4, 206–7, 213, 216
    1 Henry IV 32, 160, 209
    2 Henry IV 160, 209,
    Henry V 209,
    1 Henry VI 211
    Henry VIII 36, 200, 218, 223
    Julius Caesar 31, 34, 35, 58, 133
    King John 36, 51, 84–5, 174, 205, 218
    King Lear ix, 7, 31, 35, 43, 91, 95, 98, 100, 115, 117, 119, 121, 123–4, 127, 176–7, 185, 187, 199, 205, 215
    Love's Labor's Lost 188
    Macbeth 8, 29, 31–3, 35, 36, 43, 45, 49, 51, 63, 84, 91, 92, 94–113, 116, 140, 187, 189, 208, 210, 219,
    Measure for Measure 51
    Much Ado about Nothing 177, 188
    Othello 25, 31, 33, 35, 36–9, 43–5, 47, 48, 60–63, 88, 91–5, 98, 116, 118, 120, 122, 128, 135, 153, 174, 204, 215
    Pericles 223
    Richard II 128, 172, 207, 209
    Richard III 84, 140, 213, 223
    Romeo and Juliet 43, 54, 55–6, 62, 63, 86, 89, 128, 178, 180, 185, 191, 200–201, 209, 220
    Sonnets 39, 135, 173, 176–7, 195–8, 217
    Titus Andronicus 153, 184
    The Comedy of Errors 51, 63, 66, 89–90, 174, 188
    The Merchant of Venice 31, 36, 43, 63, 83, 86, 88, 98, 153–65, 211, 213; see also Merry Merchant of Venice, The
    The Merry Wives of Windsor 128, 162
    "The Phoenix and the Turtle" 198
    The Rape of Lucrece 198
    The Taming of the Shrew 51, 98, 206, 211
    The Tempest 31, 33, 34, 36, 39, 43, 63, 100, 115, 127, 174, 177, 180, 200, 206, 209, 223
    The Two Gentlemen of Verona 51
    The Two Noble Kinsmen 199, 200

The Winter's Tale 24, 51, 223
Timon of Athens 51, 123, 205
Troilus and Cressida 133, 135, 180
Twelfth Night 25, 63, 128
Venus and Adonis 176, 198
Shakespeare Wallah 117, 119, 126
Shapiro, James 170–74, 182
Shapiro, Michael 20
Shaughnessy, Robert 181–3
Sheen, Erica 206–7
Slights, Jessica 204–5
Smith, Bruce 176–8
Smith, Emma 182
Stewart, Stanley 178–9
Stoppard, Tom 135, 147
Supple, Tim ix, 3, 66–81

Tagore, Rabindranath 40, 78, 98
Talfourd, Francis 10, 17, 20
Tanvir, Habib 4, 65

Terris, Owen 180–81
Trivedi, Poonam 215–17, 222

Vidyasagar, Chandra Ishwar 88, 90, 98

Warhol, Andy 143–4, 148
Watkins, John 210–11, 222
Wayte, William 158
Weimann, Robert ix
Wells, Stanley 9, 25
Wilder, Lina Perkins 208–10
Wilson, Robert 148
Woodliffe, Oliver 155, 157
Wooster Group, The 148
Worthen, W. B. 146, 182, 188

Yachnin, Paul 204–5
Yong Li Lan 211, 213–16, 221

Zurek, Jerzy 139, 140, 147